Screening the Hollywood rebels in 1950s Britain

Manchester University Press

Screening the Hollywood rebels in 1950s Britain

Anna Ariadne Knight

Manchester University Press

Published by Manchester University Press
Altrincham Street, Manchester M1 7JA

www.manchesteruniversitypress.co.uk

British Library Cataloguing-in-Publication Data
A catalogue record for this book is available from the British Library

ISBN 978 1 5261 5448 4 hardback

First published 2021

Typeset
by New Best-set Typesetters Ltd

Contents

List of figures — *page* vi
Acknowledgements — vii
List of abbreviations — viii

Introduction — 1
1 'Attractive and imitable': Marlon Brando and *The Wild One* ban in the UK — 39
2 'Our Teddy boys are angels': *Blackboard Jungle* fever in the classroom — 79
3 'He died in his own rebellion': James Dean and *Rebel Without a Cause* — 111
4 'A teenage revolution': Bill Haley and the rock 'n' roll cinema riots — 150
5 'All-singing, all-fighting man': Elvis Presley as a rock 'n' roll rebel — 183
6 Conclusion: the rise of the Angry Young Men — 227

Filmography — 238
Bibliography — 240
Index — 254

Figures

1.1	Marlon Brando in *A Streetcar Named Desire* (1951)	*page* 44
1.2	Marlon Brando in *The Wild One* (1953)	57
2.1	Publicity materials featuring Glenn Ford and Eleanor Powell (uncredited photographer, *Modern Screen*, January 1944, p. 53)	95
2.2	Vic Morrow, Dan Terranova and Paul Mazursky in *Blackboard Jungle* (1955)	97
3.1	James Dean, Ann Doran and Jim Backus in *Rebel Without a Cause* (1955)	118
3.2	Natalie Wood and James Dean in *Rebel Without a Cause* (1955)	126
4.1	Publicity photo of Bill Haley and the Comets (Wikimedia)	152
4.2	Bill Haley and the Comets in *Don't Knock the Rock* (1956)	167
5.1	Elvis Presley in *Jailhouse Rock* (1957)	189
5.2	Elvis Presley in *King Creole* (1958)	207
6.1	Billy Fury interviewed in *Billy Fury at the ABC Plymouth* (1962)	232
6.2	Cliff Richard in *Serious Charge* (1959)	233

Acknowledgements

I would like to thank Mark Glancy in the History department at Queen Mary, University of London, whose academic rigour and expertise guided the initial research which underlies this book. Thanks are also due to Joanna Cohen, Mark White, Matt Jacobsen, Lucy Bolton and Sue Harris, in the History and Film Studies departments at QMUL, who gave helpful feedback on early draft chapters and offered moral support and advice when needed. I am indebted to Helen Hanson, at Exeter University, and Tamar Jeffers McDonald, at University of Kent, for greeting my project with so much enthusiasm, advising me to write this book and suggesting improvements to the manuscript. Special thanks to Hollie Price, a friend and colleague at QMUL, for generously sharing her advice on publishing and licensing and offering her unwavering support. Thanks to the students at QMUL, who asked when my book was due to be published so that they could read it! Also, I appreciate the assistance of staff at the BFI Reuben Library, Senate House Library, and the British Library.

I gratefully acknowledge the help from various staff at the publishers during the completion of this book, and from my anonymous reviewers, whose reports offered valuable insights on draft versions.

I am especially grateful to my family and friends for their untiring encouragement, love of classic movies, good humour and generosity throughout the ups and downs of my completing this project. I couldn't have asked for a better 'supporting cast' than Stella, Chris Marco, Chris K., Maria, Marotta, Isabella, Julius, Martin, Juliette, B.N.H. and Arthur.

Abbreviations

BBC	British Broadcasting Corporation
BBFC	British Board of Film Censors
BFI	British Film Institute
ITV	Independent Television
MGM	Metro-Goldwyn-Mayer
NFT	National Film Theatre
NUT	National Union of Teachers
UNESCO	United Nations Educational Scientific and Cultural Organization

Introduction

Certain Hollywood stars of 1950s cinema were enormously influential in British youth culture of the period. These alluring and confrontational representations of masculinity gave expression to the changing mood of a rising generation. The power of teenage consumerism redirected the economy to produce the consumables – and the film stars – young people most desired. Several American actors idealised masculine rebellion by starring in Hollywood films that glamorised juvenile delinquency. Their images linger in the public imagination: Elvis Presley's photo as the 'jailbird' Vince Everett furnishes many a barber shop window in London; and novelty lighters decorated with the 'incendiary' image of James Dean as rebellious teen Jim Stark can still be picked up at Camden market. Recently, a credit card commercial promoting quintessential American jeans showed the surly, leather-clad Marlon Brando as Johnny Strabler dismounting a Triumph Thunderbird.[1] In part, this book attempts to deconstruct the mystique enshrouding these iconic rebels and account for why such images have endured for so long.

From the earliest inception of Hollywood's star system, cinema audiences have been interested in movie stars. These celebrity personae have been assiduously developed and sustained through studio publicity departments, film criticism and fan materials as well as the films themselves. In the 1950s, a new type of method acting reimagined film performance with a searing psychological realism and, as a result, reconfigured Hollywood stardom. Several 'rebel' films produced by Hollywood between 1953 and 1958 were the first to explore post-war juvenile delinquency within the context of an attractive, multi-dimensional masculinity. This book explores the impact that these American films about juvenile delinquency had in Britain when the 'youth problem' was considered a particularly prominent social issue. In addition, it considers the legacy that the three very influential Hollywood stars Marlon Brando, James Dean and Elvis Presley had on British popular culture.

This study was born of a desire to understand an extraordinary episode of film censorship when the British Board of Film Censors (BBFC) took the decision to ban *The Wild One* (Laslo Benedek, 1953), a prestigious Hollywood film starring Marlon Brando.[2] Brando plays Johnny Strabler, a truculent motorcycle rebel, who is effectively unpunished for manslaughter, in a film originally intended to offer a commentary on the de-individuation of mindless gang violence. In truth, it was no more violent than earlier gangster films, popular with British audiences and given the BBFC's approval. However, with Brando as the Black Rebel gang leader, *The Wild One* was interpreted as an amoral tale of anarchy and iconoclasm. Inadvertently, it introduced cinema audiences to a new type of anti-hero: the charismatic juvenile delinquent or – as coined by the media of the time – the 'crazy mixed-up kid'. In quick succession, Hollywood recognised the currency of this trope and produced a series of films that exploited the fascination with delinquent youth. Therefore, in addition to its analysis of *The Wild One*, the principal case studies in the book are: *Blackboard Jungle* (Richard Brooks, 1955), *Rebel Without a Cause* (Nicholas Ray, 1955), *Rock Around the Clock* (Fred F. Sears, 1956), *Jailhouse Rock* (Richard Thorpe, 1957) and *King Creole* (Michael Curtiz, 1958).[3]

The inclusion of *Rock Around the Clock*, which does not engage with juvenile delinquency, is essential for a number of reasons. First, the song *Rock Around the Clock*, performed by Bill Haley and his Comets, had featured in *Blackboard Jungle* and subsequently became a number one hit record in Britain in 1956 – the first ever to sell a million copies. As a result of the hit song, Haley became a star of two Hollywood films and made a successful nationwide tour of Britain. As I show in Chapter 4, it was *Rock Around the Clock*, ostensibly a musical biography of Haley's rise to fame, which incited the actual juvenile delinquency among Britain's Teddy boys and girls so feared by the BBFC. The so-called teenage 'cinema riots' of 1956 provide a fascinating *outré* example of the generational differences between filmgoers. Furthermore, a re-examination of Haley's *Rock* film usefully segues into the delinquent film roles of the rock 'n' roll performer, Elvis Presley. Indeed, Presley 'inherited' the mantle of the film rebel once a significant portion of British rock 'n' roll fans found Haley's married status and conservative values less appealing.

As the book demonstrates, Hollywood machinery imbued this 'rebel' male with a glamour and kudos that resonated with younger cinemagoers. This coincided with a change in audience demographics. By the end of the 1950s and early 1960s, cinema's traditional family audiences became increasingly fragmented and, because 15- to 24-year-olds constituted a quarter of all cinema admissions, exploitative youth-oriented films were expressly made for the teenage market. In consequence, Hollywood's rebel films are among the best-remembered films of the 1950s for their depiction of insubordinate youth and for anticipating the change in cultural mood and new direction in production. Given the circulation and cultural legacy of the changing images of masculinity these film stars generated, they, themselves, form the primary focus of the book. As iconic stars of their generation, Brando, Dean and Presley have been celebrated and pilloried in the shifting discourses of popular culture. For example, Brando's early film career was distinguished by several notable performances and he was lauded as an actor of exceptional merit. Conversely, the latter part of his career was dominated by persistent rumours of professional unreliability, avarice and reclusiveness; and details of his unconventional private life were heavily publicised when he came to the defence of his son during a murder trial in the 1990s.[4] Similarly, Dean's short life has been the subject of numerous exposé biographies, such as *Rebel: The Life and Legend of James Dean* (2000) and *The Real James Dean* (2016), which have dismantled his heteronormative meanings, with his former lovers attesting to his bisexuality and promiscuity.[5] Correspondingly, Elvis Presley's later career (in the 1970s) predicates on his Las Vegas tours, his bejewelled white jumpsuits and his deteriorating physical appearance. Revelations about the singer's private life from members of his entourage circulated soon after his sudden death of a heart attack at the age of 42. These accounts centred on the singer's dependence on barbiturates and compulsive overeating. Such accounts tended to overshadow the early promise of Presley's acting career; in 2017, forty years after the singer's death, under the aegis of the Graceland estate, his former wife

Priscilla Presley, and others who knew him, participated in a series of TV programmes to restore the performer's reputation and musical legacy.[6]

Outline of the book

This book consists of five chapters, which explore the responses from British censors, critics and cinemagoers to principal films. Chapters examine the films in the order that they were released in Britain. Chapter 1 evaluates the BBFC's fourteen-year ban on *The Wild One*. My analysis of Marlon Brando's career – his method acting and his popularity with young cinemagoers – proposes that star charisma, rather than screen violence, more likely motivated the BBFC's intransigence. This chapter also explores British reactions to method acting and illustrates how Brando's fans negotiated the BBFC's ban to see their film idol. In Chapter 2, the British censorship problems of *Blackboard Jungle* are explored against its obvious attractions for teenage cinemagoers, who delighted in the film's rock 'n' roll soundtrack. The star studies of the urbane Glenn Ford and the Method-trained Vic Morrow demonstrate how the film privileged Ford as a heroic teacher and denied (young) audiences a charismatic anti-hero. Chapter 3 is concerned with the posthumous fame of James Dean, who predeceased the (British) release of *Rebel Without a Cause*. In its commentary on teenage consumerism, the chapter illustrates how the British media negotiated Dean's fascination for teenagers but distinguished British 'Deanagers' – as fans were labelled – from 'morbidly obsessive' American fans. Chapter 4 shows that the global phenomenon of *Rock Around the Clock*, the jubilant teenage anthem featured on the soundtrack to *Blackboard Jungle*, launched the Hollywood career of Bill Haley and resulted in demonstrably expressive interactions between British teenagers at local venues. These 'rock 'n' roll cinema riots', as they became known, are substantiated as the logical outcome of the film's participatory style, which resulted in an inevitable clash of generationally divided cinemagoers. Chapter 5 focuses on *Jailhouse Rock* and *King Creole* to demonstrate that Elvis Presley was promoted as a Marlon Brando type and James Dean's successor. Equally, the chapter shows that by the end of the 1950s, the 'power' of British teenage consumers had developed Presley's career around his status as an American working-class 'Teddy boy'.

Methods and approaches

In this book my ultimate aim is to arrive at a more complete understanding of how specific cultural phenomena are situated in cinema and social history. This entails 'disentangling' these American stars from their residual contemporary meanings using primary source material. In so doing, I argue that Hollywood stardom per se is only one piece of the conundrum and there are yet unexplored, alternative histories: in this case, a British history. By taking this approach, the book is interested in a transatlantic cultural dialogue; it shows that US and British culture of the period informed each other in complex ways. In my conclusion, for example, I argue that the Beatles phenomenon of the 1960s was influenced by these American rebel stars. To remap this cultural dialogue, I draw from the influential work of Janet Staiger (1992) and Barbara Klinger (1997) who argue against films having 'immanent' meanings and show that historical audiences have a more dynamic relationship to film by creating their own understanding from prevalent social and critical discourses. In their respective books, *Interpreting Films* and *Melodrama and Meaning*, Staiger and Klinger recover 'lost' historical audiences through an evaluation of critical reviews and commentary, publicity and promotional materials surrounding particular films.[7] In her later essay on reception studies (1997), Klinger proposes that, while no 'total history' is ever possible, an analysis of cinematic practices, authorship, production, star journalism and fan culture, among other contextual considerations (re)generates a range of social and cultural discourses surrounding a film in a given period.[8]

On the basis of Staiger's and Klinger's scholarship, James Chapman, Mark Glancy and Sue Harper promulgated a 'new film history' that encourages students and researchers to evaluate films as texts, through an appraisal of *mise en scène*, and as cultural documents, by sourcing a broad range of primary sources to contextualise them in specific historical moments. Gaining momentum since the mid-1980s, new film history has shifted away from the 'traditional' film history that tended to focus on an 'aesthetic' evaluation of cinema's rare 'masterpieces' (film-as-art); and the reflectionist model (film-as-social-mirror), which oversimplified the relationship between film and its social context.[9] In 'The New Film History' (1986), Thomas Elsaesser asserts that films should be interpreted as 'cultural artefacts' because they are shaped by a range of economic, industrial and technological practices. A film is unlike a novel, argues Elsaesser, and should be appraised for its visual and aural qualities – that imbue it with a particular style – in addition to its discernible narrative elements.[10]

However, a critical analysis of *mise en scène* raises specific concerns for the historian because it requires a particular set of skills. In this, the work of James Walters and Tom Brown, Douglas Pye and John Gibbs (and the many contributors to their respective edited collections) demonstrate the range of interpretative practice available to film scholars and film historians.[11] The rationale here, then, is to apply an investigative model that emphasises how film form – technical, narrative and stylistic elements – works to produce intellectual and emotional effects in the viewer. This method proves most suited to the central questions I raise, namely, to reconstitute the dynamic relationships between specific American stars and their British audiences and, thereby, recover these 'lost' voices of the past. Given my socio-cultural concern, I take a 'neoformalist' approach that focuses on the aspects of *mise en scène* most commonly debated by the censors, critics and filmgoers themselves. For these reasons, I make observations on the interrelation of narrative, visual and aural elements that operate to 'privilege' the lead actor in his role as a juvenile delinquent. In the case studies that follow, I assess how close-ups and blocking (where actors are positioned in relation to the camera), dialogue and music, lighting and costuming, and performance style – the method acting of Brando and Dean, and the 'natural' acting of Haley and Presley – produce and enhance screen charisma.

Close-ups are particularly significant because they establish an intimacy between actors and audiences. In recognition of how screen and stage acting (and stardom) differ, Alexander Walker describes the potency of the cinematic close-up as 'isolating' and 'concentrating' a player's personality and looks, which, therefore, offers audiences a glimpse of his uniqueness.[12] Similarly, V. F. Perkins attributes a voyeuristic aspect to the close-up that overcame the usual embarrassment and respectability of post-war life: 'We can stare at screen characters, invade their most private actions and reactions, with an openness and persistence which decency forbids us to extend to the couple in the next row.'[13] Lastly, in providing a material dimension to *mise en scène*, I evaluate the wrangles for creative control between the British censor and the Hollywood studios – which resulted in multiple deletions, overdubbing and other modifications – that 'imposed' a British standard on each case study film, and produced its distinctive visual and aural qualities.

Determining agency and process in film production requires a careful examination of a broad range of primary sources. Unlike contemporary films, which are widely debated, critiqued and informally reviewed on social media, recovering cinema's 'lost audiences' requires robust archival methods. Sarah Street, who has examined British cinema, usefully frames her historical research around specific concerns. Street asks questions on the *type* of document it is (a diary, a memoir, a statistical survey, a governmental report, a poster or other ephemera), its authorship and agency; and where the document ranks in an archival scheme.[14] By focusing on the British reception of these classic Hollywood films, there exists the immediate challenges of transposing American film texts to British cinema culture. My evaluation has, of necessity, negotiated two (often opposing) sets of social and cultural documents from the home culture (America – as represented by Hollywood) and the host culture (Britain). Richard Maltby surmises that the 'semantic complexity' of a film or other artefact of popular culture is 'lost' when exported to a host culture.[15] According to Maltby, the transcultural 'exchange' of an artefact is first characterised by an oversimplification of its uses or value and a reinterpretation according to the new 'cultural matrix' before it is subsumed into the host culture. Similarly, this study critiques the relatively fixed notions of US and British culture of the period by investigating the meanings these rebel films generated in Britain and exploring how they were subsumed into British youth culture. As discussed in Chapter 5, British teenagers created their own home-grown 'rebels' in the careers of Tommy Steele and Billy Fury, who were refashioned around aspects of Hollywood's delinquents but looked and sounded like the 'boy next door'.

The Hollywood films concerned with juvenile delinquency have an enduring legacy, largely because the screen rebels were played by iconic stars relevant to young audiences. Thomas Doherty argues that American films became increasingly 'juvenilized' in the late 1950s because teenage themes and tropes became commercially viable and popular with this demographic.[16] Similarly, Amanda Klein locates the rebel films in an American film cycle responsive to contemporary social issues in the USA.[17] In more recent years, the production histories of *Rebel Without a Cause* and the legacy of James Dean's emblematic portrayal of teenage angst have been of scholarly interest as subsequent generations of filmmakers assimilate and reimagine the trope.[18] One film historian encourages teachers to use *Rebel* to contextualise American courtship in the mid-1950s.[19]

This book aims to contribute to our understanding of transnational reception studies, which is a new and exciting field of inquiry that unpacks films and renegotiates parameters of stardom and fandom. In his analysis of the British 'pop' film, Andrew Caine examines the vicissitudes of journalistic reaction to Elvis Presley and, in so doing, uncovers the burgeoning rivalry that existed between the established music magazine *Melody Maker* and the fledgling *New Musical Express*.[20] Mark Glancy's account of Hollywood and the Americanisation of Britain includes a reception study of *Grease* (Randall Kleiser, 1978) that demonstrates that key elements of the 1950s rebel films were reimagined as 'high camp' to promote the film to British audiences in the 1970s.[21]

In my investigation of how key films were consumed by historical audiences and how publicity set up audience expectations, primary arguments are not developed around quantitative data. Nonetheless, scholarly work in this field has been instructive. For example, Annette Kuhn (2002), conducted an oral history with British cinemagoers of the 1930s, and argues that viewing contexts – dingy 'fleapits' or picture palaces – affected the audience's responses to films as well as the film narrative.[22] In what has long been considered an essential study in fandom, Jackie Stacey's work on British fan behaviours in relation to their favourite Hollywood star was based on the data she collated from detailed questionnaires and personal commentaries.[23] Significantly, both these studies challenge previous theories about gullible and impressionable (generally female) film fans 'duped' by the artifice of the Hollywood star system. In challenging these notions, this book revitalises the discourses around American stars of the 1950s and demonstrates the agency of younger British fans. For example, teenage boys and girls were proactive in setting up their own unofficial Elvis Presley fan clubs across the country.

Direct interaction between audiences and films during screenings has generally gone unrecorded. The new film historians have demonstrated that 'lost' responses may be recovered through fan letters, polls and surveys, memoirs, and promotional materials in the trade press and in studio pressbooks. Pressbooks were compiled to serve commercial interests for film industry personnel, but they also offer an invaluable glimpse into how studios anticipated and set up audience expectations of stars and genre. Additionally, I utilise informal correspondence held in the BBFC archives that record a film examiner's experience of watching a film with the paying public. In such cases, one of the censors would attend a screening with family or friends to gauge public reaction to a particular film and verify whether any deletions – in a time of celluloid – had been noticed. These handwritten correspondences have proved illuminating for encapsulating immediate responses from audiences in 'direct' contact with the principal films; they also offer impromptu opinions from the censors. Significantly, these 'examiner notes' validate or dismantle first suspicions about films and demonstrate the variance between cinemagoers merely a few London boroughs apart. Where written accounts require supplementary material or do not exist, televised interviews and transcripts may provide missing information and contribute impressionistic accounts of films and film stars. Broadcast interviews have been particularly useful in my research on Elvis Presley's career, where well-known British performers share their early admiration for the singer with an unprecedented candour incongruent to the prohibitive climate of the 1950s.

Disagreement among film historians demonstrates the different approaches and some of the challenges to current reception methodology. Eric Smoodin, for example, disregards critical reviews from his film histories for revealing more about individual critics and the generic conventions of criticism and less about actual audiences.[24] However, Andrew Spicer, in his study of 'typical' men in British cinema, infers that the 'interest, alarm or offence' expressed by film critics was the likeliest audience response.[25] Klinger and Staiger also validate journalistic commentary for performing an important 'taste-making' function and guiding audiences in 'how' – if not necessarily 'what' – to think when they evaluate films.[26]

When considering journalism as a sociological phenomenon, Pierre Bourdieu's work is instructive. The 'journalistic field', according to Bourdieu, dominates high and popular culture because of its de facto monopoly on the 'instruments' of production and diffusion of information. By these means, journalists, who do not produce art or cultural artefacts themselves, nevertheless control 'public expression'; they control how ordinary citizens access the media and, therefore, control how scholars, artists and writers – the veritable 'producers' of culture – access the 'public space' of mass circulation.[27] To apply Bourdieu's theories specifically to the film histories and star studies in this book is fruitful. To varying degrees, British journalists in the 1950s worked to 'control' how Hollywood films were consumed by British audiences whether through mild ridicule, by giving poor reviews or by making unfavourable comparisons to British films. By 'controlling' the means of public expression, journalists also exerted their influence on 'public existence' or rather, could determine which American actors or performers became stars in Britain.

The emergence of the teenage consumer by the mid-1950s required subtle renegotiation of this journalistic 'power'. Bill Haley, for example, was subjected to unflattering commentary until rock 'n' roll became popular with the royal family. Similarly, in the extraordinary circumstances that created James Dean's 'death cult', British journalists were obliged to accommodate the thousands of young fans, who wanted to participate, so that their publications remained relevant to an ever-growing teenage readership. Furthermore, by the end of the decade, British performers popular with teenagers were given unprecedented access to media platforms. Cliff Richard, for example, then a rising star who had left school to work in a factory, was given a weekly column in the prestigious *Picturegoer* magazine.

In this book, as for any reception study, breadth is paramount. I examine film reviews from both popular (metropolitan) daily papers and quality broadsheets to reconstitute a range of interpretations on specific films. In this study, to discount film reviews – a staple in every popular and quality newspaper – would be counterproductive at a time when readership was enormous. In the early 1950s, daily newspapers in Britain were affordable to all and their circulation was higher – relative to population – than that of any other country.[28]

The validity of fan materials as primary sources has also divided opinion. While Staiger and Klinger attribute a 'taste-making' function to professional film critics, they eschew fan literature as a reflection of editorial policy rather than of actual filmgoers' responses. By way of contrast, Anthony Slide's historical overview of American fan magazines regards these as the 'arbiter' of 'taste' within the wider discourses of journalism and popular culture.[29]

Fortunately, Slide's frustrations of incomplete or missing editions of fan magazines did not hamper this project. The British Library and the British Film Institute Reuben Library hold complete collections of a range of fan publications, such as *Picturegoer*, *Films in Review*, *Photoplay* and *Picture Show.* In particular, *Picturegoer* has been an invaluable source in recovering fan responses for the period because it was Britain's most popular weekly fan publication throughout the decade. Between July and December 1950, *Picturegoer* subscriptions peaked at 548,329, stayed well above 400,000 until mid-1957, and only showed evidence of decline in 1959 when subscriptions dipped below 300,000.[30] An appraisal of a variety of fan materials, such as readers' letters, audience surveys and questionnaires, vox pops and popularity polls, maps out the range of meanings and pleasures British cinemagoers took from Hollywood films.

Fan materials can also be utilised to reconstruct a public persona. For example, Tamar Jeffers McDonald has reconstructed Doris Day's stardom from fan publications, and argues that these materials do more than promote films in the run-up to new releases; they maintain the intimacy of the star–fan relationship.[31] In like manner, Lucy Fischer and Marcia Landy assert that audiences are interested in the 'star text' – an amalgamation of a star's on- and off-screen life – and place high importance on 'gossip' columns in fan magazines.[32] In fact, scandalmongering, characteristic of the tabloid journalism popularised in exposé magazines such as *Confidential* (1952–78), also featured in British fan journalism, albeit in milder form and, therefore, has a place in historical stardom. Hollywood scandal is also an indicator of wider social concerns, as argued by Adrienne L. Mclean, because it challenges notions of acceptable and conventional public/private behaviour, confronts proper/immoral conduct and (re)defines gender, family relationships and film art.[33] For these reasons, I consider the frequency of a star's appearance in the film fan magazines; how he compared to his contemporaries; and which of the 'key interests' (or 'gossip') concerned journalists and titillated readers. For example, Brando's early career was marked by the media's lascivious interest in his dating history and a fascination with his refusal to get married at a time when such individualism appeared transgressive.

Stardom of the Hollywood rebels

The book focuses on how specific American stars were received in Britain. To recover the stardom of these leading men, a wide appraisal of primary sources including but not limited to popularity polls, social surveys, publicity materials, film reviews, popular fan magazines, and memoirs can reconstruct the 'star text'. Looking historically at stars inevitably intersects with star studies since an understanding of how iconic personalities function in wider society requires a workable model of inquiry. A number of film scholars have developed theories around fan consumption of star identities that prove useful here. Edgar Morin's early study is a good starting point for thinking about stars of the post-war period.[34] Morin distinguishes between the 'apotheoses' of actors of the classical Hollywood period and method actors such as Brando and Dean, whose good/bad and ideal/everyday binaries and 'anti-star' behaviours 'humanised' stardom for later audiences.[35] More recently, Richard Dyer and Paul McDonald have developed Morin's work by arguing for the economic functions stars fulfil in selling their films (representing capital, investment and outlay) and endorsing a range of other commodities.[36] Indeed, this book argues that the rise of teenage consumerism in post-war Britain was largely responsible for the sustained popularity of the 'rebel' stars. For example, Elvis Presley's persona – offensive to parental authority – was lucratively branded and marketed to his enormous teenage fan base and could potentially 'sell' everything from pin-up portraits and records to the bunches of bananas that embellished one of his co-star's dance costumes.

In my detailed textual analyses of the case studies, I develop arguments on the interrelated aspects of *mise en scène* that create star 'charisma'. In unpicking these ideas further, Dyer's assertions on screen charisma as a cultural phenomenon prove useful: 'Stars matter because they act out aspects of life that matter to us; and performers get to be stars when what they act out matters to enough people.'[37] Dyer's argument is pertinent because it defines stardom as time-sensitive – a star is considered 'charismatic' for as long as he or she negotiates the tensions of social and cultural discourses. This does not mean that an obscure or less popular (former) star will not engage new audiences when they acquire new or different meanings. For example, Martin Shingler has used Staiger's historical-materialist approach to 'recover' Bette Davis's stardom around her role as Margo Channing in *All About Eve* (Joseph L. Mankiewicz, 1950) and demonstrates that it mobilised feminist readings in the 1950s and enjoyed a resurgence in the 1970s when it was reappropriated by gay audiences for its 'camp' qualities.[38] In Brando's case, the young method actor came to the attention of Hollywood producers because of his extraordinary effect on theatre audiences during the two years he played Stanley Kowalski on Broadway. By all accounts, his acting was startlingly nuanced and unpredictable and, off-screen, his unorthodox behaviour appeared starkly oppositional to the mundane aspects of suburban living and corporate business. However, when *The Wild One* was eventually granted a certificate in 1968, it was because Brando's popularity – and 'charisma' – had dwindled to the extent that the British censors believed the film was no longer relevant to young audiences.

Stardom has been shown to be polysemic in structure in that it is developed and sustained by multiple media platforms. Paul McDonald, who integrates industry studies and star studies, challenges 'the charismatic theory' of enigmatic individuals and, therefore, brings additional points to bear upon the studying of film stars. McDonald argues that, although a gifted performer will bring his or her talent (their raw material) to a screen role, charisma is the 'industrialized cultural production' of a team of dedicated, but inconspicuous, personnel including screenwriters, lighting technicians, makeup artists, cameramen and publicists.[39] Thus, beyond any analyses of *mise en scène*, McDonald's industry focus informs my examination of promotional materials and publicity around stars. In 1947, Warner Brothers produced a screen test of a young Brando – then known only to his theatre audiences – which shows him performing a scene for *Rebel Without a Cause*, eight years before the film was actually produced with James Dean in the lead role. At this point of his career, Brando bears all the marks of a newcomer and appears relatively gauche and self-conscious before a movie camera.[40] Within a few years, Brando had benefited from the build-up of Hollywood's publicity machinery, and the professional experience gained in working closely with prestigious directors such as Elia Kazan and Joseph L. Mankiewicz, so that by the time *The Wild One* was debated and subsequently banned in Britain, the actor was regarded as one of Hollywood's most charismatic leading men.

If charisma may be understood as the product of this collective, industrialised output – partly conferred by *mise en scène* – types of masculinity specific to the period may be explored through close textual analysis of the key films. Cinema in the post-war period brought its own peculiar concerns in the representation of masculinities. After the social disruption of the Second World War, the return to civilian life for millions of servicemen meant that women were once again subsumed into the domestic sphere. At the same time, Freudian theories, originally confined to the treatment of traumatised servicemen, began to flourish and become familiar staples of American popular culture. Discourses around sexuality placed enormous emphasis on the 'sex element' both in choosing a suitable mate and throughout married love.[41] While gender roles were ostensibly reaffirmed, the Kinsey reports (on men, 1948 and on women, 1953) disclosed the high incidence of homosexual activity between men, and destabilised many preconceived notions of normal and deviant sexual practices. The social historian Beth L. Bailey observes that Kinsey's work reverberated through American society and gender binaries were no longer regarded as 'natural traits, proceeding casually, masculinity from maleness, femininity from femaleness, but as identities that must be acquired, earned and constantly demonstrated'.[42]

The 'crises' of femininity and masculinity that Bailey describes inevitably played out in the representation of gender in film. Entitling his book *Masked Men*, Steve Cohan argues for the performative aspects of masculinity characteristic of Hollywood films of the 1950s that worked to reaffirm heterosexuality and hegemony during a veritable 'national crisis' of 'American manhood'. The 'problem' of any such reaffirmation, as Cohan points out, is that when an actor is placed before the camera he is invariably positioned as 'spectacle' because he is validated for his good looks and body rather than for his 'impersonation of agency'.[43] Brando, Dean and Presley were among a younger cohort of actors that Cohan defines as 'boys who would not be men'; whose arrested development was founded upon their neurosis, ambivalence and strong homosocial attachments. Seemingly, this 'diminished' status of perpetual adolescence was an industrialised means of negotiating their obvious differences to the stalwart masculinity of mature 'men' like John Wayne and Gregory Peck.

Steve Neale's essay on the 'masculine spectacle' proves equally useful here. Neale subverts Laura Mulvey's essay on the gaze, 'Visual Pleasure and Narrative Cinema' (1975), to apply questions of 'identification, looking and spectacle' to cinematic images of men and male spectators.[44] I draw on Cohan's and Neale's work in the following chapters to evaluate images of masculinity offered by the rising generation of American actors. Against such considerations, my star studies demonstrate the antipathy of British censors and critics when confronted with Dean's unfamiliar performative emotionality, and Presley's overt display of sexuality expected of (and tolerated in) female stars. Interestingly, the unprepossessing Bill Haley was a star name but – as neither the juvenile delinquent nor the romantic lead – was generally not privileged by *mise en scène* to the same degree. Nor was he subjected to the sustained pillory of the British press.

Cinema has been described as 'an industry of desire' whose stars invite contradictory, multiple and shifting identification with audiences.[45] Maltby argues that a cultural history of cinema should account for both Hollywood's actual audiences and those discursively constructed by a movie's address.[46] There can be little doubt that Hollywood's rebel characters, with their self-governing philosophies and self-conscious style, motivated strong identification with gay and lesbian audiences. Indeed, the heteronormative conventions of Hollywood's rebel films are malleable and may be destabilised to fruitfully produce alternative readings. To this end, Graham McCann provides a queer perspective on *The Wild One* and *Rebel Without a Cause*, by reading 'against the grain' of the narrative, and sustains his arguments against Brando's and Dean's real-life bisexuality.

Drawing on the literary works of Charles Baudelaire and Albert Camus, McCann argues that Johnny Strabler (Brando) is a marginalised outsider, a dandy with mannered speech who merely affects the aesthetic pose of masculine bravado, and rejects Kathy not because he is a freewheeling rebel but because he is homosexual. By similar means, McCann argues that Jim Stark (Dean) is another confused and alienated outsider figure, whose personal struggle for self-identity is motivated by disdain for his parents 'arbitrary' gender roles.[47] Indeed, Jim Stark's friend Plato (Sal Mineo) has been credited as the silver screen's first 'openly' homosexual character, 'coded' by the pin-up of Alan Ladd he keeps in his locker. Further, under Nicholas Ray's direction, Plato's hero-worship of Jim continually blurs the homosocial-romantic attraction between them.

In his book on queer culture, Dyer historicises James Dean and Marlon Brando in gay iconography for respectively displaying the qualities of the boyish youth and the rugged muscleman so admired by underground homosexual groups.[48] In her work, *Imagining Masculinities* (2013), Katarzyna Kosmala demonstrates that visual art offers a space where the binaries of gender and sexual identities may be contested. Thus, lesbian academia has theorised that Dean's characterisation of Jim Stark is gender-fluid and argues that his striking physical appearance both informed and influenced the development of the urban American 'butch'.[49] While marginalised groups of the 1950s may have adapted filmic iconography for their own uses and pleasures, Claudia Springer contends that Cold War politics created a mistrustful social and cultural climate of rigid conformity that ultimately mainstreamed film production. The Hollywood studios and the American media appropriated oppositional subcultural forms – such as the biker gangs depicted in *The Wild One* – so long as such imagery and concepts were first stripped of their subversive power before their consumption by American teenagers. By these means, rather than viably offer audiences multiple identification and diversity, Brando's and Dean's bisexual histories were rebranded as virile heterosexuality and their cinematic 'rebellion' was muted in films with 'recuperative closures'.[50]

With my emphasis on representations of American masculinity, I am arguing for the pleasures these rebel stars offered British audiences which national stars were not yet able to fulfil or rather fully express. Notions of typical post-war 'Britishness' were developed and sustained across multiple media platforms (in film, TV and literature). In his overview of popular entertainments, Jeffrey Richards argues that the British Everyman displayed a mixture of good sportsmanship, tradition, sincerity and the proverbial ‘stiff upper lip’.[51] It is difficult to pinpoint when ‘Britishness’ became so indelibly associated with the stiff-upper-lip attitude recognisable to foreign audiences. Thomas Dixon argues that this emotional reserve was expected during the patriotic keep-calm-and-carry-on mentality of the Second World War, and diverted the British away from the highly celebrated emotionality that characterised earlier generations.[52] Similarly, the respondents in Geoffrey Gorer’s social study of English character (1955) used this reserve to safeguard their privacy and agency.[53] What I emphasise here, then, is that this self-sacrifice and emotional restraint, which came to characterise an older generation, was challenged by the exuberance of a new generation of post-war teenagers. Rather than actually be the unwitting victims of ‘Americanisation’, as some commentators claimed, the younger generation was often misunderstood (even demonised) for embracing aspects of American popular culture in anticipation of their own national heroes and teenage folklore.

As a comparative history, the book draws attention to British cinema commentary on juvenile delinquency. However, the neutrality of standard British film characters was disrupted by the Angry Young Man trope. The ‘Angry’ ethos gained momentum after John Osborne’s play, *Look Back in Anger* (1956) proved a critical success and generated a media sensation. Later adapted for the screen, the story focused on the character Jimmy Porter, a highly educated but frustrated working-class man. Porter’s anger is directed at the complacency of the upper classes and at his middle-class wife. Eventually, Porter’s feelings of alienation envelop him and he almost destroys his marriage by having an affair with his wife’s best friend. Following Osborne’s success, the ‘Angry’ term became media shorthand to describe a group of post-war working- and middle-class playwrights, artists and novelists who challenged deferential attitudes to the establishment.[54] The Angry Young Man appeared in the British New Wave cinema that flourished at the end of the 1950s and into the 1960s. Therefore, Hollywood’s rebel trope not only anticipated the Angry trope but was identifiably different and offered British audiences other pleasures. Hollywood romanticised its rebel characters; they were young and vulnerable, and unscarred by the Angry Man’s psychosexual problems. Realised by method actors, whose stuttering and mumbling sustained emotionally rich performances, the American trope also lacked the truculent verbosity of this newly defiant British male.

Historical contexts

Situating this reception study of Hollywood films in post-war Britain invariably confronts the discourses of Americanisation. In his historical analysis of the American jukebox in post-war Britain, Adrian Horn argues that defenders of 'high' culture – namely, the BBC, local magistrates and schools – were ideologically opposed to 'the creeping commercialism' of American mass-cultural techniques.[55] Underpinning these elitist concerns was the fear that the popularity of American mass media would render British traditions and culture unrecognisable; and the young and uneducated were considered particularly susceptible to its influences.[56]

Resistance to Americanisation has taken both explicit and implicit forms. Early objectors to American influences on the arts included the highly renowned novelist George Orwell and Frank and Q. D. Leavis, who criticised Hollywood films and American-style pulp fiction in a series of lectures and publications in the 1930s and 1940s.[57] Margaret Dickinson and Sarah Street have chronicled how foreign governments initiated protective legislation to protect their national cinemas and generate revenue for domestic film production.[58] In Britain, the Cinematograph Films Act of 1927 (modified in 1938 and repealed in 1960) was designed to stimulate investment in domestic production and eventually create a self-sustaining industry. In summary, this legislation stipulated that a proportion of films shown in cinemas should be British films, which qualified if they involved British film personnel or were shot in Britain or in the British dominions. In effect, the Act attempted to promote and emulate Hollywood's successful business model of vertical practice (that is, monopolising production, distribution and exhibition) among British studios, distributors and cinema chains.

In the 1950s, concerns about Americanisation inevitably focused on working-class teenagers. This demographic spent their considerably large disposable income on a range of mass media exports from the USA and were, therefore, seen to openly embrace aspects of

American culture. Richard Hoggart's book *The Uses of Literacy* (1957) challenged the mass-produced American-style fiction then popular with a younger British readership. While not directly aimed at the detrimental effects of Hollywood films, like his literary predecessors, Hoggart objected to the passivity and suggestibility of cinema's youngest audiences. He famously admonished the National Service recruits as 'juke-box boys' because they gathered in their local milk bar, posturing like surly American film stars, rather than participating in the more traditional leisure activities espoused by generations of working-class communities.[59]

Given this context, I explore how these particular Hollywood films about juvenile delinquency became a feature of the Americanisation discourses in Britain. As the most visible, prolific and popular form of exported American culture, Hollywood films were prominent in social debates on high and low art, mass media techniques and their effects on receptive audiences.[60] Pierre Bourdieu's theoretical work, *Distinction* (1984), extends our understanding of how sociocultural hierarchies are sustained. According to Bourdieu, the 'habitus' – one's disposition based on deeply ingrained beliefs, habits and tendencies – determines the cultural tastes of a particular social group. Furthermore, high and low art is differentiated by an elite group which has accumulated 'cultural capital' (that is, education) and, therefore, gains access to social and economic capital. In this way, conforming to particular taste patterns that distinguish between high and low art – the sublime and the vulgar – serves to 'classify the classifier' and maintain and legitimate social identity and class difference.[61] In essence, then, working-class groups might devise their own taste preferences but these define themselves in terms of the dominant aesthetics of the elite.[62]

To apply Bourdieu's concepts specifically to the post-war period, we can identify the elite groups that promoted hegemonic forms of high or respectable culture and opposed, for example, working-class tastes for rock 'n' roll (over jazz). Indeed, the British film censors fulfilled their mandate for moral guardianship and 'cultural education' when critiquing entertainment with direct appeal to the unsophisticated teenage consumer. Motivated by generational and class differences, the censors worked diligently to 'reduce' the imitability – invariably the 'gratuitous' appeal of American sex, violence and glamour – of our case studies. Similarly, the critics of *Sight and*

Sound hierarchised films according to their framework of 'credible' social realism and (method) acting to distinguish their taste palette from young working-class audiences and from critics reviewing films for the popular dailies. Again, Bourdieu's theories are instructive for observing that 'the journalistic field' is characterised by the 'various actors' who struggle for the domination, transformation and preservation of a domain.[63] In the 1950s, the cineaste critics used the 'power' at their disposal – their superior knowledge of film's formal and philosophical aspects – to elevate particular film genres and diminish other popular forms.

Method acting

Based on the innovative principles of the Russian actor Konstantin Stanislavski, by the end of the 1940s, the Method was regarded as an incontrovertibly American style of acting. The Group Theatre of New York had been developing its performance techniques since the 1930s and their work became the foundation for the Actors Studio, established in 1947, by Cheryl Crawford, Robert Lewis and Elia Kazan. As is well known, Marlon Brando and Elia Kazan collaborated professionally on a number of projects beginning with a celebrated Broadway production of Tennessee Williams' play, *A Streetcar Named Desire* (1947) with Brando in the lead role of Stanley Kowalski. When Kazan later adapted the play for the screen, Brando reprised his role as the rough-edged Polish-American car mechanic; and method acting became the benchmark for realistic screen performance.

Brando's implementation of the Method within specific performances has already been investigated.[64] This book emphasises how method acting polarised British responses because it was informed by psychoanalytical techniques not yet familiar (or widely endorsed) in Britain. Unpacking Brando's highly visceral performance style illustrates the marked differences between his acting and that of classical Hollywood and British theatrical traditions. Furthermore, the display of male vulnerability displaced precepts of (screen) masculinity and upset the delicate balance of British sensibilities and emotional restraint. Virginia Wexman argues that method acting created the Hollywood rebel trope and the type of star that came to the fore in the 1950s. According to Wexman, films fashioned around the neurosis and introspection of the method actor's personality promoted the idea that masculinity was in crisis and blurred the star's public and private persona.[65] As I show, method acting elicited a range of responses in the post-war era: it was largely censured by the British censors, revered by the majority of film critics – particularly those associated with specialist cinema journals – and reverberated with the younger cinemagoer.

The British Board of Film Censors

The British Board of Film Censors (BBFC) was founded by members of the film industry in 1912, primarily to ward off interference from local authorities. In 1917, the board began to operate according to a set of guidelines or 'concerns' known more generally as T. P. O'Connor's '43 Rules of the BBFC'. At this fractious time of war, the guidelines were partly motivated to uphold issues of national security. In 1926, these 'concerns' were reinstated, though not modernised, and became known as the Codified Grounds for Censorship. The Hollywood censors, known formally as the Production Code Administration (PCA), did not follow guidelines but rather enforced the Motion Picture Production Code (1934); a statutory code devised and enforced to protect commercial film interests. The Code came in response to the wave of hostility and lobbying from conservative and religious groups across the USA after a series of damaging scandals and the increasingly mature content of American films. Ostensibly, then, because the British censors were governed by a set of guidelines, rather than a statutory code, they were less restricted and emphasised their relative freedom in being able to evaluate a film on its individual merits.

Despite the flexibility proffered by O'Connor's guidelines, the British censors shared a highly conservative outlook. The President of the BBFC, Sidney Harris, was a Victorian, born in 1876; he and his secretaries, Arthur Watkins and his successor John Trevelyan, though self-professed cineastes, maintained professional and personal links to the Home Office.[66] Indeed, regardless of the status of the BBFC as a non-governmental agency, created for the protection of the film industry, the examiners reflected official policy on all matters.[67]

Protecting children from the 'false values' of Hollywood films about juvenile delinquency – the 'harmful effects' of sex and violence – was a recurring preoccupation. According to Maltby, foreign censors consistently foster these notions of superiority around their home culture and resurrect any practicable 'other' in need of their stringent protection.[68] Similarly, in his study of Hollywood's gangster genre, Ross McKibbin observes that British censors would tolerate controversial themes in domestic cinema but were predisposed to eliminate *American* sex, *American* violence and *American* politics from Hollywood films shown in Britain.[69]

In the 1950s, films were regulated through a classification system with some minor differences to current regulation. As for today, the 'U' (Universal) certificate conveyed a film's suitability for everyone. Closely aligned with the PG (Parental Guidance) category, the previous 'A' certificate relied on parental discretion but (unofficially) conveyed a film's 'unsuitability' for younger audiences. Further restrictions were imposed by stipulating that parents or a bona fide adult must accompany children to watch 'A' films. Given the passing trend for Hollywood's horror films, the X certificate, introduced in 1951, replaced the H (Horror) certificate, and was intended to protect children from the increasing sex and violence in American films. Negotiations between Hollywood studio executives and the British censors frequently debated the X certificate, which barred the under-16s rather than the under-18s. Producers disliked it not only for restricting their audiences but also because the major British cinema chains would not book X-certificate films. As individual chapters show, once the Hollywood studios had modified their films, they petitioned the British censors for an A certificate. However, there were additional complications and annoyances in granting an A certificate to a 'borderline' film: common knowledge that parental discretion was rarely exercised dissuaded the censors from reclassifying such films.

When the board faced the challenge of Hollywood's rebel films of the 1950s, other marked differences became apparent, given the differing ideologies of the respective censor boards. The PCA was under enormous pressure from the powerful lobbying of the Catholic League of Decency (established in 1933), which scrutinised and proscribed the sexual content of American films. The BBFC's main concern was screen violence: was it sensationalised and 'exploitative' and, therefore, likely to be imitated? Inevitably, these stipulations worked against the case study films, which aimed to explore the pertinent themes of juvenile delinquency with veracity. As a result, British audiences of the 1950s only ever saw scrupulously modified versions of these American films.

Teddy boys and teenage consumers

Working-class Teddy boys – or Edwardians as they were first called – became central to the British film censors' concerns. A survey of the wider discourses on youth (and youth subculture) has demonstrated why the term 'Teddy boy' became synonymous with 'juvenile delinquent' and the ways in which they were 'scapegoated' for Britain's social decline in the 1950s.[70] Indeed, revisionist post-war historians such as Selina Todd, Hilary Young and Nick Thomas have shown that negative stereotypes of affluent teenagers originated in the media, and find evidence of intergenerational cooperation between working-class parents and children.[71]

However, the dislocation of the Second World War had wrought many changes: the rising generation and juvenile delinquency had become a matter of topical and urgent debate. In the USA, the Senate Subcommittee on Juvenile Delinquency (1953) was established; in Britain, social research debated the juvenile delinquency 'syndrome' as a delayed consequence of childhood neglect in the war years.[72] Between the 1930s and the mid-1950s, crimes against the person rose by 6 per cent every year and by 11 per cent thereafter, with the sharpest incline in the 17–21 and 14–17 age groups.[73] The notorious clash on 24 April 1954 involving fifty young men at St Mary Cray station in Kent was much publicised and characterised the 'Teddy boy' as a social problem. The *Orpington & Kentish Times* headline summarises the details of the incident: 'Gang battle at railway station: Edwardian Youths in half-hour fight: Wooden stakes, sand-filled socks as weapons'. As well as describing their improvised weaponry, local and national press brought attention to the battlers' Edwardian suits with velveteen collars and drainpipe trousers. Throughout the mid-1950s, the press frequently covered local gang fights, scuffles and disturbances between Teddy groups with the result that they became synonymous with immorality and reckless violence. Cinemas, amusement arcades, dance halls and cafes similarly became 'menacing' public spaces because they attracted young people and offered them opportunities to loiter. The demoralising influences of popular amusements on adolescent mischief have an older history: the Teddy boys were the successors of earlier expressions of teenage rebellion and exuberance.[74]

Scholars of the Centre for Contemporary Cultural Studies were among the first to evaluate Teddy subculture. Richard Hoggart became the centre's first director when it was founded at the University of Birmingham in 1964. One topic of concern was how rapid post-war redevelopment and rehousing projects in urban areas had dismantled working-class communities. Phil Cohen, for example, argues that high-rise schemes in London's East End isolated the nuclear family, removing the essential extended family ties and 'articulated communal spaces' – such as the local corner shop and pub – that had 'informally regulated' the wider community. In addition, Cohen asserts that post-war economic recovery benefited skilled workers in the high growth sectors of the new advanced technology but deprived early school leavers, who would once have joined their fathers in a smaller specialist trade, of all but intermittent and mundane work in the service industries.[75] Indeed, T. R. Fyvel's study of juvenile offenders (1963) considers Teddy boys to have been largely recruited from the unskilled workforce who were excluded from a post-war process of embourgeoisement through longer education and securing a regular income.[76]

Part of the Teddy boy's visibility was his garish appearance and accumulation of possessions, which contrasted sharply to his lowly social status and Britain's continuing austerity. Harry Hopkins, a contemporary historian, describes Teddy fashion as the 'defiant uniform' that unified gangs and distinguished Teds from other teenagers.[77] In other words, this embellishment of Edwardian dress could be regarded as both a subversion of post-war rationing (abolished in 1954) and as a misappropriation of the foppish, aristocratic male persona. More recently, British cultural scholars have recognised that American-style fashion choices became sartorial codes of 'cultural resistance' adopted by working-class youths in search of identity and kinship. Dick Hebdige describes the expensive, exaggerated style of the Teddy boys as an antidote to 'the drab routines of school, the job and home'.[78] Similarly, Tony Jefferson regards the Teddy boys' extravagant attire, their camaraderie and territorial attitudes as their 'attempt to defend, symbolically, a constantly threatened space and a declining status'.[79]

Part of this disenfranchised status found expression in racially motivated attacks against immigrants. 'The hard-core Teds were frightening and horrible', recalled the jazz musician George Melly, observing a new kind of criminality amongst them that was 'neither obligatory nor even necessary'.[80] In North London, Teddy boys frequently vandalised Greek-Cypriot-owned cafes and attacked small business owners. In August 1958, clashes between white Teddy boys and black residents erupted in St Ann's in Nottingham, an area already notorious for racial name-calling and the vandalism of private homes. Apparently sparked by growing prejudice to inter-racial relationships, the St Ann's riots attracted hundreds of white 'sightseers' who wanted to witness the trouble for themselves.

Following these incidents in St Ann's, the local and national press warned that similar outbreaks of violence would likely follow in West London because it was another hotbed of racial tension. In fact, Oswald Mosley's Union Movement and Colin Jordan's White Defence League enjoyed popular support for their 'keep Britain white' campaigns in this economically deprived area. 'Kensington has a colour problem whether you care to admit it or not', observed one reporter, and explained, 'it must exist where people of greatly differing outlook, emotions and appearances are living side by side'.[81] Despite the advice offered by local magistrates, there was no increase in police presence in the Notting Hill area. On 24 August, nine white Teddy boys filled the boot of their car with homemade weaponry, and drove through the Kensington area seeking out unaccompanied black residents to attack. Violent racial clashes continued for several days until police reinforcements moved in to restore order. British Pathé news denounced the riots as a 'shameful episode' and narrator Bob Danvers-Walker called for level-headedness: 'Opinions differ about Britain's racial problems but the mentality which tries to solve them with coshes and broken railings has no place in the British way of life.'

Significantly, official commentary on the Notting Hill riots laid emphasis on an uneducated 'British hooligan class' rather than attending to the root causes of racism.[82] According to eyewitness testimonies, Teddy boys were the main instigators of the Notting

Hill violence, but they were spurred on by middle-class political agitators and by complacent police, who harboured their own racial prejudices. Furthermore, hordes of white onlookers amassed wherever the attacks took place.[83] To have wholly accepted that Britain had a 'colour problem' would arguably have aligned the country with the segregationist policies of the Southern United States and South Africa. In September 1958, when the teenage culprits of the first Notting Hill disturbances were brought to trial at the Old Bailey they were given heavy fines and unprecedented four-year sentences – presumably to deter other hooligans or, rather, as the media termed it, to 'de-teddify' them. In his final summation, Mr Justice Salmon delivered an emotive and condemnatory sentence:

> It was you men who started the whole of this violence in Notting Hill. You are a minute and insignificant section of the population but you have brought shame on the district in which you live and have filled the whole nation with horror, indignation, and disgust.[84]

The exemplary harsh sentencing made front page news across the country, usefully exposing the organised gang mentality behind the brutal attacks. However, because it confined the disturbances to a select few thugs, it failed to address the underlying causes of racial tension. Indeed, racism remained an ugly feature of Teddy boy subculture: in May 1959, another gang of white youths – never named or brought to justice – attacked and killed Kelso Cochrane, an Antiguan-born carpenter, in London's Paddington area.

Two high-profile murder cases were directly referenced by the British censors in their evaluation of the Hollywood rebel films. These incidents indelibly positioned the Teddy boys as the impressionable 'other' in their heavy-handed censorship of contemporary films. In November 1952, the notorious murder of PC Sidney Miles involving the 19-year-old Derek Bentley and the 16-year-old Christopher Craig realised an older generation's worst fears about an increasingly disaffected, irresponsible youth. PC Miles was 42 years old, married with a young family, and had gained recognition for his service in the Royal Army Medical Corps. He was shot dead by Craig when he intervened during the teenagers' botched robbery of a Croydon warehouse but, as is well known, it was the older Bentley who was eventually hanged for his involvement in the crime. Replete with schoolboy camaraderie, the iconography of Hollywood gangsters, and a grave miscarriage of justice, the sordid Craig–Bentley case later inspired the film *Let Him Have It* (Peter Medak, 1991). During Craig's trial, the media forged a portrait of a schoolboy murderer that resonated with the BBFC's gravest doubts about showing films that sensationalised violence to 'impressionable youngsters'. During his trial, Craig was described as a gun-obsessed low achiever, whose illiteracy led to an all-too-frequent cinemagoing habit and a 'desperado complex' among his peers. '[Craig's] education was the synthetic lore of the American gangster film,' commented a *Daily Mail* journalist, 'his heroes were the desperate characters of the cheap comic strip'.[85] Across the nation's front pages, experts and commentators attempted to understand the teenagers' motives while making observations on the garish sports jackets and pleated trousers – the emergent Teddy boy 'look' – favoured by both defendants. The second highly publicised crime involving Teddy boys was the 'Clapham Common Murder' of July 1953. The victim was 17-year-old John Beckley, who had insulted the appearance of another teenager from a rival gang of Teddy boys. Having made a casual but offensive remark, the outnumbered Beckley was hotly pursued by the gang before being dragged from a bus and fatally stabbed in full view of bystanders, who did nothing to intervene. The Clapham murder, mentioned by name in the BBFC files, did much harm: it conflated South London gangs, Teddy boy regalia and indiscriminate violence in the public imagination.

High-profile crimes were few in reality but the media's focus on minor affrays and anti-social behaviour between competing gangs perpetuated what soon became known as 'the Teddy boy problem'. Resolving this prominent social issue polarised public opinion. On the one hand, staunch conservatives supported longer National Service, stringent corporal punishments, and naming (and 'shaming') the families of Teddy boys and girls in the press. Lord Goddard, a former Lord Chief Justice, for example, believed that media attention was glamorising the petty criminal and proposed the reintroduction of more traditional methods. 'I think it is an awful pity that the stocks cannot be used for the Teddy boy, whom nothing cures as quickly as ridicule', Goddard told the Somerset and Bath Association of Magistrates.[86]

Throughout the 1950s, regular cinemagoing remained a favourite pastime for most teenagers while their parents and married friends preferred staying in to watch TV, a medium that had gained new respectability after Queen Elizabeth II's coronation was televised live on 2 June 1953. As this book shows, the BBFC were pessimistic about the average Teddy boy in the cinema audience and, in their prescriptive 'nanny' role, restricted viewing pleasures by desensationalising contemporary themes in Hollywood films. This pessimism, however, was not theirs alone and can be further explained by the wider discourses on youth. UNESCO felt compelled to draw on the expert opinion of hundreds of academics from around the world to examine how children and adolescents were affected by their 'persistent' liking for cinema because 'great and growing importance is attached to the problem of film and youth'.[87] Similarly, government reports, sociological studies, health education literature and Conservative Party pamphlets cohere to a negative view of the post-war teenager overall. Such literature demonstrates that the rise in juvenile offences was believed to be the result of the affluence, materialism and social permissiveness encouraged by the welfare state and sustained by ineffectual parenting.[88] Indeed, respondents in Gorer's social survey of the mid-1950s cited a lack of parental discipline as the primary reason for the increase in juvenile delinquency.[89]

Alongside this officious commentary, alternative views of Teddy boys and girls began to proliferate in a series of friendlier editorials in popular news magazines, such as *Picture Post*, and newspapers favoured by teenagers, such as *Daily Mirror*. Liberal and progressive groups, recognising that teenagers were naturally exuberant rather than collectively intent on misbehaviour, suggested that routine and structure would deter 'potential' juvenile delinquents. As such, local youth clubs were formed to provide diversional, largely homosocial, after-school recreation. In fact, the Albemarle Report (1960) legitimised such initiatives in its recommendations for a range of extra-circular activities under the supervision of specialist social and health care professionals. Those who came into regular contact with young people, such as vicars and youth workers, realised that adopting Teddy fashion was for some teenagers a statement of personal style rather than a declaration of maleficence.

We Are the Lambeth Boys (Karel Reisz, 1958), produced by the Free Cinema group of filmmakers, offered a sympathetic portrait of the Teddy boys and girls who frequented a South London youth club.

They were shown to be a raucous but friendly group who valued one another and shared common interests in fashion, cinemagoing and dancing. In Birmingham, an inner-city youth leader, a local Teddy boy and a prominent Quaker petitioned for greater tolerance and less victimisation of Teds. These aims were formalised in a proposed National Association of Teddy boys (NATB) with a charter, advertised in the following way: 'Calling all Teds! Are you fed up with being criticised? Are you tired of being called hooligans when the majority of you are decent working lads?' The main objectives of the charter aimed to establish recreational youth centres 'for Teddy boys run by Teddy boys' and renounce misbehaviour and hooliganism among their members.[90]

Throughout this book, there is greater emphasis on Teddy boys rather than girls, which is the inevitable outcome of research rather than a conscious decision to marginalise the feminine aspect of Teddy culture. Teddy girls were involved in petty crime such as theft and minor disturbances rather than the serious crimes involving young men. As Louise Jackson argues in *Policing Youth*, girls were most likely reprimanded through the informal sanctions of school, or by their parents, for their involvement in low-level aggressive behaviour.[91] Teddy boys, invariably, attracted more mainstream interest than Teddy girls for reasons already outlined. Nonetheless, Amy Helen Bell, who has used photos to examine Teddy fashion, argues that Teddy girls consciously adopted a bold Neo-Edwardian style to achieve their own 'androgynous, improvised and customised' look.[92] Fortunately, Ken Russell produced a unique photographic essay, 'The last of the Teddy girls' (*Picture Post*, 4 June 1955) when he was forging a reputation as a freelance photographer. This series of photos shows a group of stylish teenage girls posed against the post-Blitz rubble of London's East End and testifies to the feminine participation in Ted culture. Russell recognised his contribution when he recalled that '[n]o one paid much attention to the Teddy girls before I did them, though there was plenty on Teddy boys', adding that he found the girls to be 'proud. They knew their worth. They just wore what they wore.'[93]

The lingering mythology around teenagers of the 1950s has given them an unrivalled prominence in the public imaginary. Dominic Sandbrook offers a pragmatic explanation for the increased attention focused on post-war teenagers. According to Sandbrook, these wartime 'baby boomers' were simply greater in number, conspicuous because they were concentrated in new towns and suburban developments, and remained in education longer than their predecessors.[94] Larger numbers of teenagers inevitably resulted in greater spending 'power'. In 1959, the economist Mark Abrams' *The Teenage Consumer* was the first comprehensive study of teenage spending in Britain.[95] Abrams' calculations for mid-1958 revealed that the teenage wage earner was drawing approximately 8½ per cent of all personal income in Britain, which showed that teenage spending had doubled to £900 million since 1939.[96] Subsequent post-war histories and sociological studies have challenged aspects of Abrams' work. David Fowler, for example, argues that teenage consumerism was already strong before the Second World War.[97] Other historians consider Abrams' definition of a teenager as anyone unmarried and aged between 14 and 24 too 'vague'; and Pearl Jephcott's study of teenage spending in Scotland demonstrates the bias of his figures toward male teenagers in London and the southeast.[98]

This book is more concerned with the type of teenage spending that showed marked growth and for this reason Abrams work is valuable. Over 60 per cent of British teenagers were found to visit the cinema at least once a week as opposed to 13 per cent for the rest of the population; and boys had as much as £5 (girls somewhat less) for discretionary spending on leisure products such as films, magazines and records.[99] Of equal importance, approximately 90 per cent of all teenage spending was conditioned by working-class tastes since middle-class teenagers were still in school or in college.[100] These are significant findings when evaluating the special position of cinema culture within the lives of young working people and examining the oppositional attitudes of educated elites to this newly powerful teenage demographic.

In effect, teenage spending favoured consumables and leisure that gave immediate pleasure but had little lasting value. This book argues for the consumer power of the working-class teenager in sustaining the popularity of the American stars under discussion. The emergence of this hedonistic, predominantly working-class, teenage consumer was celebrated in a number of contemporaneous novels and essays. Peter Laurie considered this social transformation to be a rudimentary, but perceptible, nationwide teenage 'revolution'. According to Laurie, the rising generation were better educated, earned higher salaries and could grasp the mass media. These young people, then, were finally able to abandon the insular and bleak 'I'm alright, Jack' mentality of a highly suspicious older generation.[101] Colin MacInnes, whose observational writings richly capture this transformative teenage mood, argues for the enormous influence of young working-class consumers on the direction of popular culture. 'Youth has money, and teen-agers [*sic*] have become a power', MacInnes contended.[102]

Throughout the book, I raise questions about the new meanings these Hollywood films acquired in Britain, as the secondary host culture. To explain the stringency of British censorship, I ask questions about negative attitudes to the USA in general. In its comparative function, the book contrasts British cinema's treatment of juvenile delinquency with Hollywood's rebel films. As a British reception study of American films, this book widens the context of extra-cinematic culture by examining how several emblematic Hollywood icons influenced British popular culture.

Notes

1 'Priceless', MasterCard 2009.

2 The BBFC's refusal to grant the film a certificate was commonly referred to as a 'ban' in the British media. In effect, their action 'barred' the film from general release and local authorities were required to override this decision to have the film shown in their boroughs.

3 For all case studies, I quote the year of US film production rather than the date of the film's release in Britain.

4 Marlon Brando's son Christian was charged with manslaughter after he accidentally shot and killed his half-sister Cheyenne's boyfriend at his father's home in Beverly Hills. Marlon Brando's court appearance in his son's defence marked the end of a long reclusive period. The media focused on Brando's morbid obesity and the salacious details of his unorthodox polyamory.

5 Donald Spoto, *Rebel: The Life and Legend of James Dean* (New York: Cooper Square Press, 2000), and Peter L. Winkler (ed.), *The Real James Dean: Intimate Memories From Those who Knew Him Best* (Chicago: Chicago Review Press, 2016). Earlier biographies include David Dalton, *James Dean: The Mutant King* (Chicago: Chicago News Press, 1983) and *James Dean: Rebel Life* (London: Plexus, 1985).

6 *The King* (Eugene Jarecki, 2017) and *Elvis: The Searcher* (Thom Zimny, 2018) are two such documentaries that have re-examined Presley's musical heritage as a metaphor for the American Dream.
7 Janet Staiger, *Interpreting Films: Studies in the Historical Reception of American Cinema* (Princeton, NJ: Princeton University, 1992), p. 8. Barbara Klinger, *Melodrama and Meaning: History, Culture and the Films of Douglas Sirk* (Bloomington: Indiana University Press, 1994).
8 Barbara Klinger, 'Film history terminable and interminable: recovering the past in reception studies', *Screen*, 38:2 (1997), pp. 107–28.
9 James Chapman, Mark Glancy and Sue Harper (eds), *New Film History: Sources, Methods, Approaches* (London: Palgrave Macmillan, 2007), pp. 1–11.
10 Thomas Elsaesser, 'The new film history', *Sight and Sound*, 55:4 (Autumn 1986), pp. 246–51.
11 James Walters and Tom Brown (eds), *Film Moments: Criticism, History and Theory* (London: Bloomsbury Academic, 2010); Douglas Pye and John Gibbs (eds), *Film Style and Meaning: Detailed Studies in the Analysis of Film* (Manchester: Manchester University Press, 2005); John Gibbs, *Mise-en-scène: Film Style and Interpretation* (London and New York: Wallflower, 2002).
12 Alexander Walker, *Stardom: The Hollywood Phenomenon* (Harmondsworth: Penguin, 1974), p. 5.
13 V. F. Perkins, *Film as Film: Understanding and Judging Movies* (London: BFI, 1975), p. 72.
14 Sarah Street, *British Cinema in Documents* (London: Routledge, 2000), pp. 6–9.
15 Richard Maltby, 'Introduction', in Richard Maltby and Melvyn Stokes, *Hollywood Abroad: Audiences and Cultural Exchange* (London: BFI, 2004), p. 2.
16 Thomas Doherty, *Teenagers and Teenpics: The Juvenilization of American Movies in the 1950s* (Philadelphia: Temple University Press, 2002).
17 Amanda Klein, *American Film Cycles: Reframing Genres, Screening Social Problems and Defining Subcultures* (Austin, TX: University of Texas Press, 2011).
18 J. David Slocum, *Rebel Without a Cause: Approaches to a Maverick Masterwork* (Albany, NY: State University of New York Press, 2005); Claudia Springer, *James Dean Transfigured: The Many Faces of Rebel Iconography* (Austin, TX: The University of Texas Press, 2007).
19 Michael Lewis Goldberg, 'Rebel without a cause: using film to teach about dating in the 1950s', *OAH Magazine of History*, 18:4 (2004), pp. 38–42.

20 Andrew Caine, *Interpreting Rock Movies: The Pop Film and its Critics in Britain* (Manchester: Manchester University Press, 2004).
21 Mark Glancy, 'The sixth-form was never like this: *Grease* (1978) and the American 1950s', in *Hollywood and the Americanization of Britain: From the 1920s to the Present* (London: I. B. Tauris, 2014), pp. 215–45.
22 Annette Kuhn, *An Everyday Magic: Cinema and Cultural Memory* (London and New York: I. B. Taurus, 2002).
23 Jackie Stacey, *Star Gazing: Hollywood Cinema and Female Spectatorship* (London: Routledge, 1993).
24 Eric Smoodin, '"Compulsory" viewing for every citizen: "Mr Smith" and the rhetoric of reception', *Cinema Journal*, 35:2 (Winter, 1996), pp. 3–23.
25 Andrew Spicer, *Typical Men: The Representation of Masculinity in Popular British Cinema* (London: I. B. Tauris, 2001), p. 3.
26 Staiger, *Interpreting Films*.
27 Pierre Bourdieu, *On Television and Journalism*, trans. Priscilla Parkhurst Ferguson (London: Pluto Press, 1998), p. 46.
28 Arthur Marwick, *British Society Since 1945* (Harmondsworth: Penguin, 1982), p. 169.
29 Anthony Slide, *Inside the Hollywood Fan Magazine: A History of Star Makers, Fabricator and Gossip Mongers* (Jackson, MS: University Press of Mississippi, 2010), pp. 9–10.
30 Circulation figures courtesy of Mark Glancy and the Audit Bureau of Circulations.
31 Tamar Jeffers McDonald, *Doris Day Confidential: Hollywood, Sex and Stardom* (London: I. B. Tauris, 2013), p. 36, 133–4.
32 Lucy Fischer and Marcia Landy (eds), *Stars: The Film Reader* (New York and London: Routledge, 2004), p. 4.
33 Adrienne L. McLean in Adrienne L. McLean and David A. Cook (eds), *Headline Hollywood: A Century of Film Scandal* (New Brunswick, NJ: Rutgers University Press, 2001), p. 5.
34 Edgar Morin, *The Stars* (New York: Grove Press, 1960).
35 *Ibid.*, pp. 14, 19, 99 and 109.
36 Richard Dyer, *Stars* (London: BFI, 1979), especially pp. 10–11 and *Heavenly Bodies: Film Stars and Society* (Basingstoke and London: Macmillan Education Ltd, 1987); Paul McDonald, *Hollywood Stardom* (Chichester: Wiley-Blackwell, 2013) and *The Star System: Hollywood's Production of Popular Identities* (London: Wallflower Press, 2000).
37 Dyer, *Heavenly Bodies*, p. 19.
38 Martin Shingler, 'Interpreting *All About Eve:* a study in historical reception', in Melvyn Stokes and Richard Maltby (eds), *Hollywood*

Spectatorship: Changing Perceptions of Cinema Audiences (London: BFI, 2001), pp. 46–62.

39 Paul McDonald, *Hollywood Stardom* (Chichester: Wiley-Blackwell, 2013), pp. 13–14.

40 The screen test may be viewed at: www.youtube.com/watch?v=j2lRdkNGDcY (last accessed 11 March 2020).

41 Jeffrey Weeks, *Sex, Politics and Society: The Regulation of Sexuality Since 1800* (New York: Longman Group Ltd, 1981), p. 210.

42 Beth L. Bailey, *From Front Porch to Back Seat: Courtship in Twentieth Century America* (Baltimore and London: The Johns Hopkins Library, 1988), p. 98.

43 Steve Cohan, *Masked Men: Masculinity and the Movies of the Fifties* (Bloomington and Indianapolis: Indiana University Press, 1997), xvi.

44 Steve Neale, 'Masculinity as spectacle: Reflections on men and mainstream cinema', in Ina-Rae Clark and Steve Neale, *Screening the Male: Exploring Masculinity in Hollywood Cinema* (Oxford: Routledge, 1993), pp. 9–22.

45 Christine Gledhill (ed.), *Stardom: Industry of Desire* (London and New York: Routledge, 1991), p. xi.

46 Melvyn Stokes and Richard Maltby, *Identifying Hollywood's Audiences: Cultural Identity and the Movies* (London: BFI Publishing, 1999), p. 3.

47 Graham McCann, *Rebel Males* (London: Hamish Hamilton, 1991), pp. 8–10.

48 Richard Dyer, *The Culture of Queers* (London: Routledge, 2001), p. 163.

49 For an involved discussion of James Dean's influence within lesbian culture see Sue Golding, 'James Dean: The almost-perfect lesbian hermaphrodite', in T. Boffin and L. Fraser, *Stolen Glances: Lesbians Take Photographs* (London: Pandora, 1991).

50 Springer, *James Dean Transfigured*, p. 29.

51 Jeffrey Richards, *Film and British National Identity: From Dickens to Dad's Army* (Manchester: Manchester University Press, 1997), pp. xii, 3 and 10–11.

52 Thomas Dixon, *Weeping Britannia: Portrait of a Nation in Tears* (Oxford: Oxford University Press, 2015), pp. 230–48.

53 In conjunction with a popular Sunday paper, *The People*, the English anthropologist Geoffrey Gorer selected 5,000 completed questionnaires from a total of 10,000 for his psychoanalytical survey of social attitudes. See *Exploring English Character* (London: Criterion Books, 1955), pp. 288–9.

54 A useful account of the Young Angry Man discourse is given by Peter Lewis, *The Fifties* (London: Book Club Associates, 1978), pp. 158–86.
55 Adrian Horn, *Juke Box Britain: Americanisation and Youth Culture, 1945–60* (Manchester and New York: Manchester University Press, 2009), pp. 70 and 75.
56 Arthur Marwick, *Culture in Britain* (Oxford: Basil Blackwell, 1991), pp. 56–7; Dick Hebdige, *Hiding in the Light* (New York and London: Routledge, 1988), p. 47.
57 Q. D. Leavis, *Fiction and the Reading Public* (London: Chatto & Windus, 1939); F. R. Leavis, 'Mass civilization and minority culture' (1930), in John Storey, *Cultural Theory and Popular Culture: A Reader* (London: Pearson, 2007), pp. 12–20. In his essay, George Orwell objected to the 'false values' conveyed in Hollywood films which characterised the 'Cleft Chin Murder'. 'Decline of the English Murder' was first published in *Tribune*, 15 February 1946. Available at: http://orwell.ru/library/articles/decline/english/e_doem (last accessed 10 October 2018).
58 Margaret Dickinson and Sarah Street, *Cinema and State* (London: BFI, 1985).
59 Richard Hoggart, *The Uses of Literacy: With a New Introduction by Andrew Goodwin* (New Brunswick and London: Transaction Publishers, 1992), pp. 189–90.
60 For a wider examination of discourses of Americanisation and Hollywood films over the course of eighty years, see Glancy, *Hollywood and the Americanization of Britain*.
61 Pierre Bourdieu, *Distinction: A Social Critique of the Judgement of Taste*, trans. Richard Nice (London: Routledge, 1984), pp. 6–7.
62 *Ibid.*, p. 41.
63 Bourdieu, *On Television and Journalism*, pp. 40–1.
64 Paul McDonald, 'Public bodies, private moments: method acting and American cinema in the 1950s', PhD thesis, Warwick University, 1997.
65 Virginia Wexman, *Creating the Couple: Love, Marriage and Hollywood Performance* (New Jersey: Princeton University Press, 1993), pp. 160–6.
66 Sidney Harris was knighted in 1947 in recognition of his contribution to protective legislation for children; in 1949, John Trevelyan was given an OBE for his contribution to educational initiatives.
67 Vincent Porter, *On Cinema* (London: Pluto Press, 1985), p. 93.
68 Richard Maltby, 'D for disgusting: American culture and English criticism', in Geoffrey Nowell-Smith and Steven Ricci (eds), *Hollywood & Europe: Economics, Culture, National Identity* (London: BFI, 1998), pp. 104–15 (pp. 109, 114 and fn. 27).

69 Ross McKibbin, *Classes and Cultures: England 1918–51* (Oxford: Oxford University Press, 1998), p. 341.
70 Stanley Cohen, *Folk Devils and Moral Panics* (London and New York: Routledge, 1972); Robert J. Cross, 'The Teddy boy as scapegoat', in *Doshisha Studies in Language and Culture*, 1–2 (1998), pp. 263–91.
71 Selina Todd and Hilary Young, 'Baby-Boomers to 'Beanstalkers': making the modern teenager in post-war Britain', *Cultural and Social History*, 9 (2012), pp. 451–67; Nick Thomas, 'Will the real 1950s please stand up? Views of a contradictory decade', *Cultural and Social History*, 5 (2008), pp. 227–36.
72 See for example, M. E. Bathurst, 'Juvenile delinquency in Britain during the war', in *Journal of Criminal Law and Criminology*, 34:5 (Article 1, 1944), pp. 291–302; T. R. Fyvel, *The Insecure Offenders: Rebellious Youth in the Welfare State* (London: Chatto & Windus, 1963), p. 51.
73 Home Office figures are quoted in Fyvel, *The Insecure Offenders*, p. 19; Marwick, *British Society Since 1945*, p. 144.
74 Nineteenth-century youth subcultures were also targeted in the press as symptomatic of cultural decline and a 'new' affluence in the young. See Geoffrey Pearson, *Hooligan: A History of Respectable Fears* (London: Macmillan, 1983), p. 33.
75 Phil Cohen, 'Subcultural conflict and working-class community', in Stuart Hall, Dorothy Hobson, Andrew Lowe and Paul Willis (eds), *Culture, Media, Language: Working Papers in Cultural Studies, 1972–79* (London: Routledge, 1980), pp. 66–75 (pp. 67–8).
76 Fyvel, *The Insecure Offenders*, p. 122.
77 Harry Hopkins, *The New Look: A Social History of the Forties and Fifties in Britain* (London: Secker & Warburg, 1963), p. 457.
78 Dick Hebdige, *Subculture: The Meaning of Style* (London and New York: Routledge, 1979), pp. 46–51 (p. 50).
79 Tony Jefferson, 'Cultural responses of the Teds: the defence of space and status', in Stuart Hall and Tony Jefferson (eds), *Resistance Through Rituals: Youth Subcultures in Post-War Britain* (London: Hutchinson, 1976), pp. 81–6 (p. 81). For an insightful discussion of how the American drape suit was assimilated into British fashion but remained a signifier of Hollywood influences, see also Steve Chibnall, 'Whistle and zoot: The changing meaning of a suit of clothes', in *History Workshop Journal*, 20:1 (1 October 1985), pp. 56–81.
80 George Melly, *Revolt into Style: The Pop Arts in the 50s and 60s* (London: Allen Lane, 1970), pp. 37 and 32.
81 *Kensington and West London Times*, 29 August 1958.

82 For an informed account see 'Coloured people in Great Britain: summary of press news and comment, September 1958 (UK/43)', a seventeen-page document issued by the Institute of Race Relations. Available at: https://cdm21047.contentdm.oclc.org/digital/collection/tav/id/4835 (last accessed 2 April 2020).

83 For a fuller description and an evaluation of the riots in Nottingham and London see Tony Moore, *Policing Notting Hill: Fifty Years of Turbulence* (Hampshire, UK: Waterside Press, 2013), pp. 37–56; Edward Pilkington, *Beyond the Mother Country: West Indians and the Notting Hill White Riots* (London: I. B. Tauris, 1988).

84 'Four-year terms for nine "nigger-hunting" youths', *The Times*, 16 September 1958; 'You started this violence – judge tells gaoled gang', *Daily Mirror*, 16 September 1958.

85 Unnamed reporter, 'Gang-boss Craig trained other boys to become gunmen', 12 December 1952, *Daily Mail*, pp. 1–2, 8–9 (p. 2).

86 'Stocks for Teddy boys – Goddard', *The Observer*, 5 May 1963, p. 3.

87 'The influence of the cinema on children and adolescents: an annotated international bibliography', UNESCO, 1961, Reports and Papers on Mass Communication, No. 31, p. 5.

88 For example see Conservative Political Centre, 'Youth astray: being a report on the treatment of the young offenders' (1946); and King George's Jubilee Trust. Council, 'Citizens of tomorrow: a study of the influences affecting the upbringing of young people' (London: Odhams Press Ltd, 1955).

89 Gorer, *Exploring English Character*, pp. 208–9.

90 'A Teddy boys' charter: no victimisation, no violence', *Manchester Guardian*, 31 October 1958, p. 7.

91 Louise Jackson, *Policing Youth, Britain 1945–70* (Manchester: Manchester University Press, 2014), p. 98.

92 Amy Helen Bell, 'Teddy boys and girls as neo-flâneurs in post-war London', *The Literary London Journal*, 11:2 (Autumn 2014), pp. 3–17 (p. 6).

93 Sean O'Hagan, 'The fabulous 50s … as seen by Ken Russell', *The Observer* [online], 14 March 2010. Available at: www.theguardian.com/artanddesign/2010/mar/14/ken-russell-photography-interview-ohagan (last accessed 4 April 2020).

94 Dominic Sandbrook, *Never Had It So Good: A History of Britain from Suez to the Beatles* (London: Abacus, 2006), p. 435.

95 Mark Abrams, *The Teenage Consumer* (London: London Press Exchange Ltd, 1959).

96 *Ibid.*, p. 7.

97 David Fowler, *The First Teenagers: The Lifestyle of Young Wage-Earners in Interwar Britain* (London: Woburn Press, 1995).

98 Horn, *Juke Box Britain*, p. 93; Bill Osgerby, *Youth in Britain Since 1945* (London: Wiley, 1998); Pearl Jephcott, *Time of One's Own* (London: Oliver & Boyd, 1967), p. 55.

99 Abrams, *The Teenage Consumer*, pp. 9–10 and 14.

100 *Ibid.*, p. 13.

101 Peter Laurie, *The Teenage Revolution* (London: Antony Blond, 1965), p. 13. 'I'm alright, Jack' is a phrase believed to have originated in the Royal Navy. It was adopted as a pejorative phrase that conveyed acting solely in one's own interest to the detriment of others. It was later used as the title of a film, starring Peter Sellers: *I'm All Right Jack* (John Boulting, 1959).

102 Colin MacInnes, *Absolute Beginners* (London: MacGibbon & Kee, 1959) and *England, Half English* (London: MacGibbon & Kee, 1961).

1

'Attractive and imitable': Marlon Brando and *The Wild One* ban in the UK

> If anything, the reaction to the picture said more about the audience than it did about the film.
>
> Marlon Brando, *Songs My Mother Taught Me*, 1994[1]

> I would say let it be seen. It is so far removed from anything that could possibly happen in this country that it borders on farce.
>
> John Watney, *Sunday Dispatch*, 1954[2]

In April 1955, *The Wild One*, starring Marlon Brando, premiered at the Rex Cinema in Cambridge. This was no ordinary screening, since the film had recently been denied a certificate by the British Board of Film Censors (BBFC), who took the unanimous view that general exhibition would prove pernicious to the more impressionable among Britain's teenagers.[3] *The Wild One*, which told the story of a nomadic group of law-breaking motorcyclists, arrived in Britain during a period of heightened concerns about the violent nature of Teddy boy gangs. The decision taken by the BBFC did not deter Leslie Halliwell, the manager of the Rex and an erudite film essayist. Halliwell had petitioned Cambridge magistrates to grant the film a local X certificate because he believed that Brando was 'an actor whose every appearance is a major screen event'.[4] Having received the approval of the local watch committee, Halliwell's petition met with mixed responses from other Cambridge residents. Frank Hardy, a local youth club leader, commented: 'It's alright showing it in Cambridge. We have a low juvenile delinquency rate. But in some places it could be a harmful influence. I wouldn't show it in Liverpool, for instance.'[5]

Given the short distance between Cambridge and London, Halliwell was 'besieged' by requests for party rates from film enthusiasts and motorcycle clubs across the country. London sophisticates and celebrities, such as the former music hall star Beatrice Lillie and the film actor Jon Pertwee, joined Teddy boys and bikers at the much-publicised film screenings. When hordes of motorcyclists were met by Cambridge police at this small, specialist cinema in one of Britain's safest and most respectable towns, it appeared to some residents that life was beginning to imitate art. News reporters were quick to point out, however, that the police presence was intended to uphold residential parking regulations rather than contain an 'invasion' of revellers.

This chapter explores and illuminates this most compelling, landmark episode of film censorship and examines why the BBFC decided to ban *The Wild One* from general exhibition. The film's commentary on recreational violence was an obvious point of contention given the board's opinions of young, receptive cinemagoers. However, this scenario provides an incomplete and simplified version of events. The censors described Marlon Brando as 'attractive, admirable, [and] imitable' and I argue that this is the more persuasive and plausible reason for the film's ultimate fate.[6] As a newly emerging 'anti-star', Brando was offering British audiences a range of meanings connotative of his tough looks, 'unorthodox' acting style and off-screen anti-Hollywood behaviour that had never yet been encountered in the USA or in Britain.[7]

In *The Wild One*, Brando takes the role of Johnny Strabler, the leader of the Black Rebel Motorcycle Club. The Black Rebels are disqualified from entering a rally because of anti-social behaviour and, to show their disapproval, steal a prize statuette. They mockingly award the prize to Johnny, who straps it onto his motorcycle. From there, the gang rides on to Wrightsville, so named, presumably, to suggest its ordinariness and respectability. Once there, the Black Rebels start drinking and become boisterous and unruly. The situation worsens when the Beetles, a rival gang led by Johnny's nemesis, Chino (Lee Marvin), arrive. Taunting and jeering escalate into a brawl between the arch rivals. Needless to say, Johnny wins. When a local resident attempts to drive through the fracas, his car is overturned and Chino is arrested by the local sheriff, Harry Bleeker (Robert Keith). However, the ageing Bleeker is somewhat ineffectual and lacks manpower, with the result that the gangs continue to cause havoc as the night progresses.

Johnny takes a liking to Bleeker's daughter, Kathie (Mary Murphy) and tries to persuade her to go riding with him. In the meantime, a local group of townsmen arm themselves and plan to take matters into their own hands. With phone lines cut, and a building set alight, the gangs' antics appear to be out of control. At one point, Kathy is terrorised by a several motorcyclists and Johnny intervenes to rescue her (presumably from an attempted rape) and then tries to seduce her himself. Frustrated by her resistance and then confused by her submission, Johnny decides that he will leave town instead. Johnny rides off but is captured by vigilantes and severely beaten. When he manages to escape with Kathie's help, one of the vigilantes throws a tyre lever at his back wheel and Johnny falls off his bike. The riderless motorcycle careens into the crowd, killing an innocent bystander – a kindly old man who had been amused by the biker gangs. Johnny is picked up and detained by police. Kathie and her father, who have witnessed the events, come to Johnny's defence and explain that the killing was accidental. Johnny is exonerated and released after being issued with a warning against future misbehaviour. Moments before Johnny finally leaves town, he silently drinks a cup of coffee in the local cafe. Kathie watches him but he refuses to make eye contact with her. Without saying a word, he retrieves the (stolen) statuette from his jacket pocket and places it on the counter, pushing it toward her and leaving it there. They share an enigmatic smile; he exits.

The Wild One had been inspired by actual events that took place at the American Motorcycle Association rally in Hollister, California, in 1947, when hundreds of drunken motorcyclists overwhelmed local police. The story was then fictionalised by Frank Rooney and published in *Harper's Magazine*, under the title, *Cyclists' Raid* (1951) when it attracted the attention of Stanley Kramer, a film producer known for his interest in pithy contemporary stories. Together with the director Laszlo Benedek and the screenwriter John Paxton, Kramer oversaw the adaptation of Rooney's story with the aim of developing a star vehicle for Marlon Brando. For one, Rooney's story uses frequent and deliberate military allusions to describe the motorcycle gangs, thus denying any individual character an especial distinction. Second, Kathie, herself – rather than the old townsman killed in the film – is the tragic victim of a motorcycle jaunt that goes awry by an unidentified assailant among the 'standardized figurines' of the motorcycle gang.[8] Interestingly, Rooney's original story title, *Cyclists' Raid* was first modified to the more sensational, though generic, *Hot Blood* before the studio agreed on *The Wild One* in the singular, perhaps drawing on the 'untameable' qualities that inflected Brando's previous performance as Stanley Kowalski.[9]

Contrary to the glamour and vibrancy that Brando brought to the role of Johnny, the American novelist Hunter S. Thompson, who spent a year among California's Hell's Angels, described an alternative version of the events at Hollister. His account of minor injuries, a few fines and jail time for incidences of indecent exposure are hardly consistent with the thrilling action of *The Wild One*.[10] Notably, Thompson surmised that Brando's brooding and sensitive portrayal of Johnny provided the Hell's Angels with the 'lasting romance-glazed image' they identified with, despite the fact that Lee Marvin's characterisation of Chino, memorable for his pantomimic behaviour and eccentric clothing, was closer to the truth. Photos of the Boozer Fighter motorcyclists featured in the *Life* magazine article, 'Cyclists' holiday' (21 July 1947), of the original Boozer Fighter gang demonstrate their ordinariness and emphasise the somewhat ridiculous aspects of their members.

The rebel star: the construction of charisma

Brando's early stardom in Britain was significant to the BBFC's gravest concerns: *The Wild One* allied an established and popular method actor with reckless juvenile delinquency. What 'dangers' did Brando's stardom represent? One British critic perceived the actor's uniqueness as his innate ability to project an undercurrent of 'protest' both on and off the screen.[11]

Brando's spectacular rise from the Broadway stage to Hollywood leading man was well documented in the British media with a mixture of curiosity and awe. Early studio biographies developed Brando's star meanings around his humble beginnings and wayward adolescence; his serious commitment to the theatre and his reluctance to work in Hollywood.[12] The British *Film Review* annual of 1951–52 introduced Brando as a transgressive and unorthodox young actor, who 'left military school to dig ditches', enjoyed playing the drums, and was already earning the enormous salary of $300 on Broadway.[13] Juxtaposed with the standard studio portraits of the other 'rising stars', Brando's photo shows him (typically) absorbed in reading a script and paying no attention whatsoever to the photographer.

From the outset, Brando's anti-Hollywood rhetoric ingratiated him with those British film reviewers and commentators who criticised Hollywood's dominance in cinema and its exploitation of stars.[14] Thus, the actor gained the respect and admiration of the erudite film essayists of *Sight and Sound* and *Monthly Film Bulletin*, who championed good cinema as a credible and influential art form. The chief editor, Penelope Houston, considered Brando's look, sound and manner to emblematise 'an effortless contemporaneity', which endeared him to a young generation of cinemagoers.[15] Among the critics in the popular press, Brando's childish pranks, his unwillingness to court favour, his absorption in Shakespeare, and his candidness about his high earnings were interpreted as evidence of his being a 'sincere non-conformist'.[16]

In the lead-up to *The Wild One*, Brando was known for several striking method performances, which became the benchmark for realistic and credible acting. Brando had learned his dramatic craft from Stella Adler in New York, whose approach to acting was based on Konstantin Stanislavsky's teachings. As suggested in my introduction, method acting did not uniformly suit British tastes. The disparities between the British and American imaginary at this time are partly explained by contrasting attitudes to Freudian theories. After the Second World War, Freud's practices were assimilated into American mainstream culture, proving so popular and influential that Hollywood interwove psychoanalysis into its modern stories and melodramas.[17]

Brando's contemporaneity hinged on his multifaceted performance style, which broke from earlier acting traditions. Where the Method championed experiential and excessive passions, fervent public displays of emotion were less characteristic of British acting. After an acclaimed two-year run as Stanley Kowalski in Elia Kazan's Broadway production of *A Streetcar Named Desire* (1947–49), Brando made his film debut as a paraplegic army veteran in

Figure 1.1 Male pin-up: Marlon Brando became associated with the raw masculinity of Stanley Kowalski, the character he portrayed in *A Streetcar Named Desire* (1951). The role became the benchmark for realistic method acting; Brando earned kudos from the critics and became popular with film fans.

The Men (Fred Zinnemann, 1950). Consistent with his method training to create an inner world for his screen characters, Brando learned to use a wheelchair and fraternised with wounded veterans during pre-production so that he could create as realistic a portrait as possible. It is significant that Brando's screen debut divided opinion among the British reviewers. Some interpreted his performance as 'glum' or 'unlikeable'; others applauded him for his lack of histrionics and for bringing a searing realism to the role that 'surged' through cinema like a 'blood transfusion'.[18] Despite these mixed reviews, when Brando reprised the role of Stanley Kowalski in the film *A Streetcar Named Desire* (Elia Kazan, 1951), his performance was received with universal approval and familiarised audiences with the Method.

Streetcar's author, Tennessee Williams, had personally approved Brando's casting and celebrated the potent combination of Brando's remarkable talent with Kazan's direction. According to Williams, Brando managed to mitigate Kowalski's brutality to 'the callousness of youth' and, importantly, swayed the audience's allegiances.[19] To Brando's detriment, perhaps, he was to be persistently associated with the role of the volatile but sensual Kowalski; it characterised his stardom and informed subsequent film promotion.[20] To unpack Brando's performance further, it is worth comparing the film to Laurence Olivier's West End production of *Streetcar*, starring his wife Vivien Leigh as Blanche. Premiering at London's Aldwych Theatre in October 1949, *Streetcar* was a prestigious and hotly anticipated event that offered British theatregoers the adult realism of the Broadway 'smash' and the glamour of the revered Lord and Lady Olivier. Under Olivier's direction, the production was adapted to showcase Leigh's talents 'to the fullest' in a performance that foregrounded Blanche's vulnerability and fragility.[21] In addition, Olivier wanted his production to offer audiences a 'new reading' of Kowalski that was wily rather than 'apelike', and 'slightly subtler' than Brando's incarnation.[22] The role was taken by the American actor, Bonar Colleano, familiar to British audiences for his many character roles. For the most part, critics applauded Olivier's production for Leigh's sensitive portrayal of Blanche, and Colleano's 'powerful' and intelligent account of Kowalski.[23] The outspoken diarist and theatre critic Kenneth Tynan disagreed, arguing that the miscast Colleano had reduced Kowalski to 'a lean, zingy, gum-chewing

GI stationed outside Warrington', who lacked the essential sex appeal Brando had brought to the role.[24]

Following his success as Kowalski, Brando was offered the equally prestigious role of Mark Antony in MGM's production of *Julius Caesar* (Joseph L. Mankiewicz, 1953), which boasted a predominantly British cast of highly acclaimed Shakespearean actors. Whatever his experience of the Broadway stage, Brando was concerned about the challenges of unfamiliar Shakespearean verse-speaking and took action to improve his diction. John Gielgud, who was cast as Cassius, marvelled at the hours the younger actor spent practising the recordings made by Laurence Olivier and Maurice Evans.[25] In the final reckoning, American critics applauded Brando for losing his '*Streetcar* accent' but the British critics were divided in their opinions. In general, they praised his impressive physique and glamour but considered his voice altogether inadequate for Shakespeare.[26] To some degree, the elitist British critics displayed the expected attitudes and behaviour that cohere with Bourdieu's theories on habitus and its predetermination of cultural taste patterns. Straightforward acceptance of Brando's modern (and American) interpretation of Shakespeare would arguably have diluted an exclusive field of acting tradition established and coded as British. Gavin Lambert, for example, urged readers of the journal *Sight and Sound* to overlook the 'rough edges' of Brando's vocal performance and enjoy the extraordinary 'electricity' he generated.[27]

On the other hand, bringing Shakespeare to mass audiences in a lavish but faithful screen adaptation elevated the status of Hollywood cinema. Lionel Collier, who had disliked Brando in *The Men*, awarded him *Picturegoer* magazine's 'Seal' and emphatically declared: 'Even if he'd done nothing else this would have entitled him to take his place along with the screen's best actors.'[28] Similarly, the Council of the British Film Academy generously rewarded Brando: he received the medallion for Best Foreign Actor of 1953. Thus far, Brando's prestigious career had created a niche in Hollywood acting and the performer had brought an unsurpassed sensual glamour and naturalism to every one of his roles. His landmark performances and his method acting established a highly influential style that others would copy, with James Dean and Paul Newman among his earliest imitators. This impressive portfolio of film and stage work created widespread anticipation for his next role as Johnny Strabler.

Banned: the British censors and *The Wild One*

The Wild One dramatised the lifestyle of motorcycle gangs, already familiar to Californians where open spaces and long stretches of highway encouraged weekend roaming. Not only was the subject matter far removed from British realities, an explanatory title and Brando's voiceover emphasised that it could 'never happen again in a million years'. Indeed, long before despicable crimes became synonymous with the Hell's Angels, the incident at Hollister was notable for being out of the ordinary. Thus, the BBFC's ban of *The Wild One* was one of the most astonishing aspects of its censorship history largely because, in theory, the X certificate – introduced in 1951 – permitted filmic treatments of adult themes. This is not to suggest that the BBFC never banned Hollywood films – they did. However, prestige productions were not generally denied a certificate after cuts had been made. *Island of Lost Souls* (Erle C. Kenton, 1932) was a notable exception: it was banned in Britain for twenty years. It, too, boasted an all-star cast, including the revered character actor Charles Laughton, and was made to high production values. However, its commentary on blasphemy and scenes of horrific vivisection proved unpalatable to the British censors for a host of moral and religious reasons.

The Wild One's screen violence was the main thrust of the censors' arguments when they discussed their ban with the media. This explanation perplexed the majority of discerning British cinemagoers because they had encountered worse violence in Hollywood's gangster films. The Production Code Administration's (PCA) main concern was to proscribe sexual impropriety – rather than screen violence – because it was the red flag of the American Catholic League of Decency. The former secretary of the BBFC, John Trevelyan, recalled that he and his fellow examiners often encountered excessively violent American films already granted the PCA's 'seal' of approval.[29] When submitted to the BBFC in January 1954, *The Wild One* had already undergone substantial changes – such as 'toned down' violence and the insertion of a condemnatory preface – to obtain the PCA's seal.[30] As was customary, the PCA and Columbia studio benefited from their ongoing correspondence throughout the pre- and post-production processes. Inevitably, the BBFC's involvement in these conferences was both unfeasible and unwelcomed by Hollywood. When met with *The Wild One*, the PCA's modifications did nothing to placate the board's members.

The BBFC's prestige and reputation lay in making value judgements on acceptable mass entertainment. As explained in the Introduction, they functioned as a purely advisory body to local licensing authorities but could exert their authority by other means. In a decade when cinemagoing still constituted the most popular form of mass leisure, they could limit a film's exhibition to those aged 16 and over with an X certificate. Ostensibly, the X certificate encouraged production of specifically adult entertainment. Yet it also implicitly 'controlled' the content of British films at the pre-production stage when the mere threat of an X certificate resulted in abandoned film projects. This was primarily because X certificate films were excluded from the major circuits – the ABC and Rank cinema chains – and, therefore, proved financially impracticable for British film producers to pursue.[31] The X certificate was equally ignominious to Hollywood producers, who did not want restrictions placed on their most lucrative and dependable foreign market.

In the case of *The Wild One*, the BBFC exercised their ultimate power by banning the film. While T. P. O'Connor's '43 rules' had been updated and extended in the BBFC's Codified Grounds for Censorship, both documents proscribed excessive violence and imitable methods of criminality.[32] *The Wild One* breached too many of these recommendations by showing scenes of excessive drunkenness, knuckle fights, offensive vulgarity, and impropriety in dress and conduct. It further disparaged 'public characters and institutions' and failed to decisively show that 'crime does not pay'. In effect, the Black Rebels – and Johnny in particular – were all framed sympathetically through narrative devices and *mise en scène*.

The BBFC's formal records and informal correspondence around the film reconstruct their low opinion of teenage Teddy boys, who were considered highly susceptible to re-enacting the reckless violence and misbehaviour they saw on screen. Similarly, the examiners held other concerns about unsophisticated teenage girls, whom they believed harboured 'secret' desires for over-glamorised screen criminals. From its very first scenes, *The Wild One* establishes the ways that Johnny appeals to both genders. Despite the obvious maturity of the cast, the Black Rebels are bound together by the raucous behaviour, shared slang and mutual admiration of adolescent camaraderie. For example, the gang mocks the onlookers at an organised rally and boasts that Johnny's daredevil riding skills surpass those of any of the contenders. As well as establishing these strong homosocial ties, Johnny's sexual self-assuredness is conveyed by his confident swagger and elaborate costume, and established in scenes with female characters. There are shades of Kowalski's misogyny in Johnny's rough treatment of his ex-girlfriend, Britches (Yvonne Doughty). In one scene, Britches tries to win back Johnny's affections by hinting at a romantic encounter they had shared: 'What do you want me to do', Johnny sneers, pushing her aside, 'buy you flowers?'

This aloofness to attractive women appears outdated and sexist to modern viewers but it presumably conferred Johnny's enviable bachelor status at a time when strict social morality governed sex and marriage. Britches (an American word for 'trousers' no less) was a sexually experienced woman and, therefore, did not overly concern Sidney Harris, the president of the BBFC. Harris wanted to 'protect' Kathie, the virginal *ingénue*, because she represented the impressionable girls in British audiences. In their love scene, when Johnny violently seizes Kathie and kisses her, she initially resists and then submits to him. Harris took this as a typical example of 'the morbid attraction which young toughs have for immature girls'.[33]

At the time of the ban, the BBFC Secretary Arthur Watkins gave a series of press releases to offer cinemagoers the facts: 'Brando's film' could not be granted an X certificate because it would encourage juvenile delinquency in teenagers of 16 years and above.[34] As extant records prove, the decision to ban the film was actually a protracted and contested business that divided opinion. Initially, examiners debated further cuts for an X certificate, adding an explanatory prologue or epilogue, or inserting additional courtroom scenes where the motorcycle gang is substantially punished.[35] Sir David E. Griffiths, President of the Kinematograph Renters' Society, encouraged examiners to opt for 'judicious cutting' thus making the film suitable for adults and circumventing the local authorities. After all, regional watch committees, made up of several magistrates, could override the BBFC, and grant a film a local X certificate if they so wished. Reminding examiners that the events in Wrightsville could 'never possibly happen' in England, Griffiths feared that a 'total ban' would be sensational publicity for the film and attract the undesirable filmgoers the BBFC hoped to repel.[36]

It becomes instructive here to compare *The Wild One*'s censorship to that of *Cosh Boy* (Lewis Gilbert, 1953), a British film about juvenile delinquency. The film relays the story of Roy Walsh, a 16-year-old Teddy boy, whose gang coshes and robs its victims. Furthermore, Roy manipulates his ineffectual widowed mother and seduces his friend's impressionable sister, Rene (Joan Collins), only to abandon her when she becomes pregnant. In the climactic final scenes, the gang shoots and wounds a police constable during a botched heist. Resonant with the urgency of real-life Teddy boy gangs, who generated enormous attention across the media and in public debates, this film placed the BBFC in a complex situation. Sensationalising criminals was anathema, but to have avoided topical subjects would have denied British cinema its didactic role in telling contemporary stories with moral endings. In spite of his horrible crimes, Roy looked and sounded like an ordinary teenager. Surely, he invited higher levels of identification for young British audiences than an American motorcycle rebel did. *Cosh Boy* was eventually granted an X certificate because it benefited from the close cooperation between the BBFC and the film's producer, Daniel Angel. Angel undertook all the changes the board asked for, suitably de-glamorised Roy by overdubbing any offensive dialogue that mocked public figures and removing the tawdrier moments of his seduction scene with Rene. In due course, the film version pleased the BBFC because it depicted Roy as a very recognisable social type: the maladjusted – and ultimately unsympathetic – juvenile delinquent. In addition, *Cosh Boy* had originated as a West End play and, as such, had already secured a pass from the Lord Chamberlain's office, which customarily addressed all issues of theatre censorship.[37] To have denied *Cosh Boy* a certificate would have been highly irregular of the BBFC at this late stage.

Released in February 1953, *Cosh Boy* coincided with the real-life Craig and Bentley case of armed robbery and the murder of a police constable. The film's resemblance to recent events, inevitably, created a public furore. Milton Shulman, the *London Evening Standard* film critic, was of the widely held opinion that the ill-timed showing of *Cosh Boy* was 'a monumental error in [the BBFC's] taste and judgment', adding that prospective juvenile delinquents would only remember Roy's power, his sexual conquests and his distinctive fashion rather than his eventual capture.[38] Voicing similar concerns, an actual 'cosh victim' from Richmond Hill implored the BBFC to renounce and withdraw the film, commenting that, 'it seems a shame that [thugs] can have the opportunity to see how it is done on [*sic*] the pictures'.[39] Nonetheless, Sidney Harris was satisfied that *Cosh Boy* had communicated its 'strong moral note' succinctly and proficiently in final scenes that show Roy humiliated and captured.[40] Indeed, parallel editing cuts between Roy being given a well-deserved beating by his stepfather as police arrive at the front door to arrest him. Johnny Strabler, on the other hand, is not held accountable for his sexual activities or criminal behaviour: he remains a glamorised rebel who is above the law.

The Wild One was not the first American film to comment on juvenile gang life. *Dead End* (William Wyler, 1937) followed the exploits of the sharp-talking juvenile gangs of New York's poorest neighbourhoods, depicting scenes of truanting, fist fighting, the carrying of weapons and the use of bad language. Yet neither the PCA nor the BBFC hindered the production and the film's popularity inspired a film cycle (1938–39). In her analysis, Sarah J. Smith argues that the *Dead End* kids were redeemed by being portrayed as sympathetic victims of circumstance, who lived on their wits because of harsh social conditions.[41] Equally, *Dead End* unambiguously represented the themes of good versus evil and, therefore, reinforced the inherent morality approved by censors. This dualism is represented by juxtaposing two local boys who grow up choosing very different paths. Leaving behind his childhood poverty, Baby Face Martin (Humphrey Bogart) has become a ruthless gangster while Dave Connell (Joel McCrea) is the unemployed but pristine architect who hopes to regenerate his old neighbourhood. James Robertson argues that Connell fulfils the censor's moral compensation function by demonstrating that impoverished circumstances do not inevitably lead to a life of crime.[42] When contrasted with *Dead End*, it becomes apparent that *The Wild One*'s gangs – and the ambiguous Johnny in particular – do not convey these traditional dichotomies forcefully enough.

As seen, the BBFC followed a policy of recommending deletions and other modifications to ensure that films were appropriate for exhibition in Britain. In similar fashion, Hollywood censors asked that an explanatory prologue be inserted to precede *The Wild One*'s opening titles. Johnny's voiceover exonerates him from instigating the violence in Wrightsville and depicts him as taking defensive action when there was no alternative. 'How the whole mess happened I don't know', Johnny explains, 'but once the trouble was on the way, I was just going with it.' While this placated Hollywood, the British censors interpreted Brando's prologue as a reiteration of a prevalent and dangerous Teddy boy psychology. Inevitably, Johnny's glib remarks throughout the film were correlated with the worrisome 'recreational' elements that, for the public, characterised the rise in amoral urban gang crime. Most famously, when asked what he is rebelling against, Johnny retorts: 'Whaddaya got?'

With its emphasis on the dangers of the 'pack' mentality, *The Wild One* proved particularly unpalatable at a time when the press tended to demonise the Teddy boys. Despite the rarity of serious crime committed by teenagers, the frequency with which the media reported on lower level misbehaviours and petty crime reinforced the widespread notion of a 'youth problem'. The media had become fascinated with the Teddy boys' 'flagrant' disregard for moral and legitimate authority – the so-called 'organised hooliganism' that concerned the BBFC and other members of the establishment. As recounted, *Cosh Boy* had been tainted by its close association with the Bentley–Craig case. Similarly, *The Wild One*'s submission to the British censors coincided with the Clapham Common murder of 17-year-old John Beckley in July 1953 and determined final negotiations between the BBFC and Columbia. This high-profile case was a much-publicised crime.[43] The press reported that Beckley had insulted the appearance of one of the 'Plough Boys', a rival group of Teddy boys. Singled out and pursued, Beckley was eventually dragged from a bus and fatally stabbed in full view of witnesses. The press described, in painstaking detail, the victim's multiple stab wounds and this gave rise to the theory that there had been several assailants.[44] Watkins and his fellow censors were appalled by this 'atrocious' murder of a British teenager, slain in plain sight of passers-by, who did nothing to prevent it and, later, could not identify the killer.[45] For the BBFC, there were parallels to be drawn between the 'Teddy boy bullies' of the Clapham case and the motorcyclists in *The Wild One*, who commit a manslaughter that cannot be satisfactorily attributed to any individual biker.[46]

Hebdige and Jefferson have argued for the camaraderie and impeccable fashion that bound marginalised working-class Teddy boys together in territorial gangs. To have insulted the appearance of a rival Ted was not considered a trivial matter to the boys involved but rather a contravention of accepted gang lore or 'codes'.[47] Nonetheless, the media's sustained coverage of the murder trial generated a very disturbing image of London's Teddy boys. The popular dailies referred to 'the pack' of twelve boys who outnumbered and attacked a gang of four. Later, witnesses recounted hearing the 'leader' of the gang ordering the others to 'get the knives out'.[48] Within a short time, the Craig–Bentley murder trial and the Clapham case associated Teddy boys with gang life and weaponry, gaudy Edwardian suits and the hedonism of post-war leisure. For the BBFC examiners, Teddy boys lived on the margins of society and for them, *The Wild One* depicted their 'unbridled hooliganism' where 'henchmen and stooges' carried out the orders of 'an acknowledged leader'.[49]

Given the prestige of the production, an outright ban was an extreme measure. However, had *The Wild One* been cut and granted an X certificate, the censors were concerned that British filmmakers would be encouraged to produce yet more exploitative dramas about juvenile delinquency. The president of the board, Harris, held steadfastly to the lessons learned during the *Cosh Boy* episode, and now wanted to appease public concerns about the 'Teddy boy problem'. According to Harris, *The Wild One* would condone future attacks on 'young and old alike' and, unlike *Cosh Boy*'s compensatory ending, Brando and his Black Rebels were made to 'appear rather clever fellows rather than silly and dangerous young fools'.[50] As far as the British censors were concerned, *The Wild One* was unsalvageable: it depicted a gang of outsiders causing mayhem and manslaughter in a small, law-abiding town. In response to Columbia studio's missive, the BBFC vindicated their ban by listing Johnny's multiple offences: 'larceny, malicious damage to property, false imprisonment, assault and battery, insulting behaviour, reckless driving, and whatever federal offence it is to break into a government telephone exchange and prison and [take] control [of] them'.[51] Furthermore, these acts went virtually unpunished. After Johnny's involvement in heavy drinking, a jailbreak, an attempted seduction and a manslaughter, the police chief's final warning is discernibly mild: 'I don't know if there is any good in you … But I'm going to take a big, fat chance and let you go.' Given the discursive surround of the film, such leniency appeared inexcusable to the board.

'Hot blood': Brando in *The Wild One*

In this close textual analysis of *The Wild One* I want to demonstrate how the camera privileged Brando and, therefore, glamorised juvenile delinquency. A useful working definition of *mise en scène* is the structuring and framing of what the audience sees and how we are invited to look at it.[52] *Mise en scène* is one of the collaborative industrial practices used by filmmakers to enhance personal attributes that help construct star charisma.[53] From the outset, *The Wild One* incorporates formal elements to build audience anticipation for Brando's arrival. The opening shot shows us a deserted road, and we hear Brando's explanatory voice over the jazz soundtrack. As Helen Hanson argues, the Hollywood soundscape is the 'invisible' feature that provides 'the narrational modality of the film', and voiceovers, in particular, create an intimacy with the audience.[54] Given these points, the overall effect of sound, music and Brando's voiceover in the opening sequence of *The Wild One* has multiple functions. First, his voiceover identifies this as *his* story. Further, his voiceover is underscored by sensual jazz, which anticipates the love theme and sets up his romantic allure. As the jazz segues into an orchestral score, the distant hum of motorbikes grows into a cacophonous roar of engines as a group of speeding bikers fill the frame. The orchestral score crescendos to convey greater urgency, and is synchronised to the first medium shot of Brando riding his motorbike. At this point, the camera zooms in for Brando's close-up and his name appears, preceding the film's main title. These combined elements identify this as Brando's film and firmly establish that our viewpoint will be restricted to Johnny's experience of the events that follow.

Notoriety and censorship problems have both reimagined and maligned *The Wild One*. However, Brando was originally attracted to the role of Johnny because he admired Stanley Kramer, a respected film producer known for serious and affective realism. *The Wild One* was intended to entertain and comment on contemporary violence in all its forms: from the gang mentality of the bikers to the vigilantism of the townsfolk.[55] In marked contrast, the BBFC examiners believed that *The Wild One* had limited appeal and should only be seen by specialist audiences of educationalists, sociologists and those concerned with the problems of juvenile delinquency.[56]

The earlier evaluation of Brando's career aimed to show that his skill and method acting elevated the ordinary characters he played. In the same way, the actor's popularity and realistic performance glamorised the violence of *The Wild One* as well as endorsing a new type of non-conformist masculinity. Indubitably, part of this allure and glamour is achieved by Johnny/Brando living by his own rules. For instance, Johnny's inscrutable reaction to the police chief's closing statements, and his indifference to being released, demonstrates his truculence towards any form of authority. In their first cafe scene together, Johnny explains the pleasures of his unconventional, nomadic lifestyle to the provincial Kathie: 'We just go.'

The restless mobility trope of the film deserves further comment because it also romanticises Johnny (and his lifestyle). During the Depression, a small number of solitary American drifters rode motorbikes in search of employment. In the post-war period, unattached war veterans and others unwilling or unable to conform to suburban lifestyles and middle-class values formed motorcyclist clubs and associations. Such groups that prized this new-found freewheeling mobility inspired the Black Rebels and Beetles. Later, these gangs organised themselves into nationwide 'chapters' and lived by their own tough, vengeful code of retaliation and violence. Of these groups, the Hell's Angels became notorious, presenting a problem for police and an enduring and morbid fascination for the public.[57] Given these points, Johnny's motorbike symbolises more than his mobility: it represents his resistance to materialism and conformity. Drawing parallels between Brando and Johnny, British fan magazines described the actor's passion for motorcycling – Brando rode a similar model to the Triumph Thunderbird shown in the film – which substantiated his demonstrable riding skills. In addition, riding a motorbike symbolised his defiance of another of Hollywood's conventions of stardom. Rather than be driven around Los Angeles by a chauffeur-driven Cadillac as would befit the average Hollywood star, Brando preferred to ride onto the set, sporting motorcycle paraphernalia.[58]

As the BBFC stated, it was unlikely that British motorcycle gangs would adopt the lifestyle of their American counterparts in the ways described. To begin with, the USA's sheer vastness encouraged American motorcycle groups to drive hundreds of miles at the weekend – something that British motorcyclists could not hope to recreate. Nonetheless, the fact that Brando rode a British-made Triumph on-screen aroused concern among British riders, who were keen to watch *The Wild One* but were relieved that the film would have a limited release. Surprisingly, then, the Official Triumph Owners' Club of Great Britain fully supported the BBFC's ban in the belief that the antics of the Black Rebels would constitute a 'death blow' to their club and convince the public that all British motorcyclists were 'mad and dangerous homicidal maniacs'.[59]

Complementary to the restless trope symbolised by his motorbike, Hollywood marketed *The Wild One* on the aesthetic pleasures of Brando's motorcycle paraphernalia. In many ways, the transgressive meanings of Johnny/Brando are crystallised in his striking costume, which popularised the film poster. The novelist Ray Gosling, then a grammar school boy in Manchester, confirms that the poster was in circulation despite the film ban, and reverentially describes Brando's regalia as 'moving' and enormously 'influential' to young people.[60]

Given his acknowledged leadership of the Black Rebels, Johnny enjoys a number of privileges not extended to the rest of the gang. For example, he is the only Rebel known by a recognisable Christian name, with other gang members answering to unconventional nicknames, such as 'Crazy' and 'Pigeon'. Furthermore, Brando's prominence is distinguished by his distinctive, authoritative biker cap, which is, symbolically, knocked off when he is attacked (and emasculated) by the town vigilantes.

Parallels can be drawn between the style of the 'uniformed' Black Rebels and the 'uniform' of Britain's Teddy boys. Brando's peaked cap, leather jacket, gloves and boots distinguish him as a member of a close-knit group whose allegiances and lifestyle place him firmly outside mainstream society. The care and attention that Johnny and his Black Rebels take in maintaining their unconventional appearance also denotes their uncommon vanity. Teddy boys became a topic of discussion for their gaudy suits, patterned waistcoats, fluorescent socks, tight drainpipe trousers and colourful ties that gave them a conspicuous visibility and differentiated them from the older generation. In *Family Doctor*, Dr McAlister Brew and T. R. Fyvel, in his sociological study of juvenile offenders, argue that the extreme dandyism of Teddy boys was established to impress one another and to attract potential girlfriends.[61]

Adding more than just visual interest to *The Wild One*, Brando's clothing has the powerful effect of subverting conventional masculine codes and conveying a bolder sexuality. Brando's black leather jacket and denim jeans – associated with rugged, manual labour and outdoor pursuits – are juxtaposed to the small-town male characters who wear bland and conventional suit jackets, long-sleeved shirts and ties.

Sloan Wilson stereotyped this American middle-class male in *The Man in the Grey Flannel Suit* (1955) and described him as the de-individualised conformist embedded in the anonymising corporate world. Conversely, the fashion scholar Rebecca Arnold defines an 'ultra-style' as the display of strong visual codes of counterculture values among groups involved in 'ultra-violence'.[62] If set against

Figure 1.2 Brando's striking costume in *The Wild One* (1953) introduced audiences to the paraphernalia of California's motorcyclist clubs. Groups like the Boozer Fighters identified with Brando's glamour and mystique rather than with Chino's comicality (Lee Marvin, bottom right).

these contexts, both the fictional characters in *The Wild One* and Britain's Teddy boy gangs appear to have wielded this sartorial elegance as a bold, visual expression of their rebellion and their dissatisfaction with previously defined social parameters.

Recalling the British censor's main objections, Brando was considered an overly 'attractive' Johnny, who was likely to encourage imitation among younger audiences. In his sociological survey of cinema, Andrew Tudor maintains that cinema's youngest audiences experience the strongest projection and identification with their favourite film stars.[63] Given that Brando was 29 years old when he played Johnny, it is remarkable that Wrightsville's townsfolk refer to him and his Black Rebels as 'kids'. As improbable as it seems, the economist Mark Abrams and the novelist Peter Laurie also referred to unmarried people in their twenties as 'teenagers' if their lifestyle or behaviours were frivolous and unrestricted by financial commitments. Therefore, Johnny's attitude to life, his lack of social responsibility, and his attachment to a group of friends are elements that would have endeared him to young audiences. Further, Johnny and the Black Rebels refer to themselves as 'cool' and not 'square'.

Determining what makes an individual 'cool' is not straightforward. One thesis defines 'cool' as a highly individualistic and hedonistic code that disregards or rejects the mores of contemporary society.[64] Applying these ideas to the film's character (and Brando himself), we can arrive at only one conclusion: Johnny is 'cool'. Venerated by the gang, rejecting family ties and abjuring from marriage, pursuing hedonism in its various forms, staying 'loose' and carefree – unlike Kathie and the townsfolk – Johnny has a strong sense of self and will not compromise his desires. Playing out a veritable wish-fulfilment scenario of adolescence, Johnny confronts and challenges all figures of authority. He has the poise and arrogance to push back at the local sheriff, issuing him with a gruff warning: 'Hey, nobody tells me what to do!' Furthermore, Brando and the Black Rebels are bound together by the 'white hipster's' rhythmic and colloquial dialect –'cool' because it is adopted from marginalised black jazz culture and not mainstreamed until the Beat generation gained momentum.[65] This unfamiliar patois proved an additional source of bafflement to those in authority (the police) and the ordinary citizens of Wrightsville. Hedonism appears to motivate the Black Rebels' bad behaviour and was, therefore, evocative of the new type of violence among Teddy boys. As documented, their intensified gang life, use of improvised weapons, and fighting over 'territories' was motivated 'for the giggles', that is, as a recreational form of amusement or diversion.

Traditionally, heroic characters become role models because they display the necessary range of emotionality that appeal to their (youngest) audiences. In cinematic terms, sympathetic characters are those whom the audience closely identify with and care about. In her assessment of 1950s cinema, Penelope Houston argued that Brando was among those emerging stars whose direct appeal to the youth market was their endearing vulnerability.[66] In *The Wild One*, audience sympathy is invariably aroused when Johnny is ambushed and held captive by the town vigilantes. Having been restrained by several armed men, Johnny sustains a horrible beating. Refusing to show any weakness, he tells them: 'My dad used to hit me harder than that.' It is only when Johnny has escaped his captors, and is alone, that he allows himself to weep silently (again, a suitable narrative device that elicits our sympathy).

Ambivalence in juvenile delinquents was considered bad practice when young filmgoers were considered highly suggestible. In fact, Brando's sensitive performance was capable of 'eliciting sympathy for crooks', which directly contravened the BBFC's guidelines. When Arthur Watkins watched *The Wild One* with London's National Film Theatre members, he was greatly affected by Brando's emotive performance. 'One could also feel a certain sympathy for Johnny,' Watkins reported, 'not as a sleek villain but as a rather pitiful, confused person who learnt his lesson by the end of the film.'[67] This 'insuperably sympathetic' quality in Brando's acting was problematic because it confused the ethical issues and glorified Johnny, who should have been understood as 'a thug'.[68] Therefore, it was Brando's ability to elicit sympathy and inspire identification – through method acting techniques – which created ambivalence in all his characters as fully dimensional individuals that surely influenced the censor's ban.

Creating the brand: selling Brando in Britain

My Introduction outlined how new film historians reconstruct the unrecorded responses from 'lost' audiences. Evaluation of extra-cinematic materials, such as the weekly listings in trade journals and fan magazine polls, can be utilised to indicate a star's popularity. In 1954 and 1958, Brando ranked in *Kinematograph Weekly*'s top ten 'Best Individual Performances' and among its 'Most Popular Stars' list for 1957 – remarkable because he was the only American nominee among older, established British stars, popular with family audiences.[69] In *Picturegoer*'s annual awards poll, which drew thousands of votes from readers for their favourite individual performances, Brando secured top ten positions in the 1952 and 1958 polls, and first place in 1954 for his performance as Terry Malloy in *On the Waterfront* (Elia Kazan, 1954), which also won him a Best Actor Oscar (1955). The story of Terry Malloy provided Brando with another vehicle: the method actor played a rough-edged, inarticulate and aggrieved ex-boxer, who challenges the racketeers of the New York docks. *Picturegoer* applauded his 1954 win as a 'magnitude of triumph' for securing Brando two thousand votes more than the runner-up, the very popular Rock Hudson.[70] Naturally, *The Wild One* could not feature in the *Picturegoer* poll because of its limited exhibition. Nonetheless, Penelope Houston regarded Brando's performance as Johnny to be grounded in 'persuasive authenticity' and preferred it to his Terry Malloy, which she considered full of method acting's 'flashy effects'.[71]

Fan articles and promotional materials can be utilised to reconstruct the meanings and pleasures Brando held for his fans. Serving primarily to promote Brando's films, fan literature also sustained an extra-cinematic rhetoric between his film releases. British fan materials offer an alternative history of Brando to complement his meanings as a Hollywood icon. Throughout the 1950s, British journalists deliberated on the actor's avoidance of publicity and speculated on his non-conformist lifestyle.[72] Further, Brando's remarkable good looks and complex performances offered British audiences a new type of cinematic masculinity less clearly defined by British stars of the period. Andrew Spicer's work on men in British cinema singles out Dirk Bogarde and James Kenney as the notable sexy-sadistic juvenile delinquent types. However, British fan materials did not examine the private lives of Bogarde and Kenney with the same rigour that Brando's persona merited. Across the fan magazines, Brando was distinguished by his method acting, his physicality and an open discussion of his command of huge salaries (by British standards). Furthermore, Bogarde's 'delinquent' or 'bad boy' period was short-lived since he enjoyed more enduring success as the genteel and middle-class Dr Simon Sparrow in several of the very popular *Doctor* films (directed by Ralph Thomas), a series of whimsical British comedies that began in 1954. Arguably, it was not until Albert Finney's memorable 'rebel' performance as the factory worker and playboy, Arthur Seaton, in *Saturday Night and Sunday Morning* (Karel Reisz, 1960) that a British actor matched Brando's realistic portrayal of rugged, working-class masculinity.

In *Photoplay* and *Picturegoer*, journalists appeared to be preoccupied with Brando's transgressive off-screen behaviour and romances. That many of these articles are accompanied by advertising for beauty products suggests that Brando enjoyed a large female following. Donovan Pedelty, *Picturegoer*'s American correspondent, had introduced Brando to British audiences as the actor with a 'gladiator build' and the 'face of a poet'.[73] In addition to his remarked-upon aesthetic, Brando proved popular for his forceful acting and his 'brooding' intensity. The journalist Elizabeth Forrest declared that she would 'queue in a blizzard' for a Brando performance because 'all good women adore a brute'.[74] Similarly, ordinary female cinemagoers described their infatuation with his 'superb acting', and were keen to heartily congratulate Hollywood on their 'discovery'; predicting that he would be 'a number one "rave" for a wide feminine age group'.[75]

This ongoing preoccupation with Brando's sexual charisma is evidence of a fascination for the actor. The *Picturegoer* columnist, Henry Gris, surmised that Brando was 'the most extraordinary star in filmdom'.[76] Uncommon at the time, Brando's readings as 'unorthodox and unpredictable' and 'bohemian' were structured around his predilection for playing bongos, frequenting jazz clubs in (the predominantly black area of) Harlem, owning a pet racoon and dating ordinary, multinational women rather than Hollywood starlets.[77] When juxtaposed with rhetoric around other male stars of the period, Brando's uncompromising attitudes encouraged British journalists to discuss the actor's *sex* life rather than his love life. This rhetoric was sustained by Brando's much-publicised refusal to get married and his candidness about his sexual promiscuity – he had earned a reputation for 'courting' several women at the same time. This unconventional private life plus a flagrant defiance of the proverbial studio build-up forged an altogether new type of personality.[78] General interest articles in the specialist publication *Films and Filming* and the family-oriented *Picture Post* may not have focused on the gossip surrounding Brando's romances per se but they, too, tried to expose the nature of the 'private' man and invited speculation on Brando's faith in psychoanalytical treatment.[79]

Publicity portraits or 'stills' are also worth analysing because they provide a visual display of Brando's career transition. Early on, Brando was photographed on the set or 'at home', and standard set-ups show him posed at the piano, reading a book, playing chess, selecting records or cuddling his pet racoon. These 'relaxed' romanticised and idealised images are typical of promotional materials surrounding actors of the earlier classical Hollywood period.

On the other hand, Brando's promotional photos as Stanley Kowalski signify a distinct change and present a new type of screen masculinity. In these pin-ups – which continue to dominate internet searches on the actor – Brando conveys a bold, sexual energy by holding the gaze of the onlooker. Elements such as his sullen expression and his tousled hair evoke the hot, sultry climate of New Orleans; his T-shirt indicates his status as a manual worker. Brando's costuming in undergarments also functions to display his muscular arms and broad chest. Richard Dyer asserts that such pin-ups invite the spectator to notice 'hard' muscles as a signifier of the beauty/power duality of male strength, effort and exertion.[80]

Allusions to Kowalski were unremitting in publicity surrounding Brando's later films. Poster art for *Julius Caesar*, for example, opportunely displays Brando's muscularity in a Roman toga – other actors are depicted fully clothed – which enhances his eroticism whilst also evoking Kowalski's physicality. Connotative of method acting and his bohemian lifestyle, Brando's unconventional representation of masculinity – as an object of public speculation, adulation and fantasy – provided the basis of studio marketing for *The Wild One*, which drew on these established intertextual meanings. Promotional lobby cards for *The Wild One* generally depict him in action: he is shown looming over his co-star Lee Marvin in their fight scene or rough-handling Mary Murphy in a moment of sexual conquest.

Similarly, the poster campaign for *The Wild One* revolves on Brando's sexualised physicality. The theatrical poster centres on

Brando's face in close-up, presiding over other less prominent artwork, such as a dangling pair of female legs and a fight, which suggest the additional compensations of sex and violence. Various taglines emphasise the actor's 'raw' masculinity and magnetism and include: 'Brando is the only man who can play ... *The Wild One*' and 'Brando is a man driven wild by his own hot blood.' Drawing on Brando's intertextual meanings, he is shown without the peaked biker cap that Johnny wears throughout the film; and an insert of Johnny's love scene with Kathie is presented as an attempted rape, arguably to evoke Kowalski's sexual assault of his sister-in-law Blanche.

In like manner, the trailer capitalises on *The Wild One*'s sensational themes. The voiceover introduces the film as 'the story of a gang of hot-riding hot-heads who ride into, terrorise and take over a town led by that *Streetcar* man, Marlon Brando'. Excerpts are taken from Johnny's fight scene with Chino and his love scene with Kathie that is opportunely edited to reinforce the idea that an attempted rape is imminent.

This survey of photographic and promotional materials draws attention to how Hollywood sustained and exploited Brando's unconventional screen eroticism. Given the polysemic nature of stardom, a study of the *mise en scène* of Brando's key performances demonstrates how the 'gaze' was turned to him. Laura Mulvey's well-known essay on 'the gaze' argues that formal and technical devices enhance the 'looked-at-ness' of women in cinema to position them as the passive objects of heterosexual male desire.[81] As foregrounded in my Introduction, Steve Neale argues for the 'male as spectacle' in cinema – filmic moments when men rather than women are positioned as the object of the gaze but are feminised as a result.[82]

Unpacking this aspect of Brando's performances offers additional perspectives on the actor's stardom. Indeed, re-evaluation of *A Streetcar Named Desire* demonstrates that Brando's masculine 'beauty' overshadows that of Blanche, framed as frail and fading, and his screen wife Stella (Kim Hunter), who wears a succession of dowdy, loose-fitting costumes. Kowalski's volatile temper and the eruption of drunken fist fights with his gambling cronies doubly function to display Brando's raw physicality. Later films, including *The Wild One*, would ensure that this virulent masculinity was facilitated – even 'punished' – in brutal fight scenes in which Brando's clothes could be (excusably) ripped and torn to reveal flesh.[83] If Neale's assertion that the 'male as spectacle' is negotiated by his 'feminisation', then Brando's excessive emotionality appears to function in this way. A pertinent example would be the now classic scene of Kowalski's reconciliation with his wife. Kowalski is shown returning from a drunken brawl, disoriented and anguished; he calls, 'Stella! Stella!' before falling to his knees at the foot of the stairs. At the point of Kowalski's submission, Stella runs down the stairs to embrace him and is positioned higher in the frame than Kowalski to magnify her 'power' and emphasise his weakness. Through this camerawork, and Brando's whimpering and wailing, Kowalski is arguably reduced to a vulnerable and 'feminised' infant.

The Wild One also offers Brando as 'spectacle' in multiple shots when he dominates the frame without the mediating looks of other screen characters. This necessary mediation was a technique, achieved by cross-cutting between characters, which disavowed a homoerotic gaze among audiences. A striking example of Brando as a 'feminised' object of desire, then, is the full body shot that shows Johnny first entering Kathie's bar. The camera focuses on Brando's languorous parade in the empty space around the jukebox – the cut to Kathie's quizzical look does not happen immediately. This rugged but emotional cinematic masculinity distinguished Brando as a remarkable actor. Dyer has observed that Brando, and many of his contemporaries, possessed an alluring dual register of 'tough-but-childlike' and 'mean-but-vulnerable' qualities.[84] Evocative of Kowalski's unpredictability, *The Wild One*'s Johnny displays a spectrum of emotion. In one scene, Johnny, beaten up by the town's vigilantes, finally escapes his pursuers to find sanctuary in a secluded spot. In a tangible display of male–female duality, Johnny weeps beside his motorbike, in an unflinching close-up, enhanced – and 'beautified' – by the use of moonlight. Such filmic moments appear to endorse what Neale considers the essential 'feminisation' of the male as spectacle.

Similarly, Steve Cohan argues that Brando's sensitive, boyish character marked a transition from the rugged and mature American screen men of the 1940s.[85] Robert Muller's contemporaneous essay recognised the change in Hollywood men and compared the proliferation of 'Brando Boys' – introverts with 'complexes' – to the uncomplicated 'beefcake' or 'dream boys', like Tony Curtis and

Rock Hudson, whose personae sustained earlier notions of screen masculinity.[86]

The ban: British critics and filmgoers

In 1954, the BBFC understood the ramifications of its ban: it would now be at the discretion of local authorities to ask magistrates to grant *The Wild One* a local X certificate. After the first such decision was taken in Cambridge, several local watch committees also chose to overrule the BBFC. Perhaps with respect to traditional rivalries between their respective universities, Oxford magistrates upheld the BBFC's ban despite the fact that it shared Cambridge's low incidence of juvenile delinquency.[87]

Following its three-week run at the Rex in Cambridge, there were subsequent showings to general audiences. *The Wild One* was booked for a six-day engagement at the New Theatre, Maesteg (Wales), and the Royal Hippodrome, Belfast, from 16 May 1955. In addition, the film played for five weeks at the Grand Central, in Glasgow, beginning 15 January 1956, and had limited three-day runs at local cinemas in Lanarkshire county between October and November 1956. The film was booked in London four years later, when it played for three consecutive days from 14 March 1960 at La Continentale Cinema on Tottenham Court Road. This reluctance to show the film suggests that the BBFC's gravest misgivings about *The Wild One*'s negative influences concerned London's Teddy boys. Their attacks on immigrants and 'territorial' fights kept them in the news and branded them as the most notorious in the country. In December 1958, PC Raymond Summers was fatally stabbed while trying to intervene in a drunken brawl between rival gangs outside a dance hall in north London. The culprit, Ronnie Marwood, was a local scaffolder with alleged connections to the Nash Brothers, one of London's organised crime families. The Notting Hill race riots of August and September 1958 exposed the inherent racism of Teddy boys; and in May 1959, a Teddy gang ambushed and killed West Indian Kelso Cochrane.

Several petitions by Columbia studio to persuade the BBFC to overturn their original decision were rejected. As a pertinent commentary on contemporary violence, the examiners recommended that local film societies should show *The Wild One* to their adult-only members. However, since these events required advance planning and permissions, private screenings were slow to materialise. Approximately fourteen local film societies across the United Kingdom showed the film between December 1956 and February 1958, including those at Anglesey, Bolton, Canterbury, Edinburgh, Worthing and York. *The Wild One* premiered at London's National Film Theatre on 29 August 1957 with Arthur Watkins and the film's director Laszlo Benedek in attendance. During the question and answer forum that followed the screening, Benedek told his audience that he had sincerely wanted to make an adult-themed film and was deeply saddened and confused by the BBFC's ban.[88]

Certainly, *The Wild One* polarised opinions and opened up a public debate on the value (and scope) of film censorship. The widespread support for the BBFC ban came from older cinema patrons – youth leaders and parents – who expressed strong disdain of the 'nasty' film. Concerned by the seemingly insurmountable problems of juvenile delinquency, these individuals argued that the film would 'put ideas into teenagers' heads' and encourage 'brute force' and 'a lack of decency'.[89] On the other hand, Brando's fans, who anticipated his every appearance, were disheartened by the BBFC's decision. One Lincolnshire filmgoer called the ban 'stupid' and felt denied of the opportunity to watch another of his idol's 'brilliant' performances.[90] Another discerning filmgoer reprimanded the BBFC for an illogical decision: 'Does the censor really believe that young people, having seen the film, will race to the nearest motor-cycle, and roar off in groups to terrorise the first village they find?'[91] Similarly, an erudite NFT member accused the BBFC of underestimating *The Wild One*'s philosophical qualities – 'bravely' depicting the alienation of 'ordinary mortals' – and creating 'an unhealthy aura' around a commendable and otherwise innocuous film.[92]

British fan publications invited their readers to participate in the debate but also advised a show of restraint and equanimity. In *Picturegoer*, Lionel Collier insisted that cinemagoers respect the British censor's decision because his judgement was 'the best and most enlightened in the world'.[93] Nonetheless, some ordinary filmgoers expected and demanded more information; their letters demonstrate an underlying dissatisfaction with having their film choices made for them by a small team of individuals working without a code. One Portsmouth resident advocated for a policy of transparency in the BBFC's modus operandi because its decisions affected the cinemagoing public and the future of Britain's filmmakers.[94] In confidential correspondence, Arthur Watkins and the secretary of Bristol University's Film Society also exchanged ideas about the value of film censorship. Whilst happy to engage in the debate, the discussions concluded with Watkins' reassertion that *The Wild One*'s depiction of violence was not 'artistic' but inserted purely for 'mere sensationalism'.[95]

Many of the teenagers who saw the film at the Rex in Cambridge believed that *The Wild One* would be valuable in encouraging a dialogue about juvenile delinquency.[96] When asked about the film's purported brutality, the majority held the opinion that *The Wild One* contained milder violence than the Westerns and gangster films they were already familiar with – all passed with an A certificate. If taken at face value, these opinions appear to contradict the BBFC's decision to ban the film. What must be emphasised here, however, is that these opinions were taken from Cambridge undergraduates and middle-class teenagers not known for their altercations with police. Indeed, these same youngsters reiterated the BBFC's projections about showing the film in deprived areas (Liverpool was cited) where Teddy boy 'problems' often took on more tangible expression.

In addition to the discourses generated in the fan magazines, the BBFC's ban of a prestige production opened up the debate in the national press. *Daily Express* readers were invited to comment and demonstrated, in equal measure, praise for Brando's exceptional performance but criticism for its undesirability to impressionable teenagers.[97] On behalf of the *Sunday Dispatch*, John Watney invited several well-known personalities to a private screening and relayed the panel's mixed views to his readers. The Labour MP and former Minister of Defence (1950–51), Emanuel Shinwell, who had grown up in the impoverished East End, credited the film for being 'realistic' and for alerting Britain to some of the dangers of America's localised violence. He wanted the film passed. William Brown, an independent MP for Rugby, opined that the film should be passed because he was wary of all censorship. Ursula Bloom, a popular novelist, suggested the Teddy boys were 'bad enough' and both she and the final panellist, the actor Donald Gray, agreed that the film should be banned.[98]

In as much as cinema's survival depended on its innovation, the BBFC's mandate was to protect the youngest audiences from sensationalised depictions of contemporary life. Sidney Harris anticipated a media backlash when the *Daily Express* film reviewer David Lewin reported on confidential censorship matters divulged to him by Max Thorpe, the Columbia studio executive.[99] In January 1955, Lewin rallied support for *The Wild One* by describing Brando's 'astonishing' performance and urged the censors to reconsider because the film could be used as 'a top talking point wherever teenagers try to act tough'.[100] It remains a point of conjecture whether Thorpe had actually breached confidentiality in relaying his dealings with the BBFC to the press. More likely, Thorpe, like Lewin, considered realistic film treatment of contemporary issues to be valuable social documents. Gavin Lambert, the co-founder of the radical film magazine *Sequence* (1949–51), similarly, found the censors' decision short-sighted because sex and violence were 'unavoidable facts' of modern life.[101] Hollywood's frank commentary on adult themes was one means of challenging the competition mounted by a burgeoning television industry, then restricted to family oriented entertainment. Given that every film was an enormous financial risk, *The Wild One*, as a topical commentary, was profitable only for the short time it was relevant to audiences.

Amid these contradictory opinions, Dilys Powell proved a rare exception in unequivocally advocating the BBFC's ban. The well-respected Powell had served as the *Sunday Times* film critic since 1939 and her tenure had secured her a position of power and influence. Despite commending Brando's 'extraordinary' performance – and perhaps because of it – Powell believed the film would corrupt the nation's youth. Given its scenes of indiscriminate violence, Powell drew parallels between the brutality and uniformity of the Black Rebels to 'Hitler's young SS thugs'.[102] Why did Powell refer filmgoers back to a horrific but recent episode of political and military history? Powell's review unequivocally finds the amorality of the Black Rebels akin to the marauding Teddy boys, known for their inter-gang violence but also for their attacks on racial minorities.

Certainly, it was a striking and ugly comparison that fully vindicated the BBFC's decision to ban the film. It also drew attention to British fascist groups, such as the Union Movement and the League of Empire Loyalists which – though they never gained a substantial parliamentary foothold – gained popular support in racially diverse communities after the British Nationality Act (1948). Such groups lobbied to 'keep Britain white' and challenged the government's policies on Commonwealth immigration, espoused anti-Semitism and racial purity. As described in the Introduction, racist attacks by Teddy boys were particularly rife in areas where white working-class communities lived in close proximity to West Indian immigrants. Sidney Harris was quick to personally thank Powell for 'enlightening the public' on the BBFC's dilemma's in banning a film with 'so fine an actor in the leading role'.[103]

Issues of censorship around *The Wild One* had instigated lively debate across a range of British audiences. The BBFC's proscriptive measures to prevent 16- to 20-year-olds from viewing the film are better understood when contextualised against the change in the cinemagoing publics of the post-war years. By the mid-1950s, 15- to 24-year-olds constituted a quarter of all cinema admissions. A drop in audience attendance and the construction of fewer new cinemas concentrated filmgoing into metropolitan areas. As a result, audiences were primarily young, single working-class people – a demographic that numbered approximately five million. Between 1956 and 1957, 63 per cent of British 16- to 24-year-olds went to the cinema on a regular basis, outnumbering older demographics – such as those with young families – whose leisure patterns had changed most noticeably.[104] As Harper and Porter point out, an increasingly youthful market was satisfied by Hollywood's production of youth-oriented films at a time when British film producers had not yet found a successful teenage formula.[105] The dearth of British cinema catering to this fragmenting family audience meant that Hollywood films anticipated and filled the niche for contemporary and relevant films.

Conclusion

At the centre of a troubled and contested censorship, *The Wild One* comprises an important episode of 'British' cinema history. In his memoir, John Trevelyan explained the ban as the only means to thwart the misleading 'message' of *The Wild One*: in effect, that 'crime pays' and relieves the monotony of an otherwise mundane existence. In preventing the 'message' being disseminated to 'the irresponsible class of adolescent to be found in too many of our large cities', the board was vindicated of encouraging further Teddy boy violence.[106] This chapter has argued that the 'messenger' was as problematic as the 'message': Brando glamorised juvenile delinquency by endorsing a challenge to legitimate authority both on and off screen. *The Wild One* arrived in Britain during an epoch of intense social change, amidst the emergence of the dandified Teddy boys, who, while their serious crimes were few in reality, were demonised in the press for appearing symptomatic of the nation's moral decline.

During the fourteen years *The Wild One* was banned, Columbia studio executives approached the BBFC several times to petition the examiners for a reappraisal. Throughout the 1950s, the BBFC restated that only an entirely 'new' film with a wholly 'different' outlook to juvenile delinquency would reverse original decisions.[107] In 1957, the BBFC reinstated their ban in response to a new juvenile crime wave involving urban teenage gangs, which habitually descended on rural towns to cause havoc.[108] In the mid-1960s, the film was rejected by the BBFC for its evocation of the skirmishes between the Mods and Rockers in British seaside towns.[109] It was clear from the outset that the censors would rather be criticised by cinemagoers for their stringent censorship than be reprimanded by local authorities for passing a film perceived as dangerous on 'social grounds'.[110]

By not granting *The Wild One* a certificate, the BBFC had delivered a landmark verdict. High production values and a top-ranking star were no longer a guarantee that a Hollywood film would enjoy a wide exhibition in Britain. *The Wild One* was rejected for glamorising crime and contravening the British censor's 'crime does not pay' mandate. Rather than accommodating Hollywood's new direction in socially relevant but challenging drama, the British censors held firmly to an outmoded 'hypodermic needle' theory of cinema that cast predominantly young, working-class audiences as highly suggestible and undiscerning.

The problem confronting the British censor essentially lay in the stardom of Marlon Brando. The analysis has shown that Brando's status as a credible, charismatic actor had created an overly sympathetic and compelling study of the juvenile delinquent. One critic of note, Robert Muller, lauded Brando for his 'brilliance' and because he 'taught' foreign audiences about contemporary America.[111] Sidney Harris also realised Brando's cultural relevance and contemporaneity, and remarked on his special relationship with film fans.[112] Brando's anti-star rhetoric in extra-cinematic materials and several powerful performances had imbued the actor with a verifiable and potent rebelliousness. The prototype of the rebel motor biker was to prove highly influential as a trope in popular youth culture. The long-serving *Picturegoer* critic Margaret Hinxman was one of the first to recognise Brando's single-handed influence in beginning the 'rebel cult' in films.[113] In the 1960s, the mentality of Brando's 'anarchical motor-cyclist' would be assimilated into the British rock rebel figure of popular music and counterculture.[114]

In 1968, *The Wild One* was finally granted an X certificate by the BBFC. John Trevelyan conceded that the film posed no threat as an imitable model for teenage gangs because time had reduced its 'impact'.[115] The premiere of this prestigious Hollywood production was anti-climactic: the filmic elements that singled out the contemporaneity of *The Wild One* had inevitably dissipated. British film reviewers were unanimous in denigrating the anachronism of the film's language, lacklustre performances, and the unlikelihood of Brando and his Black Rebels being 'teenagers'. In 1968, the actor was middle-aged and no longer relevant to younger cinemagoers. Numerous interviews had recounted his anti-star rhetoric ad nauseum, and his credible method acting was superseded by a well-documented avarice and a reluctance to ingratiate himself with fans.[116] A series of box office failures, and a financially disastrous turn at directing (*One-Eyed Jacks*, 1961) had gained Brando a reputation for being unprofessional and uninsurable. No doubt, this reconfiguration of Brando as a jaded Hollywood personality without a sustainable fan base facilitated the reversal of the BBFC's original decision. *The Wild One* was released on VHS in the 1980s (rated PG) and first shown on British television on 28 October 1983 after the watershed.

The chapter has shown that Brando's status in the early 1950s marked him as a new and important personality. However, Brando was almost 30 when he played Johnny. His maturity and his desire for versatility steered his career towards a range of demonstrably adult roles, which would invariably distance him from cinema's youngest fans. The mantle of the young Hollywood 'rebel' was to be enduringly redefined by other 'Brando Boys' such as James Dean (Chapter 3) and Elvis Presley (Chapter 5). In adhering to the chronological structure of the book, however, the next chapter analyses *Blackboard Jungle*, the film that synergised rock 'n' roll with depictions of American juvenile delinquency and instigated stringent British censorship.

Notes

1 Marlon Brando with Robert Lindsey, *Songs My Mother Taught Me* (London: Century, 1994), p. 176.
2 John Watney, '*The Wild One*', *Sunday Dispatch*, 24 April 1954 (*The Wild One*, BFI microfiche).
3 Stephen Watts, 'Brando's fans resent Wild One ban', *New York Times*, 22 May 1955, p. 129.
4 Leslie Halliwell, 'Why I fought for the film', *Picturegoer*, 29:1044, 7 May 1955, p. 9; and *Seats in All Parts: Half a Lifetime at the Movies* (London: Granada, 1985), pp. 188–190.
5 Quoted in Lionel Collier, 'The fuss fizzles out', *Picturegoer*, 7 May 1955, p. 9.
6 Examiner's Report, 5 January 1955 (BBFC Files).
7 'A Streetcar to Hollywood', *Picturegoer*, 20:805, 7 October 1950, pp. 5–6.
8 Frank Rooney, 'Cyclists' raid', *Harpers Magazine*, January 1951, pp. 34–44.
9 'Hot Blood' was substituted because it was thought to suggest a "blood-spill" of violence. See 'Marlon Brando title again *The Wild One*', *Variety*, 192:13, 2 December 1953, p. 20.
10 Hunter S. Thompson, *Hell's Angels* (London: Penguin, 1988), pp. 77–9.
11 Donovan Pedelty, 'Brando: a hillbilly or ragged rebel', *Picturegoer*, 28:1017, 30 October 1954, pp. 14–15.
12 *The Men* pressbook (Columbia, 1950, BFI microfiche).
13 F. Maurice Speed, *Film Review 1951–1952* (London: Macdonald and Co Ltd, 1951), p. 39.
14 See for example, Michael Sheridan, 'The heart of Marlon Brando', *Picturegoer*, 36:1216, 23 August 1958, p. 7.
15 Penelope Houston, 'One eyed Jacks', *Sight and Sound*, 30:3 (Summer 1961), p. 144.

16 *Sunday Express*, 22 November 1953 (*Marlon Brando*, BFI microfiche). See also John Seton, 'Hollywood's bad lads', *Picturegoer*, 24:916, 22 November 1952.
17 Stella Bruzzi, *Bringing up Daddy: Fatherhood and Masculinity in Post-War Hollywood* (London: BFI, 2006); Barbara Klinger, *Melodrama and Meaning: History, Culture, and the Films of Douglas Sirk* (Bloomington: Indiana University Press, 1994). For a social context of psychoanalysis in the USA, see Elaine Tyler May, *Homeward Bound: American Families in the Cold War Era* (London: Hachette, 2008).
18 The following reviews were unfavourable: Lionel Collier, 'Coming your way: *The Men*', *Picturegoer*, 20:815, 16 December 1950, p. 18; and W. H. Mooring, 'The truth about Judy', *Picturegoer*, 20:794, 22 July 1950, p. 16. Favourable reviews included: Mary Benedetta, 'Will the women like *The Men*?' *Picturegoer*, 20:809, 4 November 1950, p. 17; and Richard Winnington, '*The Men* and the undefeated', *Sight and Sound*, 19:81 (December 1950), p. 330.
19 Tennessee Williams' letter to his agent, Audrey Wood, quoted in Brando, *Songs My Mother Taught Me*, p. 119.
20 See the chapter 'Brando: in the shadow of Kowalski' in Hollis Alpert, *Dreams and Dreamers* (New York: Macmillan, 1962), pp. 40–62.
21 Laurence Olivier, *Laurence Olivier: Confessions of an Actor* (London: Weidenfeld & Nicolson, 1982), p. 135. For a fuller account of Olivier's production and the censorship issues raised by the Lord Chamberlain's office see Philip C. Kolin, *Williams: A Streetcar Named Desire* (Cambridge: Cambridge University Press, 2000), pp. 62–70.
22 Laurence Olivier letter to Tennessee Williams quoted in Kolin, *Williams: A Streetcar Named Desire*, p. 69.
23 'At the theatre: *A Streetcar Named Desire*', *The Tatler*, 194:2520, 26 October 1949, p. 10.
24 Kenneth Tynan, *He that Plays the King: A View of the Theatre* (London: Longman Green, 1950), p. 170. Tynan may well have been referencing Colleano's memorable role as the GI deserter in *Good-Time Girl* (David McDonald, 1948).
25 John Gielgud, *Gielgud Letters* (London: Weidenfeld & Nicolson, 2004), p. 157.
26 See 'Focus: a film review', 20:228, December 1953, p. 276; 'Julius Caesar', *Monthly Film Bulletin*, 22:3, 1 January 1953, p. 172.
27 Gavin Lambert, 'Julius Caesar', *Sight and Sound*, 23:2, 1 October 1953, p. 89.
28 Lionel Collier, 'Julius Caesar', *Picturegoer*, 26:966, 7 November 1953, p. 18.

29 John Trevelyan, *What the Censor Saw* (London: Michael Joseph, 1968), p. 152.
30 Jerold Simmons, 'Violent youth: the censoring and public reception of *The Wild One* and *Blackboard Jungle*', in *Film History*, 20:3 (Studio Systems, 2008), pp. 381–91.
31 Sue Harper and Vincent Porter, *The Decline of Deference: Cinemagoing in 1950s Britain* (Oxford: Oxford University Press, 2003), pp. 221–2.
32 T. P. O'Connor's 43 rules (1917) and the BBFC Codified Grounds for censorship (1926) are reproduced in full in Sarah J. Smith, *Children, Cinema & Censorship: From Dracula to the Dead End Kids* (London: I. B. Tauris, 2005), pp. 179–83.
33 Sidney Harris letter to Sir David E. Griffiths, 7 January 1955 (BBFC Files).
34 Reg Whitley, 'At the new films: a nightmare comes true', *Daily Mirror*, 25 March 1955, p. 10.
35 'For and against', Examiner's Notes, 5 January 1955 (BBFC Files).
36 Sir David E. Griffiths letter to Sidney Harris, 17 January 1955 (BBFC Files).
37 Anthony Aldgate and James Robertson, *Censorship in Theatre and Cinema* (Edinburgh: Edinburgh University Press, 2005), pp. 79–85.
38 Milton Shulman, 'Is this the time to put thugs on the screen?', *London Evening Standard*, 5 February 1953.
39 Letter to Sidney Harris from an unnamed 'cosh victim', 19 February 1953 (BBFC Files).
40 Sidney Harris note to Arthur Watkins, 4 April 1952; Harris to Griffiths, 7 January 1955 (BBFC Files).
41 Sarah J. Smith, *Children, Cinema and Censorship: From Dracula to the Dead End Kids* (London: I. B. Tauris, 2005), p. 75.
42 James Robertson, *The Hidden Cinema: British Film Censorship in Action 1913–1972* (London: Routledge, 2006), p. 71.
43 See for example, 'Clapham Common stabbing: five youths charged', *The Times*, 6 July 1953, p. 6; 'Youths on murder charge: girl's evidence of alleged threats', *The Times*, 5 August 1953, p. 3.
44 Details of Beckley's multiple stab wounds were reprinted from the testimony of a high-ranking Harley Street pathologist called as witness. See 'Clapham Common stabbing: six youths sent for trial', *The Times*, 13 August 1953, p. 3.
45 Harris to Griffiths, 29 January 1955 (BBFC Files).
46 Examiner's note, 26 January 1955 (BBFC Files).
47 Dick Hebdige, *Subculture: The Meaning of Style* (London and New York: Routledge), p. 50; Tony Jefferson, 'Cultural responses of the Teds', in Stuart Hall and Tony Jefferson (eds), *Resistance Through*

Rituals: Youth Subcultures in Post-War Britain (London: Hutchinson, 1976), p. 81. For an alternative account of the Teddy Boy murder see: www.edwardianteddyboy.com/page6.htm (last accessed 20 June 2019).

48 Michael Davies, a 20-year-old labourer from Clapham, was convicted of Beckley's murder. See 'Edwardian suits, dance music and a dagger', *Daily Mail*, 15 September 1953, pp. 8–9. When the barristers Sasha Wass and Jeremy Dein reinvestigated the case in *Murder, Mystery and My Family* (Season 1, Episode 9, BBC, Lorna Hartnett, 2018) the charge was found to be 'unsafe'.

49 Arthur Watkins to Messrs Columbia Studios, 25 January 1954; Harris to Griffiths, 29 January 1955 (BBFC Files).

50 Examiner's report notes by NKD, 5 January 1955 (BBFC Files).

51 Note from Examiners, 26 January 1955 (BBFC Files).

52 John Gibbs, *Mise-en-Scene: Film Style and Interpretation* (London: Wallflower Press, 2002), p. 5.

53 Richard Dyer, *Stars* (London: BFI, 1979); Paul McDonald, *Hollywood Stardom* (Chichester: Wiley-Blackwell, 2013), pp. 13–14.

54 Helen Hanson, *Hollywood Soundscapes: Film Sound Style, Craft & Production in the Classical Era* (London: BFI/Palgrave, 2017), pp. 61 and 74–7.

55 Brando, *Songs My Mother Taught Me*, pp. 175–6.

56 Watkins to Thorpe, 23 July 1954 (BBFC Files).

57 Thompson, *Hell's Angels*, p. 81.

58 Pedelty, 'Brando: hillbilly or ragged rebel', p. 14.

59 W. Ronald Quennel, Official Journal of the Triumph Owners' Motorcycle Club, to Arthur Watkins, 6 May 1955 (BBFC Files).

60 Ray Gosling, *Personal Copy: A Memoir of the Sixties* (London and Boston: Faber & Faber, 1980), p. 37.

61 Dr Josephine McAlister Brew, *Family Doctor* (7 July 1955); T. R. Fyvel, *The Insecure Offenders: Rebellious Youth in the Welfare State* (London: Chatto & Windus, 1961).

62 Rebecca Arnold, *Fashion, Desire and Anxiety: Image and Morality in the 20th Century* (New Brunswick, NJ: Rutgers University Press, 2001), pp. 12 and 34–5.

63 Andrew Tudor, *Images and Influence: Studies in the Sociology of Film* (London: Routledge, 2014), pp. 83–4.

64 Dick Pountain and David Robins, *Cool Rules: Anatomy of an Attitude* (London: Reaktion Books, 2000), p. 23.

65 Norman Mailer's much reprinted essay *The White Negro* (San Francisco: City Lights, 1957) was the first to explore the white American hipster philosophy and culture.

66 Penelope Houston, *The Contemporary Cinema* (Harmondsworth: Penguin, 1966), p. 77.
67 Notes from Examiners, NKD, National Film Theatre Screening, 29 August 1957 (BBFC Files).
68 Francis Wyndham comments on the film in a retrospective article: 'Brando by Wyndham', *Sunday Times*, 3 July 1966 (*Marlon Brando*, BFI microfiche).
69 *Kinematograph Weekly*, 16 December 1954, p. 8; 12 December 1957, p. 6; 18 December 1957, p. 6 (BFI microfiche).
70 'Picturegoer awards', *Picturegoer*, 27:992, 8 May 1954, p. 7.
71 Penelope Houston, '*The Wild One*', *Monthly Film Bulletin*, 22:252, 1 January 1955, p. 88.
72 Donald Hunt, 'Two views on Brando', *Picturegoer*, 23:883, 5 April 1952, p. 9; Pedelty, 'Brando', pp. 14–15.
73 Donovan Pedelty, 'A streetcar to Hollywood', *Picturegoer*, 7 October 1950, pp. 5–6.
74 Elizabeth Forrest, 'Two views on Brando', *Picturegoer*, 23:883, 5 April 1952, p. 9.
75 Miss Grace Brown, Seven Kings, Essex, Miss Shirley Moore, Willesden, London, and J. Merrick, Bushey, Herts, 'Brando', *Picturegoer*, 23:891, 31 May 1952, p. 3; Miss Hetty Sweeney, London, E.9., 'Bravo Brando', *Picturegoer*, 29:1048, 4 June 1955, p. 3.
76 Henry Gris, 'King Beatnik: Part III: Hollywood tycoon', *Picturegoer*, 38:1276, 5 December, pp. 14–15.
77 See for example, John Seton, 'Hollywood's bad lads', *Picturegoer*, 22 November 1952, pp. 11 and 26; 'Brando goes for warmth', *Picturegoer*, 32:1124, 17 November 1956, p. 29; Bill Bailey, 'Why Brando likes cats', *Movie Secrets* (April 1956), pp. 40 and 70; Billie and Marsha Doe, 'Brando tries Tahitian love', *Movie TV Secrets* (May 1961), pp. 38–39 and 60.
78 See for example, 'No beauty! But I'm not unattractive – says Marlon Brando', *Daily Mirror*, 13 August 1954 (*Marlon Brando*, BFI microfiche); Ernie Player, 'Brando almost became the great lover', *Picturegoer*, 30:1062, 10 September 1955, 30:1062, p. 12; Peter Stuart, 'How to kiss on the screen', *Picturegoer*, 34:1179, 7 December 1957, p. 8; Henry Gris, 'King beatnik', *Picturegoer*, 38:1274, 21 November 1959, pp. 8–9; 'King Beatnik: Part II: The girls Brando dates', *Picturegoer*, 38:1275, 28 November 1959, p. 6; 'King beatnik: Part III: Hollywood tycoon', 38: 1276, 5 December 1959, pp. 14–15.
79 Robert Muller, 'Brando v America', *Picture Post*, Issue 10, 6 March 1954, pp. 17–18 and 41.
80 Richard Dyer, 'Don't look now: the instabilities of the male pin-up', in *Only Entertainment* (Oxford: Routledge, 2005), pp. 131–147.

81 Laura Mulvey, 'Visual and narrative pleasures', *Screen*, 16:3 (Autumn 1975), pp. 6–18.
82 Steve Neale, 'Masculinity as spectacle: reflections on men and mainstream cinema', *Screen*, 24:6, 1 November 1983, pp. 2–17.
83 Sean Day-Lewis commented: 'Experienced watchers of Mr Brando will know that a beating-up is obligatory in his films.' See 'Wild One dwindles into period piece', *Daily Telegraph*, 15 February 1968 (*The Wild One*, BFI microfiche), p. 19. Peter Biskind suggests that Brando is badly beaten in his films as 'punishment' for 'his raw power and masculinity', in *Seeing is Believing: How Hollywood Taught us to Stop Worrying and Love the Fifties* (New York: Bloomsbury, 1983), p. 260.
84 Richard Dyer, *Heavenly Bodies: Film Stars and Society* (Basingstoke and London: Macmillan Education Ltd, 1987), pp. 12–13.
85 Steve Cohan, *Masked Men: Masculinity and the Movies of the Fifties* (Bloomington and Indianapolis: Indiana University Press, 1997), pp. 201–63.
86 Robert Muller, 'Beefcake or Brando?', *Picture Post*, Issue 10, 4 June 1955, pp. 44, 47 and 50.
87 'Oxford cannot see *The Wild One*', *Manchester Guardian*, 14 April 1955, p. 1.
88 As recalled by Robert Dunstone in his letter to Arthur Watkins, 30 August 1957 (BBFC Files).
89 M. Seaward, Parsons Green, S.W, *Daily Express*, 24 January 1955; and 'Southsea', *Sunday Dispatch*, 1 May 1955 (*The Wild One*, BFI microfiche).
90 Brian Wood, Lincolnshire, 'A stupid ban', *Photoplay* [GB], 6:9 (September 1955), p. 4.
91 R. F. H. Davies, 'Focus: *The Wild One*', *Picturegoer*, 29:1037, 19 March 1955, p. 5.
92 Dunston to Watkins, 30 August 1957 (BBFC Files).
93 Derek Walker, 'The fuss fizzles out: spotlight on Cambridge where the film that was banned had its first public showing', *Picturegoer*, 29:1044, 7 May 1955, p. 8.
94 Clive Beech, Portsmouth, 'Explain the cuts', *Photoplay* [GB] (September 1955), p. 4.
95 Anthony Baker, Secretary of the University of Bristol Film Society, to Arthur Watkins, 24 October 1954 (BBFC Files).
96 Walker, 'The fuss fizzles out', p. 8.
97 See letters from Mrs W. Dutton, Middlesex, and M. Seaward, London SW, *Daily Express*, 24 January 1955 (*The Wild One*, BFI microfiche).
98 John Watney, 'The film they won't let you see', *Sunday Dispatch*, 24 April 1955 (*The Wild One*, BFI Microfiche).

99 David Griffiths to Sidney Harris, 19 January 1955 (BBFC Files).
100 David Lewin, 'Brando banned', *Daily Express*, 19 January 1955 (*The Wild One*, BFI microfiche).
101 Gavin Lambert, '*The Wild One*', *Sight and Sound*, 25:1 (Summer 1955), pp. 30–1.
102 Dilys Powell, 'The censor says no', *Sunday Times*, 1 May 1955, p. 7.
103 Sidney Harris to Dilys Powell, 1 May 1955 (BBFC Files).
104 IPA National Readership Survey statistics are quoted in Stuart Hanson, *From Silent Screen to Multiplex: A History of Cinema Exhibition in Britain since 1896* (Manchester: Manchester University Press), p. 103.
105 Sue Harper and Vincent Porter, *British Cinema Audiences of the 1950s* (Oxford: Oxford University Press: 2003), p. 261.
106 Watkins to R. M. Prisbram, Newcastle-upon-Tyne Film Society, 16 June 1955 (BBFC Files).
107 Watkins to Mike J. Frankovich, 21 December 1955 (BBFC Files).
108 Examiner's Notes, NKB, 13 September 1957 (BBFC Files).
109 John Trevelyan to E. J. Bryson, 31 March 1964 (BBFC Files).
110 Watkins to Messrs Columbia Pictures, 25 January 1954 (BBFC Files).
111 Robert Muller, 'Brando vs America: the wild and violent film hero, is now in the care of a psychiatrist. Will he return to films? Or is his strange and potent talent lost to us forever?', *Picture Post*, 6 March 1954, Issue 10, pp. 17–18 and 41.
112 Harris to Griffiths, 7 January 1955 (BBFC Files).
113 Margaret Hinxman, 'The world's most versatile actor: Marlon Brando', *Picturegoer*, 35:1204, 31 May 1958, pp. 10–11.
114 David Baker, 'Rock rebels and delinquents: the emergence of the Rock rebel in the youth problem films of the 1950s', in *Continuum*, March 2005, 19:1, pp. 39–54; George Melly, *Revolt into Style: The Pop Arts in the 50s and 60s* (Oxford: Oxford University Press, 1989), pp. 30–1.
115 John Trevelyan is quoted in Day-Lewis, 'Wild One dwindles into period piece'.
116 An early censure of this uncooperative 'killjoy' attitude was relayed to fans in 'Come off it, Brando!', *Photoplay* [GB], 6:11 (November 1955), pp. 14–15.

2

'Our Teddy boys are angels': *Blackboard Jungle* fever in the classroom

> It is a film which should be rejected. The scenes of violence inside the school and outside, in which young boys are involved, are quite revolting.
>
> British Board of Film Censors, March 1955[1]

> Our most brutal, ignorant spivs and Teddy boys are spotless angels compared with the New York slum kids of this disturbing film.
>
> Frank Jackson, *Reynolds News*, September 1955[2]

Blackboard Jungle (Richard Brooks, 1955) opened at the Red Hall Cinema in London's Fulham area to the usual rowdiness of local gangs of Teddy boys. Walham Green Teds jostled with their rivals, the Putney gang, to get to the front of the queue to buy tickets. Inside, the cinema manager's delay in raising the asbestos fire screen met with the unanimous jeers and whistles of both gangs. Finally, the house lights dimmed, the curtains were pulled back, and the film's opening titles appeared – 'Blackboard Jungle' scrawled on a chalk board – over which the sound of Bill Haley and the Comets' *Rock Around the Clock* was played. 'I sat there in the Red Hall stunned at the behaviour of the Blackboard Jungle delinquents', remembered Mim Scala, of the Walham gang, 'my suede shoes tapping to the compulsive soundtrack'.[3] The film showing was interrupted by the rowdy fight that erupted between the rival gangs. Teddy girls began screaming and watched one teenager slash the screen with his razor while other Teddy boys ripped up the formerly plush red seats of this faded picture palace. To the older patrons who took cover, the screen delinquency appeared to have spilled over into real life. The cinema manager and his projectionist – returning reluctantly from a nearby pub, where they enjoyed a customary drink between reels – intervened to stop the ruckus, which continued onto the street until the gangs finally dispersed to their own 'territories'.

Blackboard Jungle centres on the experiences of a newly qualified teacher, Richard Dadier (Glenn Ford), who takes a teaching position at the North Manual Trade School in an ethnically diverse catchment in New York. Commended for military service, Dadier is now happily married and wants to provide a stable home for his pregnant wife Anne (Anne Francis). From the outset, Dadier is shown to be an exponent of a progressive pedagogy, which balances meaningful teaching against a student's educational and pastoral needs. Thus Dadier is neither as cynical as the history teacher Jim Murdoch (Louis Calhern), who proposes an extreme discipline and a highly traditional pedagogy, nor does he take the person-centred approach of Josh Edwards (Richard Kiley), the philosophical maths teacher, who rewards good behaviour with poetry and music. Dadier immediately encounters disciplinary problems in the form of insulting and uncooperative behaviour from his home-room students. Given the assonance of his surname, Dadier is quickly renamed 'Daddio', which, as a slang term borrowed from Beatnik culture, is inappropriate use for a figure of authority.[4]

Two serious incidents occur in rapid succession, which set up a conflict between Dadier and Artie West (Vic Morrow), the teenage ringleader of a gang of delinquents. First, Dadier fights off a student attempting to rape a female teacher, his colleague, Lois Hammond (Margaret Hayes) in the dark recesses of the school library. The perpetrator is a thug in West's gang and is subsequently expelled. West actively seeks revenge for this, and plans to intimidate Dadier until he resigns his post. West's gang lies in wait for Dadier and Edwards to finish drinking at a local bar and, on their walk home, viciously assault their teachers in a back alley. Under cover of darkness, neither teacher can satisfactorily prove the identity of their attackers. Concerned that Dadier is at risk, Anne implores her husband to resign and take up a post in a more prestigious private school. Dadier tells her: 'I've been beaten up but I'm not beaten.' Having failed to scare Dadier away, West begins to terrorise Anne through poison pen letters and anonymous phone calls that suggest that Dadier is having an affair with Miss Hammond. As a result, she gives birth prematurely and the couple's new-born is at risk for several worrying days.

Throughout this suspenseful build-up, Dadier tries various approaches to improve classroom behaviour. He decides to befriend Gregory Miller (Sidney Poitier), who is a well-liked and respected black student and has kudos with his classmates. Dadier recognises Miller's aptitude and exhorts him to improve his grades and get involved in the annual Christmas show. During rehearsals, Dadier and Miller develop a more cordial relationship. In the climactic finale, West pulls out a flick knife and his accomplice Belazi (Dan Terranova), overpowers Dadier, leaving the teacher open to West's assault. At this point, Miller comes to his teacher's assistance. Seeing that Dadier has earned Miller's respect, several students take on Belazi, pinning him against the wall with the class flag. The denouement shows Dadier taking West and Belazi to the principal's office, announcing that they will be turned over to the proper authorities.

As the plot summary shows, this Hollywood film about juvenile delinquency did not offer audiences the charismatic screen rebel that was given narrative space in *The Wild One*. In contrast, *Blackboard Jungle*'s hero is the courageous and determined teacher who rails against, and quashes, the delinquent elements of an inner city high school. Yet this storyline did not immediately convince the BBFC that it deserved a certificate. Upholding their moral mandate to protect impressionable audiences, the board considered *Blackboard Jungle* another 'unsuitable' vehicle that transposed the juvenile delinquency of *The Wild One*'s motorcycle gangs to the students of an American high school.

In the USA, the film became controversial for generating a pessimistic image of American state ('public') education. Its depiction of the conflict and violence between teachers and students attracted cinema audiences but dismayed high school principals and local school boards, who worried that this popular film would adversely affect teacher retention and recruitment.[5] In light of the film's enormous domestic box office, academic researchers felt compelled to re-evaluate educational experiences in the New York state area.[6] Concerned that the film had the potential to damage international prestige, the US ambassador to Italy, Clare Boothe Luce, asked for it to be removed from the Venice Film Festival in August 1955.

High on the political agenda, juvenile delinquency generated enormous media interest and involved academics and psychologists in ongoing public discourses on its causes and implications. Senator

Estes Kefauver chaired the Hearings of the Subcommittee to Investigate Juvenile Delinquency to determine whether comics containing graphic violence had caused psychological harm to children.[7] *Blackboard Jungle* was the screen adaptation of *The Blackboard Jungle* (1954) by Evan Hunter, a fictionalised account of the author's personal experiences of substitute teaching in New York. Given the prominence of the 'youth problem', Hunter's novel was timely and quickly became a bestseller. The book's commentary on juvenile delinquency and marital relations made it perfectly suited to filmic exploitation. The Hollywood film industry, confronted with the growth of suburbia and the competition from television, turned to adult themes to entice audiences back to cinemas. As was standard practice, Hollywood optioned and purchased the film rights to a national bestseller or hit play because much of the word-of-mouth publicity was already in circulation. The American trade journal *Variety* correctly predicted that *Blackboard Jungle*'s 'shocker technique' of mature themes on a 'gritty topic' would generate 'explosive' box office returns.[8] Indeed, the film's production costs of $1,168,000 were entirely modest, placing the budget in the mid-range of MGM expenditure in the mid-1950s.[9] A staggering domestic box office of $5,350,000 gave the film an unexpected coup: it was the studio's top earning film of the 1954–55 season – and one of the most profitable films in its long and illustrious history.

When *Blackboard Jungle* was introduced to British exhibitors, MGM executives boasted that Hunter's timely novel was purchased while 'still in galley form' and had been recently serialised in the *Ladies' Home Journal*, then a prestigious publication with the enormous readership of five million subscribers.[10] In many ways, Hunter's book still has value for its engagement with serious and topical social issues. In the 1950s, the book was radical for exposing the harsher realities of state education, such as the racial tensions that existed between diverse student groups; and it familiarised readers with the vernacular commonly used by ethnic minorities. The widespread influence of Freud's psychoanalysis techniques may well have encouraged the book's candid and, at times perspicacious, discussion of sexual relations, explored through Dadier's fulfilling married life with Anne, and his potential for infidelity with Lois Hammond. In Britain, however, the book fell into the category of popular American fiction that alienated more established literary traditions. The *Times* and the *Times Literary Supplement* praised

Hunter's novel for raising a useful awareness of delinquency in secondary schools but penalised it for a banal and excessively sentimental style.[11] In my Introduction, I brought attention to the luminary British writers who criticised American-style pulp fiction in the interwar years. In the 1950s, Richard Hoggart and Kenneth Allsop joined their ranks in their disdain for the 'meretricious' direction of new American fiction. They observed that such fiction purported to observe contemporary life but predominantly appealed to readers through a tactical inclusion of sex and violence.[12]

Whatever the shortcomings of the book, there were a number of factors to recommend the film to the genre of social realism. For one, MGM appointed Richard Brooks, a former journalist and playwright, to write the screenplay and direct. Brooks adapted his script to take account of real-life crises in American education, such as low pay and budget deficits. In addition, Brooks took the decision to shoot the film in a black and white documentary style to add veracity. Nonetheless, MGM may not have been the best-placed studio for making a realistic film about the problems of inner-city schools. The majority of Hollywood's most lavish Technicolor musicals of the Golden Era were produced at MGM, and had earned the studio a reputation as 'the Tiffany's' of the film industry.[13] Throughout *Blackboard Jungle*'s production, the studio head Louis B. Mayer, well known as a purveyor of lush and over-sentimentalised products, complained about the stripped-back look of film sets, the dirt-smeared walls and desktops, and the rough and ragged appearance of its juvenile cast. In effect, any realism the film achieved and its key dramatic moments owe much to Brooks' tenacity, creative instinct and attention to finer details.[14]

Was *Blackboard Jungle* realistic or not? To judge this, an overview of the changes in American and British education becomes instructive. Post-war legislation had extended the scope and provision of education for all, partly addressed by the differentiation of educational needs. The North Manual Trade High School depicted in the film provides a pessimistic – though fictionalised – account of the vocational high school that had gained momentum in the USA after the Second World War. Detractors of these new educational programmes, which served predominantly underemployed and disadvantaged whites and ethnic minorities, argue that they exacerbated racial inequalities.[15] In Britain, the Education (Butler) Act of 1944 extended state-funded education for all pupils up to the age of 15 within a tripartite structure of the grammar school (with entry assessed through the 11+ exam), the secondary modern and the technical school. Advocates of the Butler Act argued that post-war British education was highly progressive for its inclusivity and, by 1947, the school leaving age had been extended to 15. Celebrating these educational reforms, the historian Harold Dent wrote, in 1952, that there was wider provision for pupils 'from different intellectual levels with no official and little actual class distinction'.[16]

The technical school, like the American vocational school, aimed to accommodate those with a higher aptitude for practical life skills rather than academic ability. As commendable as this appears on paper, the technical school was unfavourably compared to the grammar for taking pupils who had either failed or performed poorly in their 11+ exams; it was somewhat undervalued (and often bypassed altogether) because trade unions continued to provide apprenticeships. By 1964, only 186 technical schools had been implemented in England and Wales, a low number compared to the 3,906 secondary moderns and 1,298 grammar schools then in existence.[17] In spite of the positive changes made, research studies undertaken by the sociologists Olive Banks (1955) and Peter Willmott and Michael Young (1957) found that the education system underserved working-class children, who were more likely to underperform in their 11+ exams and leave school early.[18] In summary, inequalities in education could not be entirely eradicated.

'Some of the sting has been removed': the BBFC and *Blackboard Jungle*

With *Blackboard Jungle*, the BBFC encountered another example of Hollywood's violent adult-centred cinema. Catholic and conservative groups had influenced negotiations between the Hollywood censor and MGM with the result that much of *Blackboard*'s lewd sexual content had been removed while its violence remained intact.[19] Granted the PCA's seal, the BBFC initially rejected *Blackboard* for its evocation of *The Wild One* and for its depiction of 'revolting hooliganism' likely to offend adults and have a 'damaging and harmful effect' on 16- to 18-year-olds not barred from watching X certificate films.[20]

In Chapter 1, I argued that *The Wild One* was banned because Marlon Brando was considered too attractive and admirable rather than because of excessive violence. At the height of his popularity in Britain, Brando's method acting and status as a fully fledged star transformed Johnny Strabler from a despicable law-breaker into a glamorous daredevil. As a vehicle for Brando, rather than a reinstatement of the BBFC's 'crime does not pay' mandate, the film accommodated what audiences had come to expect of their idol. A charismatic Brando was allowed to dominate every scene, motivate the action, win the love of the ingénue, and ride away unscathed and effectively unpunished for another freewheeling escapade.

By drawing attention to how *Blackboard Jungle* had transferred the marauding gang violence of *The Wild One* to the schoolroom, the BBFC had a strong case for another ban.[21] Indeed, to reject another Hollywood film about juvenile delinquency held distinct advantages. Such action would strengthen the board's position as moral guardian of a younger generation of cinemagoers, and would dissuade future filmmakers from commenting on youth-oriented themes. However, on closer inspection, elements of *Blackboard Jungle* comfortably accommodate the censors' 'crime does not pay' mandate. As argued by Peter Biskind, Dadier functions as a centrist proponent of 'social control', who weeds out the incorrigible West and Belazi so that he can incorporate the 'redeemable' rebels into the system.[22] By the end of the film, the legitimate channels of authority have been reasserted by Dadier, who dispatches West to reform school and restores Miller's moral compass. These reassuring narrative elements were used to advantage during early negotiations between MGM and the British censors. Sam Eckman Jr, MGM's head of organisation in Britain, prepared well for these negotiations and attached clippings from 'All England Law Reports' (July 1954) and from *Parent Magazine* that suggested that realistic depictions of juvenile delinquency had the power to reduce crime figures. Furthermore, he referred Secretary Arthur Watkins back to the edifying 'spirit' of the film conveyed in a rolling title that preceded the opening credits:

> The scenes and incidents depicted here are fictional. However, we believe that public awareness is a first step toward a remedy for any problem. It is this spirit and in this faith in which Blackboard Jungle was produced.

It proved equally difficult to ban the film when, as Eckman pointed out, other censorship bodies in the Commonwealth (Ontario and Australia, for example) had granted the film an 'Adult Category' certificate after minor cuts. Finally, the board proved receptive to Eckman's missive and agreed to re-evaluate on the premise that MGM would accommodate any number of 'exceptions' (deletions) to obtain an X certificate.[23] As already explained, an X certificate was no guarantee that a Hollywood film would retain its 'spirit' or remain intact. Further, Eckman could never have predicted a lengthy list of deletions that resembled, according to a recent British censor, 'the manifesto of the Grand Master of the Inquisition'.[24]

Blackboard Jungle did not privilege a charismatic rebel but it provided other compensations for young audiences. The BBFC's 'manifesto' demonstrates its heightened concerns about the stimulant effects of screened violence on Teddy boys. Streamlined and dramatised by Hollywood's slick production values, which included the exciting rock 'n' roll soundtrack, the board recognised that the film cast a glamorous sheen over undesirable themes. As a result, the censors worked to dismantle *mise en scène* that conferred kudos on the classroom rebels. They scrutinised and deleted what they considered gratuitous violence and imitable 'mischief', which included any display of 'lecherous and dissolute practices', 'foul language', the use of American idiom, and 'indecorous' instances considered degrading to women and girls. Sensational moments such as the would-be rapist's perilous dive out of the library window to escape Dadier proved unacceptable. But so did subtler moments such as the boys' lascivious reactions to girls walking past the school gates, reference to someone's 'stinking sister', and a teenager coolly chewing gum and reading the *Racing News*.

As highlighted earlier, there were racial tensions in the UK that pitted white Teddy boys against minority ethnic groups. Newspaper reports told of attacks on businesses owned by north London's Cypriot community and altercations with West Indians in racially mixed suburbs. These considerations may well have been the reason why the censors removed all the racial slurs heard in the film. In addition, dialogue that evoked apathetic attitudes or encouraged recreational crime, closely associated with the disturbing Ted mentality, such as West's arrogant quips that 'crime always pays' and 'it's cheaper to steal [a car]' were deleted.

Given that the British censors drew parallels between *The Wild One* motorcycle gangs and the sustained violence of *Blackboard Jungle*, West's gang was of particular concern. In a memorable scene, Mr Edwards is putting away the prized vintage record collection he has brought in to share with his high-achieving maths students. When West and his gang show interest, Edwards explains why he has brought in his records. West manipulates the teacher's agreeable nature so that he agrees to play his records for them too. This goodwill gesture, however, is promptly answered with intimidation. While two teenagers restrain Edwards, West and his thugs toss the records across the room, letting them smash on the floor one by one. In view of its unprovoked violence against a figure of authority, this scene was expunged. British audiences saw only the aftermath of West's assault. Thus, the scene starts with the distraught Edwards surveying his broken record collection and Dadier entering the classroom to piece together what has happened.

Chapter 1 showed that the British censors' sensitivity to the screen violence of *The Wild One* coincided with a period of renewed and alarmist attention to young people. Such concerns were formalised in the BBFC Memorandum to Film Producers (1949) that targeted elements of violence then characteristic of gangster films.[25] These guidelines reduced the sensational effects used to heighten the action, such as prolonging fights scenes, showing the visible signs of pain or gore on victims' faces, and adding gratuitous sound effects to punches and blows. For these reasons, the board took exception to the long fight scene (it was 47 seconds) in which West's gang beat up their teachers in a back alley – a scene further animated by an instrumental reprise of Haley's *Rock Around the Clock*. MGM was instructed to cut the sustained action shots that depicted the intricacies of the fight. As a result, the shots that showed Edwards being 'cornered and pummelled', Dadier being restrained for 3 seconds, and all close-ups that conveyed the pain inflicted on them by their students were deleted. Most Teddy boy crimes reported by the press were knife crimes. Hence, the final scene that shows the knife fight between West and Dadier was equally highly objectionable. In a public information pamphlet, the BBFC explained that scenes involving knife crime were prohibited because they 'might suggest to the young and impressionable that you are someone if you have a knife, that a knife gives you power'.[26]

By deleting parts of the final scene, the examiners were directly interfering with the impact of the film and reducing the pleasures of the audience. Assiduously developed through Brooks' narrative, the final confrontation between Dadier and West was to play out as a thrilling and suspenseful resolution to their mutual animosity. Brooks had made several changes to the scene described in Hunter's novel to heighten the drama of the final showdown. As Hunter tells it, Dadier is the first to strike West rather than vice versa and Miller does not immediately offer his help to Dadier. The scene plays out less dramatically and rather pessimistically: Dadier's students urge him to set West and Belazi free rather than send them to the principal's office. In demarcating good from bad with more insistence, the film makes a number of alterations. West is exposed as a racist – he refers to the likeable Miller as 'black boy' – and a coward who stabs Dadier's hand while he is restrained by Belazi. Finally, with West reduced to whimpering hysteria, Belazi is pinned against a wall with an American flag by several of his classmates, an embellishment devised entirely by Brooks as a symbolic and visually interesting element of *mise en scène*.

After satisfying the BBFC's deletion list, the final version of *Blackboard Jungle* lost a total of six minutes. Eckman assumed that he could revoke the arguments that had swayed the PCA and attempted to 'angle' for an A certificate. Meeting with renewed opposition, Eckman accepted that the 'protective' X certificate was the only viable option available to MGM if British audiences were to see their film at all.[27] Nonetheless, although it was a severely modified version, *Blackboard Jungle* was met with enthusiasm and MGM's foreign earnings amounted to $2,950,000 boosting their overall profits to $4,392,000.[28]

To further explore the BBFC's policy on youth and violence, it becomes instructive to analyse the censorship of *Spare the Rod* (Leslie Norman, 1961), promoted as the 'British *Blackboard Jungle*'. *Spare the Rod* starred Max Bygraves as John Saunders, a sympathetic teacher in a tough West London comprehensive, where disciplinary problems are met with harsh corporal punishment. First submitted to the board in October 1954, the film immediately provoked harsh criticism from John Trevelyan and a second reader, Audrey Field, because it focused on the brutality of British schoolmasters against their students in a secondary modern.[29] Given the BBFC's links to the Home Office, and Trevelyan's previous role as Chief Education

Officer, *Spare the Rod* was considered an 'impolitic' project, a poor choice of entertainment, and likely to offend everyone involved in British education from the National Union of Teachers and local authorities to 'decent' parents and children.[30]

In his analysis of post-war censorship, Derek Hill disregards the nominal advantage that the British censors had in appraising films, not according to a code, but on a case-by-case basis. This policy, Hill argues, was little more than a 'haphazard' and 'habitual' fascination for meddling in other people's entertainment.[31] Indeed, there are inconsistencies in the censorship of *Blackboard Jungle* and *Spare the Rod*. According to the BBFC, *Blackboard Jungle* was granted an X certificate because it was an American film depicting American violence, and because of the compensatory character of Dadier, whose 'courage and perseverance' was a powerful deterrent against future juvenile delinquency.[32] Nonetheless, although Saunders served a similar function in *Spare the Rod*, this did nothing to assuage the BBFC's objections. Censorship issues delayed the project as deliberations about classification continued. The BBFC was unwilling to grant *Spare the Rod* an X certificate for fear that it would attract 'sordid interest' but refused to consider an A certificate because children would then be presented with a 'distorted picture' of school life.[33]

By offering serious and relevant commentary on aspects of British education, negotiations on *Spare the Rod* were delayed because of wider concerns of national pride and prestige. In fact, the film was not released until 1961. This protracted episode of censorship strongly suggests that while the BBFC disliked Hollywood's commentary on the 'youth problem' they were even less likely to sanction realistic adult drama from British filmmakers. The *Kinematograph Year Book* of 1955 shows the steady rise of X certificate films made in Hollywood – seven in 1951 and thirteen in 1954 – compared to the almost negligible number of X certificate films made by British producers. In his frank account of the BBFC's modus operandi, William Whitebait references *Spare the Rod* to illustrate how the X certificate was wielded as part of an underhand policy to shape film content.[34]

The British marketing of MGM's film

To ameliorate relations and secure an X certificate, MGM accepted the BBFC's recommendations on future marketing.[35] Of the six catchphrases MGM devised for promotional materials such as poster art, the censors vetoed any direct reference to British Teddy boys. Generic phrases were preferred and so, 'Is there no way to get through to these kids?' and 'MGM's explosive drama of a burning problem' replaced 'Schoolboy or spiv …? Teen-ager or tough …?' and 'MGM's drama of America's Teddy boys'.[36] The examiners recommended the following (muted) taglines: 'Dynamite Drama of American Youth' and 'MGM's Drama of American Youth'. Narrowing the scope of MGM's marketing to focus on American teenagers protected the examiners from potential criticism from local authorities and reasserted control over the domestic film industry. 'We have only passed *Blackboard Jungle*', stated Watkins, 'because it deals with an American problem.'[37]

Trailers were submitted to the board and vetted before they were granted the customary U certificate. The MGM trailer seen by British audiences focused on the film's violence and Dadier's married life; and the voiceover evoked the Americanisms common to pulp fiction:

> It is the frankest, the toughest, the most realistic film since *On the Waterfront*. It is fiction, but fiction torn from big city modern savagery. It packs a brass-knuckle punch in its startling revelation of those teenage savages who turn big city schools into a clawing jungle.

Given the restrictive nature of an X certificate, MGM's trailer exploited the adult-themed elements of the narrative to attract British audiences. One tantalising moment shows Lois Hammond suggesting that Dadier come upstairs to her apartment. She coyly asks: 'Ricky, can't you come up for just one drink?' The BBFC was unhappy with the suggestiveness of this scene, arguing that because it did not actually appear in the film it should be removed from the trailer.[38]

Despite the BBFC's negative impact on promotional materials, the MGM pressbook distributed to British exhibitors was replete with varied suggestions to maximise publicity, such as 'street stunts' and eye-catching foyer displays.[39] Exhibitors were encouraged to use 'attractive' and 'pretty' girls to chalk up the message, 'The most startling picture of the year!' on portable blackboards, and carry the novel around busy parts of town during their lunch hour. Another suggestion described setting up a First Aid station with a uniformed nurse or St John's ambulance attendant, supplied with smelling salts and bandages (even a stretcher) next to a plaque that read: 'Don't buy a ticket if you can't take [the excitement]!' Amidst this 'ballyhoo', MGM contributed serious alternatives. The studio offered free film prints to exhibitors who invited local councillors, youth workers and academics to special previews and post-screening panel discussions on the film's implications for juvenile delinquency in Britain.

As Klinger has argued, promotional materials such as posters create a film's 'consumable identity' and are devised around assumptions that audiences make intertextual links between media.[40] Significantly, MGM devised two rather different consumable identities to cater to American and British audiences. Thus, the American poster campaign evoked the love triangle between Anne, Dadier and Lois Hammond, with Glenn Ford consistently positioned 'between' the women. The undercurrent of sexual tension between Dadier and Lois (explored luridly in Hunter's novel) would have met the expectations of American audiences already familiar with the bestseller.

Rather than focus on sex and violence, British poster art focused on single images of Vic Morrow whose resemblance to Marlon Brando was advantageous (and is discussed in this chapter). When American and British marketing is juxtaposed in this way, it suggests that MGM assumed that British audiences would encounter the film before they read the novel.

The British press and *Blackboard Jungle* delinquents

Blackboard Jungle was brought to the attention of the British press when Clare Boothe Luce asked for it to be removed from 1955's Venice Film festival. Detached from the Cold War politics that consumed Russia and the USA, some British critics were unsympathetic to Boothe Luce's mandate to protect America's international reputation. They considered her request a 'hysterical' overreaction because the 'youth problem' was not confined to the USA.[41]

Hollywood's gradual shift to adult cinema was commercially astute yet the proverbial 'happy ending' was a tradition that the industry appeared determined to uphold. Despite its fidelity to Hunter's contemporary novel and its documentary style, *Blackboard Jungle*'s crowd-pleasing denouement divided critical opinion. The novel did not employ the film's simplistic finale. Instead, final scenes describe

Dadier's increasingly paranoid state that his 'bastard' students – Miller included – would rather see West and Belazi overpower him. For many British film critics, then, the optimistic 'happy ending' on screen disqualified *Blackboard Jungle* from social realism.

The *Daily Telegraph* reviewer was unable to suspend his disbelief over this 'most unlikely victory' and, asked, with more than a hint of condescension: 'Why are Mr Ford's boys almost illiterate while there are quite advanced equations on other blackboards?'[42] The facile ending was Penelope Houston's and Derek Hill's main criticism when reviewing the film for readers of the journals *Monthly Film Bulletin* and *Sight and Sound*, though they praised individual performances.[43] Dilys Powell in the *Sunday Times* compared performances unfavourably to *The Wild One* – a film banned with her full approval – but commended its 'honest message' of holding delinquent youngsters accountable for their misdeeds.[44] *The Spectator* critic was another who applauded the force of *The Wild One* and derided the 'easy melodrama' of *Blackboard Jungle*.[45]

As Bourdieu argues, a journalistic field is a contested territory where specialists jostle for hierarchical ranking. The quality broadsheets functioned to offer in-depth analysis of films, whereas the popular dailies, which addressed a wider readership, were less opposed to Hollywood and summarised the likeliest pleasures for audiences. The *London Evening News* critic, Jympson Harman, recognised that his generic function was to write film reviews that were equally accessible to 'a docker or a don'.[46] Therefore, critics in the popular press focused on *Blackboard Jungle*'s key dramatic moments such as the suspenseful power struggle between Dadier and West. Frank Jackson, the critic for *Reynolds News*, considered the film to be realistic and hoped that British cinema would soon depict its juvenile delinquents with the 'courageous verisimilitude' of Hollywood.[47] In the *Daily Express*, Leonard Mosley described watching 'the ghastly adolescent goons' with 'a hypnotic fascination' and considered *Blackboard Jungle* one of the 'most absorbing films' he had seen in months.[48]

Glenn Ford and Vic Morrow: their stardom in Britain

The British fan press, like the popular dailies, did not intellectualise on *Blackboard Jungle*'s social realism but discussed the plot in the hyperbolic style of the studio pressbook. Thus, critics recommended the film only to 'those with strong stomachs', and advised adult audiences that this realistic and frightening film was not 'kid stuff'.[49] Overall, these magazines promoted films by offering their readers personal interviews and photos of their favourite stars.

Glenn Ford and Vic Morrow, cast as *Blackboard Jungle*'s adversaries, dominated MGM's British marketing. In contrast to the rebel trope created by Marlon Brando, West was played as an unsympathetic and irredeemable thug, closer to the psychologically disturbed delinquents of British cinema. Tom Riley (Dirk Bogarde) in *The Blue Lamp* (Basil Dearden, 1950), for example, uses sadistic violence to dominate his girlfriend Diana (Peggy Evans) and brandishes a gun to intimidate his accomplice, Spud (Patric Doonan). Similarly, Roy Walsh (James Kenney) in *Cosh Boy* (Lewis Gilbert, 1952) bullies his mother, abandons his pregnant girlfriend and coerces two feeble-minded younger boys to carry out a series of muggings. Correspondingly, audiences were not predisposed to like or admire Artie West: he leads his gang through manipulation not charisma.

In Chapter 1, I showed how the *mise en scène* in *A Streetcar Named Desire* and *The Wild One* worked to idealise Brando's rebel characters. By way of contrast, West is not constructed as a romantic figure, and audiences are not given a backstory of parental neglect to elicit our sympathy. On the other hand, viewers are invited to share Dadier's domestic intimacy with Anne. In fact, Dadier negotiates some of the gentle-but-tough attributes of the new rebel trope: he rescues Lois from an assailant and, though badly injured himself, tends to Edwards immediately after West and his gang have assaulted them. The film also suggests that Dadier is a full-blooded male that women find sexually attractive. Dadier's flirtatious relationship with Lois is frequently explored in Hunter's book through inner monologues that describe his desire for infidelity. There are a few filmic moments that allude to Lois's sexual attraction to Dadier but his romantic status is constructed around his unwavering faithfulness to Anne. Lois finally concedes defeat when she tells Dadier: 'I'm bored and you're married.'

Dyer has argued that stardoms are polysemic and constructed by 'extensive, intertextual and multimedia [meanings].'[50] Similarly, Fischer and Landy describe this amalgamation of on- and off-screen discourses as the 'star text'.[51] Chapter 1 demonstrates that Brando's star text was informed by his film roles, gossip items in fan magazines, promotional materials and personal interviews, which, in turn, inflected 'Johnny the rebel' with realistic overtures. The fan rhetoric around Ford and Morrow duly informed their respective meanings for British audiences as established star and relative newcomer. A wider survey of Ford's earlier film work shows that he was often cast as the debonair co-star of Hollywood's most glamorous female stars. Notably, he starred as Johnny, opposite Rita Hayworth in the film noir *Gilda* (Charles Vidor, 1946). Otherwise, the urbane actor was miscast in a succession of 'tough guy' roles. In 1943, when Ford left acting for the navy, one British critic recognised the actor's 'rare talent' and hoped that he would be offered more suitable parts on his return.[52] According to British fan journalism, his casting in *Blackboard Jungle* marked the end of 'mediocre roles' and redirected his career toward 'strong-meat' characterisations.[53]

In terms of acting and performance style, the British quality press deconstructed *mise en scène*, whereas the fan magazines supplied their readers with personal or intimate details – gossip – about the 'real' people behind public personas. Ford's star text depended on the skilful manipulation of Hollywood's publicity machine, which maintained that he was a devoted husband to the actress Eleanor Powell and an attentive father to his young son, Peter; his stardom precluded the prurient 'gossip' generated by Brando's public persona.[54] As a hardworking, reliable actor, Ford offered his fans other pleasures associated with his portrayals of earnest and honest, rugged American men. Known for an understated natural style of acting, Ford made consistent but unspectacular press; he periodically featured in *Photoplay*'s competitions or paired with a glamorous co-star on *Picture Show*'s front covers. Publicity around Ford intensified to coincide with *Blackboard Jungle*'s British release. Indistinguishable articles on his happy marriage to Powell appeared in *Picturegoer* and *Photoplay* for fan consumption. Evocative of Dadier's married status in the film, stories about Ford and Powell emphasised their romantic courtship, their homely comforts and their family commitments.[55] Reporters duly mentioned other characteristics that Ford shared with his fictional character: an admirable naval record, a high level of education and sporting prowess.[56]

In all, fan materials show that Ford was well liked and respected. For example, Donovan Pedelty correctly predicted that Ford's performance would be nominated for a Best Actor Oscar.[57] In the

Figure 2.1 Publicity materials emphasised Glenn Ford's stable marriage to the actress Eleanor Powell and his military service.

Picturegoer annual awards of 1955, Ford won second place for Best Actor, with editorial comment suggesting that he was ungraciously (but inevitably) deprived of first place by fervent young admirers of the recently deceased James Dean.[58] Ford's steadfast fans shared this appreciation for the new direction of his career. One London cinemagoer believed that Dadier had 'salvaged' Ford's film career while another Londoner conferred on him the title of 'Mr X' and applauded his appearance in adult-centred drama.[59] At the same time, studio executives, no doubt frustrated by the new anti-stars in their industry, described him as the most 'competent, conscientious star on our books' and juxtaposed him with an errant and demanding Brando. To ensure that readers did not miss this detail and, arguably, to endear Ford to a younger audience, an 'unnamed' teen stated his preference: '[Ford] makes Marlon Brando look like something out of the local dramatic society – amateurish!'[60]

In contrast to Ford's urbanity, Vic Morrow, who made his film debut as Artie West, was presented as a 'two-fisted guy' from the Bronx.[61] Morrow, himself, was markedly different from Hunter's description of West as a rangy teenager, with stringy, matted blonde hair and a forehead covered in 'ripe acne'.[62] Bearing a striking and advantageous resemblance to Brando, Morrow was consigned to the stable of actors the British press had labelled 'the Brando Boys'. My survey of fan materials and studio pressbooks demonstrates that Hollywood studios routinely contracted new players who resembled established stars, presumably, because it prompted audiences to make intertextual meanings. Hence, Morrow's commonalities with Brando were emphasised throughout promotional materials. The MGM studio pressbook listed the attributes Morrow shared with the star such as method acting training, a 'serious' commitment to his craft, humble beginnings; and mentioned that his summer stock experience was gained 'playing the role created by Marlon Brando' in a touring production of *A Streetcar Named Desire*.[63]

Had Morrow wanted to develop his range and repertoire, he was hindered by reviews that discussed his portrayal of Artie West purely in terms of its fidelity to the Brando 'standard'. *Blackboard Jungle* was released the same year that Brando's performance as Terry Malloy in *On the Waterfront* (Elia Kazan, 1954) won the BAFTA for Best Foreign Actor and the Academy Award for Best Actor. The reviewers in the cineaste journals were especially derisive of Morrow's emulation of Brando. Derek Hill opined that Morrow's imitative performance failed 'hopelessly' because of 'some badly misjudged roars and shouts'.[64] Penelope Houston regarded all the '*Blackboard* delinquents' as Brando 'imitators' and criticised Richard Brooks' direction for aping 'the Kazan style of mannered naturalism'.[65] For these scholarly critics, the impactful commentary of social realist cinema depended on its innovative style and novelty, therefore, Brooks' production, in attempting to contrive the same effects, was denigrated as a pastiche.

Another function of the fan magazines was to participate in the industry's build-up of stars by introducing new players to audiences. Readers, themselves, were invited to participate in this process by voting for their favourites in popularity polls. In the 1955 *Picturegoer* awards for 'Best Newcomer' – which urged readers to 'make big stars' of the 'unknown youngsters of today' – Morrow was ranked fifth in the Top Ten for his performance as Artie West.[66] The young actor's popularity appeared to rest almost entirely on the characteristics he shared with his famous predecessor. One East London filmgoer praised Morrow for 'look[ing] like a youthful Marlon Brando'; and another from Lincoln considered him 'a boy with a *real* [sic] Brando touch [that places him] above the other imitators'. But this imitability proved less attractive to loyal Brando fans. 'What a pity stars cannot copyright their styles', complained Sheila Holmes of Hertfordshire. 'Vic Morrow's resemblance to Brando is striking enough to distract from a powerful story. Stars should go ahead and develop gestures, intonations and expressions of their own.'[67]

Figure 2.2 Artie West (Vic Morrow, right) and his high-school accomplices Belazi (Dan Terranova, centre) and Stoker (Paul Mazursky, left) in *Blackboard Jungle* (1955). Morrow's physical resemblance to Marlon Brando and his method training earned him the reputation as another 'Brando Boy'.

In as far as Morrow reminded audiences of Brando, Artie West does not conform to the charismatic juvenile delinquent type established in *The Wild One*. In fact, the pivotal character of Gregory Miller (Sidney Poitier) comes closer to the 'redeemable' rebel because of changes made when the book was adapted for the screen. In Hunter's novel, the relationship between Dadier and Miller is difficult and strained. This is aptly demonstrated by Miller's conflicted attitude to participating in the Christmas show, when he warns Dadier: 'The show's one thing, Chief, but English is another ... So don't 'spect me to go kissin' your ass in class.' Indeed, in the book, Dadier describes Miller as a 'two-headed gorgon' and is greatly troubled by never knowing if he will encounter the 'good Miller or the bad Miller' on any given day.[68] As David E. James asserts, the book describes Dadier's main antagonist as Miller but to streamline the film narrative West's role was enlarged to provide a commentary on white delinquency rather than focus on the highly complicated issues of racial difference.[69]

Brooks' screenplay and *mise en scène*, then, constructs Miller as the charismatic and sympathetic delinquent character, defensive and insolent but ultimately kind and honourable. One respondent in Palm and Cahill's social study 'Do Blackboard Jungles exist?' summarises Miller's most attractive qualities: 'I liked the Negro boy, he was good-looking and I trusted him.'[70] Poitier, himself, was singled out in superlative reviews (both British and American) but in spite of these accolades, is discernibly absent from MGM's promotional materials. Poitier's greater achievements were concurrent with the growth of the civil rights movement in the 1960s when, for example, he was the first African American to win the Academy Award for Best Actor in *Lilies of the Field* (Ralph Nelson, 1963). Moreover, Poitier's role as Miller found its logical conclusion in *To Sir, With Love* (James Clavell, 1967), when he plays Mr Thackeray, a teacher in Dadier's mould, who reforms a class of unruly East London teenagers. By 1967, Poitier's popularity with audiences placed him at the top of the Quigley poll of American exhibitors.

British audiences and Hollywood screen violence

As predicted by MGM, *Blackboard Jungle* stimulated a public dialogue on the youth issue. Tabloid features about Britain's 'jungle syndrome' coincided with the film's premiere in September 1955. John Laird, a New Zealander substitute teacher, contributed a three-part exposé, 'Jungle in the classroom', to the *News Chronicle*, in which he described pupils' low attainment, poor discipline and menacing behaviour toward staff across five London secondary moderns.[71] In May 1956, Ronald Balaam, another temporary teacher based in Hoxton, East London, was sacked by the London County Council (LCC) for airing similar concerns in an ITV interview. Balaam described how pupils threw knives around classrooms and shared the fact that parents would 'lie in wait' for him after school.[72] Similarly, John Townsend published *The Young Devils: Experiences of a Schoolteacher* (1958), his own fictionalised account of violence between students and teachers in a mixed school.

The term 'blackboard jungle' continued to provide a rhetorical lead-in to news items describing low-level disruption among adolescents, and, generally, these articles appear to be replete with hyperbole. Typically, one story referenced the film when it described a playground fight between north London schoolboys as the 'ambush' of '20 chain-swinging prefect hunters'.[73] However, the film stimulated substantive debate on whether restrictions on teachers using corporal punishment had aggravated a worsening situation. Consensus was divided on improving pupil behaviour: progressive educationalists opposed the punitive traditionalists who urged for a return to tougher sanctions. For some, capital punishment and longer National Service would remedy the situation. Others favoured extreme discipline in schools, such as reintroducing birching which had been abolished in 1948. A Gallup poll of 20 November 1954 had revealed that 40 per cent of respondents were in favour of 'whipping' ill-disciplined children compared with the 25 per cent who would punish children by taking away their privileges. L. A. Hackett, a 53-year-old magistrates' chairman, reasoned: 'I feel that the thrashing of the youngsters would very often be the right and effective punishment. We are all getting very soft towards them.'[74] A teacher from Lewisham agreed, and worried that, 'We shall go the way of America if teachers are not allowed to reintroduce reasonable discipline, and if erring parents are not awakened to a sense of responsibility.'[75]

In response to these ongoing debates, the National Union of Teachers (NUT) devised detailed questionnaires to investigate 'the blackboard jungle syndrome' and sent them out to local county councils. Ten per cent of all secondary modern schools (a random sample of 425) participated in the survey and, in addition, Fred Jarvis, the Assistant Secretary of the NUT, visited secondary moderns known to have disciplinary problems in larger towns and cities. Findings were eventually published in 'Paper re NUT Investigation into School Discipline and Behaviour in Secondary Modern Schools, 1954–1956'. In response to issues of organised gangs, the existence of Teddy boys, and the use of weaponry, less than 0.5 per cent of the sample reported actual 'blackboard jungle' classroom incidents; and only five schools reported incidences when students had brought in weapons. On this evidence, the NUT and the LCC believed that the experiences described by individual teachers, such as Laird and Balaam, were uncommon.

Official discourses fixated on parental supervision as the key factor in the youth problem. Jarvis, too, had cited ineffectual parenting as the most 'disturbing' problem faced by secondary school teachers. Gorer's social survey returned similar results with 56 per cent of respondents – particularly the married ones – choosing the statements imputing responsibility for juvenile delinquency to parents.[76] In their sociological study of education and working-class children in northern England, Jackson and Marsden concluded that parental involvement was the difference between success and failure at grammar school.[77] In conclusion, then, the serious problems reflected in the Hollywood film did not appear to reflect a British reality. 'If we hadn't had the film', Jarvis complained, 'we wouldn't have had this idea scouted around.'[78] The British media generated a more pessimistic image of America's 'blackboard jungle' youth. The *Daily Mail*, for example, reported on a Senate Committee's predictions that there would soon be two million teenagers with juvenile records for very serious crimes living in New York State.[79]

Whatever the BBFC's theories on the 'hypodermic needle effect' of films about juvenile delinquency and younger cinemagoers, there is little concrete evidence of reactive violence to *Blackboard Jungle* from British pupils. In contrast, the serious charge of a 'copycat killing' made against the film was documented in confidential correspondence between Reverend J. A. V. Burke, Secretary of the Catholic Film Institute in London, and Arthur Watkins at the BBFC. The case of a 15-year-old fatally stabbing his classmate to death to emulate the 'style' of Artie West answered the worst of the BBFC's projections of impressionable audiences and the imitability of screen violence. The fatal stabbing occurred after the teenage members of a Catholic film club had watched *Blackboard Jungle* at St Mary's College, Twickenham. Burke reported that 'the accused had changed markedly after seeing the film' and 'took on' the identity of Artie West; and killed his classmate for 'annoying' him.[80] In the correspondent's summation, the killer (suitably) fit the post-war profile of maladjusted delinquent: he was a neglected child from a broken home. Watkins firmly laid the blame on the club's irresponsible decision to screen the film to 15-year-olds not 'protected' by the X certificate.[81] With no reverberations in the press, Watkins appears to have successfully deflected any further criticism and opportunely reinforced the importance of BBFC guidelines.

Blackboard Jungle's violent themes addressed British audiences in different ways. As was customary, the BBFC examiners took notes when they viewed the film with the public to gauge reactions. These notes, which recorded whether cuts were discernible, also provide information about audiences and, indeed, the censors. On 16 September 1955, the examiner Newton K. Branch, his wife and some friends saw *Blackboard Jungle* at the Empire, Leicester Square. To his surprise, Branch witnessed a great deal of audience laughter, which, he concluded, had the effect of reducing the impact – or 'sting' – of the violence. For example, Louis Calhern's cynical remarks about teaching elicited raucous laughter, while 'nervous' laughter accompanied the violent clashes between students and teachers. Contradictory to the patriotic symbolism intended by Brooks, this audience laughed its 'hardest' when Belazi was pinned against the wall with an American flag. With regard to the BBFC deletions, Branch's friends noticed that cuts had been made to the scene of Lois's attempted rape, removing shots of the perpetrator breaking through the glass as he leapt out the window to escape.[82]

Later in the film's run, Arthur Watkins joined the audience at the Regal in Beckenham, South London. In contrast to Branch's observations, Watkins noted that gasps rather than laughter accompanied the climactic scenes. Significantly, the deletions to the attempted rape scene – intended to mute the sensationalism – had the effect of convincing the audience that 'Dadier's fists' had caused the lacerations on the boy's face rather than his sudden leap through the library window. Even at this late stage, given the substantial edits to the film shown in British cinemas, Watkins remained of the opinion that the screen violence was excessive.[83]

As Hollywood cinema increasingly turned to adult realism, so screen violence became the locus for debate among British film critics and audiences. Margaret Hinxman watched a preview screening of *Picturegoer* and warned future audiences of its 'grisly' and unnecessary violence. Equally, Hinxman held method acting in contempt because it pushed actors to dangerous and injurious excesses in their quest for realism.[84] Lady Norah Docker, a well-known socialite and film reviewer, was equally dismayed at the excessive violence in recent Hollywood films and considered *Blackboard Jungle*'s 'knifing scene' as 'coldly, calculatedly, contrivedly malevolent'.[85]

British cinemagoers responded more positively to the trend for sensationalised and stylised screen violence. One Brighton filmgoer considered *Blackboard Jungle* a realistic account of the classroom turbulence that presaged the 'savagery' in British schools. Another audience in Blackpool fell into rapt 'silence' during the thrilling suspense of good (Dadier) versus evil (West).[86] Audiences tended to enjoy the violent action of *Blackboard Jungle* and this encouraged some to demand more independence in their viewing choices. A frequent filmgoer demanded that the BBFC allow British adults to 'grow up' and watch X certificates 'uncut' as intended by the director.[87]

Following in the wake of *The Wild One*, *Blackboard Jungle* continued a growing trend of 'ultra-tough' X certificate films. As a result, *Picturegoer*'s Derek Walker and Allen Newton spent a day carrying out vox pop interviews on Hollywood violence in the cinemas, cafes and dance halls of Leeds' town centre.[88] 'I'll take murder over [Marilyn] Monroe any day', quipped one cinema manager who reported that screen violence generated excellent box office. The results of this informal survey indicated that older, married people expressed pessimistic views that directly corresponded to the BBFC's projections of imitable screen violence. Kathleen Sherwood, a waitress in her sixties, and Norman Day and Ted Pearce, middle-aged businessmen, held traditionalist views that correlated X-rated films with the misbehaviours of 'Teddy boy groups' and saw no compensation offered by the criminal's final demise. The young and unmarried, on the other hand, were more inclined to enjoy the 'thrilling' spectacle of violence. Frequent cinemagoer Betty Barrett, an 18-year-old hotel chambermaid, shared her opinion that *Blackboard Jungle* was 'good, dramatic stuff.'

Among the better-educated and infrequent filmgoers, Keith Normington, an 18-year-old college student, reasoned that 'healthy, normal-minded' people were no more affected by screen violence than by other forms of media such as TV, radio or books. The views of Doris Allen, a 20-year-old dance hall hostess, and a former cinema usherette, held to the deterrent effect of X-rated films and surmised that they effectively showed 'the horrible effects of violence and brutality'. Respondents in the survey, who worked directly with young people, did not ascribe the 'hypodermic needle' effect of screen violence. M. Ellis, a police constable at the YMCA, and the Vicar of Leeds, Canon C. B. Sampson, who encountered juvenile offenders on a regular basis, described *Blackboard Jungle* style films as a necessary form of escapism for young people and did not foresee any serious re-enactments.

In an attempt to unravel the perplexing mystique around Teddy culture, *Picture Post*'s Hilde Marchant spent time in local dance halls to observe the behaviour of boys and girls who favoured the new style. As a result, Marchant abandoned her preconceptions – and perhaps desired the same of her readers – describing these supposed juvenile offenders rather as vain, flamboyant and given to the posturing typical of self-aware teenagers.[89]

Conclusion

The Wild One and *Blackboard Jungle* were films that endeavoured to present a social problem with verisimilitude. The first fictionalised a real-life encounter between townsfolk and a gang of freewheeling motorcyclists. The second adapted Evan Hunter's fictionalised account of his personal experiences of substitute teaching. Both films presented their dramas in the black and white documentary-style of newsreel. Nonetheless, the consensus of British critics was that *Blackboard Jungle* was a pastiche of Elia Kazan's directorial style and Marlon Brando's method acting. The fact that all the *Blackboard* delinquents imitated Brando's acting style was a measure of his influence in American cinema. 'Happy endings' were standard in Hollywood films of the 1950s (and earlier). For this reason, *The Wild One* was a rare exception. It did not offer audiences the standard 'heterosexual union' expected of romance-driven narratives: Johnny leaves Kathie with a memento (his trophy) but rides away to join his motorcycle gang. In this way, the social realism of the film was not undermined by a sudden transformation of Johnny's wayward character. By way of contrast, *Blackboard Jungle*'s 'implausible' happy conclusion worked against its pithy commentary on a topical issue. Indeed, when reviewed for British television in the *Radio Times*, Philip Jenkinson reiterated many of the comments made by his predecessors. He commended Bill Haley's rock 'n' roll soundtrack and Vic Morrow for his convincing imitation of Brando but disliked the 'spurious' ending. This controversial film was screened on BBC2 after the watershed of 9 p.m. on 13 September 1972.

The narrative of *Blackboard Jungle* had constructed identifiable heroic and villainous types of the standard variety. The 'savages' in this 'jungle' had been tamed and legitimate authority was re-established by the film's close. Yet for purposes of teenage identification, narrative space had been given to young people who challenged and terrorised their stalwart teachers. Other than Artie West, the *Blackboard Jungle*'s teenagers looked, sounded and behaved like the average British Teddy boy. They slouched in jackets and jeans, perpetually groomed their over-long DA hairstyles, smoked and postured, and indulged in ribaldry among themselves and mocked figures of authority. For Mim Scala, the Teddy boy from Walham, and the novelist Ray Gosling, then at grammar school, it was the teenage misbehaviour and rock 'n' roll that lingered in the imagination. Gosling, who cared little about the plot, vividly describes 'going bananas at the screen' whenever the soundtrack punctuated the climactic moments of students 'beating up' their teachers.[90]

In censuring the imitable screen violence, the BBFC had failed to anticipate the tangible enthusiasm of young British audiences to the film's rock 'n' roll soundtrack. *Blackboard Jungle* was not a traditional MGM musical but it synergised images of juvenile delinquency with the aggression and vitality of a memorable anthem, which, as American teenagers had already proven, had the power to 'electrify' audiences.[91] Indeed, Chapter 4 examines the nationwide 'riots' that erupted around Britain when the soundtrack inspired *Rock Around the Clock* (Fred F. Sears, 1956), a film about Bill Haley's early stardom. Chapter 3, however, sustains the chronological structure of the book and analyses another major film about juvenile delinquency. *Rebel Without a Cause* (Nicholas Ray, 1955) starred James Dean as the juvenile delinquent, Jim Stark. Released so soon after the actor's tragic death, British teenagers were set to participate in an extraordinary episode of posthumous stardom.

Notes

1 Arthur Watkins, Examiner's notes, 16 March 1955 (BBFC Files).
2 Frank Jackson, 'Our Teddy boys are angels', *Reynolds News*, 19 September 1955 (*Blackboard Jungle*, BFI microfiche).
3 As recalled by Mim Scala in his coming-of-age memoir, *The Diary of a Teddy Boy: A Memoir of the Long Sixties* (London: The Goblin Press, 2009), pp. 19–21.
4 'Daddio' or 'Daddy-O', a slang term for 'man' was used informally. The Black Rebels of *The Wild One* and Buzz's teenage gang use the term in *Rebel Without A Cause*. Popularised in the 1950s by American hipsters involved in Beatnik culture, and most likely borrowed from jazz musicians, its exact origins are unknown.
5 Adam Golub, 'They turned a school into a jungle!' How *Blackboard Jungle* redefined the education crisis in postwar America', *Film and History*, 39:1 (Spring 2009), pp. 21–30.
6 Delmar C. Palm and Gilbert A. Cahill, 'Do blackboard jungles exist?', *Social Studies*, 48:5, 1 May 1957, pp. 147–52. Comparing educational experiences in different regions of New York State, the study showed a range of responses from finding the film 'absurd' to concrete examples of the *Blackboard Jungle* syndrome in schools.
7 The Hearings of the Subcommittee to Investigate Juvenile Delinquency of April and June 1954 are reprinted in full and are available at: https://archive.org/details/juveniledelinque54unit (last accessed 12 June 2019).
8 *Variety* [US], 197:12, 23 February 1955, p. 8.
9 Production costs and profits of the MGM studio can be found in H. Mark Glancy, 'MGM film grosses, 1924–1948: the Eddie Mannix ledger', *Historical Journal of Film, Radio and Television*, 12:2 (1992), pp. 127–44.
10 In 'MGM's Final synopsis: 'Who, what and why of *Blackboard Jungle*', Howard Strickling reported that the novel was adapted for the screen within two months of being published (*Blackboard Jungle*, MGM pressbook, 1955, BFI microfiche).

11 'Superstition into violence', *The Times*, 23 June 1955, p. 13; Marie Hannah, 'Bent twigs', *The Literary Times Supplement*, 2786, 22 July 1955, p. 409.
12 Richard Hoggart, *The Uses of Literacy* (Harmondsworth: Penguin, 1957); Kenneth Allsop, 'The asterisks are out: licence or liberty?', *Daily Mail*, 5 January 1960, p. 4.
13 Thomas Schatz, *Genius of the System: Hollywood Filmmaking in the Studio Era* (London: Simon & Schuster, 1989), pp. 440–62.
14 Richard Brooks, broadcast interview: *Hollywood Juillet 85*, *Cinéma Cinémas* (Claude Venture and Philip Garnier, 1985).
15 The George-Barden Vocational Education Act (1946) has attracted criticism for creating racial and class divisions. See M. L.Barlow, 'Coming of age 1926–1976', *American Vocational Journal*, 51:5 (May 1976), pp. 63–88.
16 H. C. Dent, *Changes in English Education: A Historical Survey* (London: University of London Press, 1952), pp. 42–3 and 94.
17 'Statistics of Education 1964 HMSO', quoted in W. O. Lester Smith, *The Government of Education* (Harmondsworth: Penguin, 1966), p. 108.
18 Olive Banks, *Parity and Prestige in English Secondary Education: A Study in Educational Sociology* (London: Routledge & Kegan Paul, 1955); Peter Willmott and Michael Young, *Family and Kinship in East London* (Harmondsworth: Penguin, 1969 [1957]), pp. 29 and 174–80.
19 Jerold Simmons contextualises the film's American censorship against the relaxation of the PCA's statutory code by its newly appointed director, Geoffrey Shurlock. See 'Violent youth: the censoring and public reception of *The Wild One* and *Blackboard Jungle*', *Film History*, 20:3 (2008), pp. 381–91; and 'A damned nuisance: The Production Code and the Profanity Amendment of 1954', *Journal of Popular Film and Television*, 25:2 (Summer 1997), pp. 76–82.
20 Notes by Arthur Watkins after meeting with the film editor, 29 March 1955; Watkins to Messrs MGM Pictures, 24 March 1955 (BBFC Files).
21 Examiner's Report [GRS], 15 March 1955 (BBFC Files).
22 Peter Biskind, *Seeing is Believing: Or How Hollywood Taught us To Stop Worrying and Love the 50s* (London: Bloomsbury, 1983), pp. 200–17.
23 Telephone calls and letters were exchanged between Eckman and Arthur Watkins on 3 June, 10 June and 15 June 1955. There was also a private meeting between Watkins, Eckman, the producer Pandro S. Berman and the film editor, C. G. N. Ayres in July 1955.
24 Exception Form: Third Viewing by Pres., AW, AOF, GRS, 17 June 1955. Deborah Courtnell makes this observation on the original list in her VHS Report, 21 July 1994 (BBFC Files).

25 Appendix BBFC Memorandum is printed in full in Sue Harper and Vincent Porter, *British Cinema Audiences of the 1950s* (Oxford: Oxford University Press, 2003), p. 242.
26 John Trevelyan, *Censored* (Southampton: The Millbrook Press Ltd, 1962), p. 10.
27 These final negotiations were recorded by Watkins in a report after his meeting with Eckman, 13 July 1955. Eckman conceded an A certificate in a letter to Watkins, 5 January 1956 (BBFC Files).
28 The Eddie Mannix Ledger has financial figures on all MGM films. Total earnings on *Blackboard Jungle* amounted to $8,300,000.
29 Examiner's Note, 15 March 1955 (BBFC Files).
30 Anthony Aldgate provides a detailed account of censorship issues (1954–61). See his chapter, 'The times they are a-changin'', in *Censorship and The Permissive Society: British Cinema & Theatre 1955–1965* (Oxford: Clarendon Press, 1995), pp. 13–31.
31 Derek Hill, 'The habit of censorship', *Encounter*, 15:1 (Summer 1960), pp. 52–62.
32 Watkins justified the Board's granting of an X certificate in his letter to L. Edgar Stephens, Warwickshire County Council, 1 September 1956; and Sidney Harris to Sam Eckman, 18 July 1955 (BBFC Files).
33 Audrey Field, *Spare the Rod*, Reader's Report, 4 December 1956 (BBFC Files).
34 William Whitebait, 'This censorship', *New Statesman*, 30 July 1960, pp. 153–4.
35 Examiner's Recommendations for Cuts, 26 July 1955 (BBFC Files).
36 Ernest Betts (p.p. Sam Eckman) submitted MGM's catchphrases in his letter to Arthur Watkins on 2 September 1955; Watkins sent his recommendations to Eckman on 5 September 1955 (BBFC Files).
37 *Ibid.*
38 Exception Form for Trailer, 17 August 1955 (BBFC Files).
39 *Blackboard Jungle* pressbook (MGM, 1955, BFI microfiche).
40 Barbara Klinger argues that promotional materials take on an extra-diegetic consumable significance. See *Digressions at the Cinema: Reception and Mass Culture, Cinema Journal*, 28:4 (Summer 1989), pp. 3–19.
41 See as examples, Christopher Lucas, 'Mrs Luce makes lion roar', *Daily Mail*, 29 August 1955, p. 5; 'Mrs Luce denies banning film', *Daily Mail*, 5 September 1955, p. 7; 'Festival head's offer to resign', *Daily Telegraph*, 1 September 1955, p. 8; Derek Granger, 'Violence in class, delinquency in youth', *Financial Times*, 19 September 1955; Julian Symons, 'The un-American jungle', *Tribune*, 19 September 1955 (*Blackboard Jungle*, BFI microfiche).

42 P. Gibbs, 'Good over evil', *Daily Telegraph*, 17 September 1955 (*Blackboard Jungle*, BFI microfiche).
43 Penelope Houston, '*Blackboard Jungle*', *Monthly Film Bulletin*, 22:252, 1 January 1955, p. 150; Derek Hill, 'Longer notices: *Blackboard Jungle*', *Monthly Film Bulletin*, 25:3 (October 1955), p. 147.
44 Dilys Powell, 'Unkindest cut', *Sunday Times*, 15 September 1955, p. 11.
45 'Cinema: *Blackboard Jungle*', *The Spectator*, 15 September 1955, p. 18.
46 Jympson Harman, 'Don't smother the child', *Sight and Sound*, 10:40 (Spring 1942), pp. 67–9 (p. 68).
47 Jackson, 'Our Teddy boys are angels'.
48 Leonard Mosley, 'The three Rs: ranting, rifling, rioting', *Daily Express*, 16 September 1955 (BFI microfiche).
49 '*Blackboard Jungle*', *Picturegoer*, 30:1068, 8 October 1955, pp. 16–17.
50 Richard Dyer, *Heavenly Bodies: Film Stars and Society* (Basingstoke and London: Macmillan Education Ltd, 1987), p. 3.
51 Lucy Fischer and Marcia Landy (eds), *Stars: The Film Reader* (New York and London: Routledge, 2004), p. 4.
52 M.A.C., 'Glenn Ford?', *Picturegoer*, 12:583, 26 June 1943, p. 11.
53 'Glenn Ford', *Picturegoer*, 5 May 1956; Ed O'Connor, 'You can't take him for granted', *Picturegoer*, 35:1188, 8 February 1958, p. 11.
54 Peter Ford's recent biography dismantles Hollywood's pristine image of his father, Glenn, by accounting for the actor's serial infidelities. See Peter Ford, *Glenn Ford: A Life* (Madison, WI: The University of Wisconsin Press, 2011).
55 'Glenn clocks off: all his bright lights are at home', *Photoplay* [GB], 6:12, December 1955, pp. 40–1; 'Eleanor Powell: my life with Glenn Ford', *Picturegoer*, 31:1096, 5 May 1956, pp. 10–11.
56 *Blackboard Jungle* pressbook; 'The life story of Glenn Ford', *Picture Show and Film Pictorial*, 65:1693, 10 September 1955, p. 12.
57 Donovan Pedelty, 'I'm rooting for the Oscar stakes', *Picturegoer*, 31:1083, 4 February 1956, pp. 8–9.
58 'You've proved the cynics wrong', *Picturegoer*, 31:1100, 2 June 1956, p. 7.
59 J. Browne, London, *Picturegoer*, 30:1075, 28 January 1956, p. 3; K. J. Weller, 'He's "Mr. X"', *Picturegoer*, 31:1082, 10 December 1955, p. 10.
60 'Glenn clocks off: all his bright lights are at home'. The magazine berated Brando's uncooperative 'killjoy' attitude toward editors. See 'Come off it, Brando!', *Photoplay* [GB], 6:11, November 1955, pp. 14–15.
61 *Blackboard Jungle* pressbook.

62 Evan Hunter, *The Blackboard Jungle* (New York: Dell Books, 1966 [1954]), p. 57.
63 *Blackboard Jungle* pressbook; *Vic Morrow* pressbook (The Bernard Company, 1964, BFI microfiche).
64 Hill, 'Longer notices: *Blackboard Jungle*', p. 147.
65 Penelope Houston, 'In brief: *Blackboard Jungle*', *Sight and Sound*, 25:3 (Winter 1956), p. 150.
66 Annual awards, *Picturegoer*, 31:1092, 7 April 1956, p. 9.
67 Helen Curtis, East London, *Picturegoer*, 26 November 1955, 30:1071, p. 26; William Carr, 'Brando boy', *Picturegoer*, 1 November 1958, 36:1226, p. 3; Sheila Holmes, 'Copyright needed', *Picturegoer*, 30:1071, 12 November 1955, p. 26.
68 Hunter, *The Blackboard Jungle*, p. 206.
69 David E. James, *Rock 'n' film: Cinema's Dance with Popular Music* (Oxford: Oxford University Press, 2016), p. 403, n.3.
70 Delmar C. Palm and Gilbert A. Cahill, 'Do blackboard jungles exist?', *Social Studies*, 48:5, 1 May 1957, pp. 147–52.
71 Dr John Laird, 'Jungle in the classroom', *News Chronicle*, 14–16 September 1955, pp. 10–12.
72 'TV "jungle school" teacher is sacked', *Daily Mail*, 8 May 1956, p. 2.
73 'Blackboard jungle comes to NW3', *Daily Mail*, 6 February 1958, p. 1; 'Blackboard jungle boys suspended', *Daily Mail*, 15 February 1958, p. 5.
74 Jack Greenslade, 'JP starts "blackboard jungle" row', *Daily Mail*, 19 March 1958, p. 5.
75 J. P. Pinel, London, SE12, 'The jungle comes to Britain', *Daily Mail*, 11 February 1958, p. 4.
76 Geoffrey Gorer, *Exploring English Character* (London: Criterion Books, 1955), p. 208.
77 Brian Jackson and Dennis Marsden, *Education and the Working Class* (Harmondsworth: Penguin, 1962).
78 The NUT findings and Jarvis's comments were reported in "Blackboard Jungle hunt fails here"', *Daily Mail*, 20 July 1956, p. 5.
79 '2,000,000 blackboard jungle boys set US a problem', *Daily Mail*, 27 April 1959, p. 2.
80 Reverend J. A. V. Burke and Arthur Watkins correspondence 19 and 24 September 1956 (BBFC Files).
81 Watkins to Burke, 24 September 1956 (BBFC Files).
82 Newton K. Branch, Examiner's report: Empire, Leicester Square, 16 September 1955 (BBFC Files).

83 Arthur Watkins, Examiner's report: Regal Cinema, Beckenham, 4 November 1955 (BBFC Files).
84 Margaret Hinxman, 'Let's stop this', *Picturegoer*, 29:1051, 25 June 1955, pp. 8–9.
85 Lady Docker, 'Is this brutality necessary?', *Picturegoer*, 31:1018, 14 January 1956, pp. 8–9.
86 Mrs Eva Yule, Brighton, and Miss Jean Smith, Blackpool, *Focus* letters, *Picturegoer*, 30:1073, 26 November 1955, p. 30.
87 'Censored', E. Hannaford, *Picturegoer*, 30:1078, 31 December 1955, p. 4.
88 The results of the vox pops are reported in Derek Walker and Allen Newton, 'Violence', *Picturegoer*, 31:1081, 21 January 1956, pp. 6–7.
89 Hilde Marchant, 'The truth about the 'Teddy boys' and the Teddy girls', *Picture Post*, Issue 9, 29 May 1954, pp. 25–27.
90 Ray Gosling, *Personal Copy: A Memoir of the Sixties* (London and Boston: Faber & Faber, 1980), p. 32.
91 In their *Blackboard Jungle* pressbook, MGM urged British exhibitors to promote the song 'at all opportunities' because of its demonstrable impact on American audiences.

3

'He died in his own rebellion': James Dean and *Rebel Without a Cause*

> I still have the feeling that our 'X' may appear too heavy handed a category for the rubbish that this picture undoubtedly is.
>
> Arthur Watkins, Secretary of the BBFC, 1955[1]

> I can't forget James Dean ... I hope that *Rebel Without a Cause* will not be shelved because of his death.
>
> Miss S. E. Manly, 'Remembered', 1956[2]

'Dean Display Dominates Dilly!' declared the Warner Brothers pressbook for *Rebel Without a Cause* (Nicolas Ray, 1955).[3] Indeed, an enormous 60 ft over-the-canopy image of James Dean had been hoisted above the marquee of the Hollywood studio's Piccadilly cinema. Looming over the Eros statue, the actor's compelling image, in a red jacket and blue jeans, looking defiantly over his left shoulder, had anticipated the great metaphor for what British censors and parents feared – Dean's towering, all-powerful influence as a teenage delinquent on young, impressionable British fans. When the film premiered in January 1956, Dean's image figured prominently in publicity; yet the charismatic, handsome leading actor was already dead. He had been killed in a car crash in September 1955.

This chapter constructs a new film history of *Rebel Without a Cause* using the historical-materialist methodology proposed by the film scholars Janet Staiger (1992) and Barbara Klinger (1997). This exploration of the film's transnational reception documents how British teenagers participated in a death cult for a unique Hollywood star. Chapters 1 and 2 analysed the reasons for the stringent censorship of *The Wild One* and *Blackboard Jungle*. When the BBFC encountered *Rebel Without a Cause* it activated a new set of concerns. Firstly, Dean played an affluent teenager, Jim Stark, whose delinquent behaviour alleviated the boredom and frustration of an emotionally unfulfilling home life. Clearly, he had little in common with the sociopaths of British cinema's commentaries such as *The Blue Lamp* (Basil Dearden, 1950) and *Cosh Boy* (Lewis Gilbert, 1953). Hollywood's engagement with the topical subject privileged an emergent anti-hero at a time when British censors were attuned to the 'public anxiety' about juvenile delinquency in society.[4] Secondly, like Marlon Brando, Dean was a method actor, who displayed a spectacular emotional range hitherto unknown in male stars. As the chapter illustrates, the combination of Dean's personal attributes, the precocious wisdom of his rebellious screen character, and his own sudden death secured him an unprecedented position in the hero-worship of British (and international) teenagers.

Rebel Without a Cause centres on 17-year-old Jim Stark, who is inebriated, lying face down in the street, and playing with a toy monkey in opening scenes. Soon, Jim is arrested and taken to the local police station for drunk and disorderly behaviour. Whilst waiting for his parents (Ann Doran and Jim Backus) and maternal grandmother (Virginia Brissac) to pick him up and take him home, Jim spies Judy (Natalie Wood). Judy is an attractive teenager being evaluated by Inspector Ray Fremick (Edward Platt), a compassionate juvenile probation officer. Plato (Sal Mineo) is the story's most emotionally disturbed delinquent: he has been called in for killing a litter of puppies. As the rich son of neglectful parents, Plato is attended only by his black housekeeper (and main caregiver) and after his interview with Fremick notices Jim. Jim is soon assessed by Inspector Fremick before his family are also invited into his office. An ugly row ensues, and we learn that Jim's family has moved him to Los Angeles for a fresh start. On his first morning of school, Jim makes friends with Judy and later Plato. The whole class visit the Griffith Observatory and afterwards Jim is harassed by Judy's boyfriend Buzz (Corey Allen) and forced into a knife fight. Watched by Buzz's gang and other high school students, the fight is eventually broken up by security guards. Having failed to establish a clear 'winner', Buzz challenges Jim to a 'chicken run' in which the contenders will drive (stolen) cars towards a cliff edge to see who will jump clear first in a battle of nerves. That night, the dare goes awry and Buzz is killed when he fails to free himself from his vehicle and Jim, the victor, consoles Judy.

When Jim tells his parents that he wants to report the tragic accident to the police, they try to dissuade him. Disgusted by their amorality, Jim argues with his mother and begins a fistfight with his dad before tearing out of the house. Arriving at the police station to make a full confession of his part in the tragedy, Jim is confronted by Buzz's gang who tell him that they will avenge their friend's death. Later that night, Judy, Plato and Jim hide out in a deserted mansion in the outskirts of the city. During the dreamlike playfulness they indulge in, Jim and Judy find consolation in one another and fall in love. Finally included in a 'family', Plato finds the 'parental nurture' he has been denied. But the happy idyll is soon disturbed when they are discovered by Buzz's gang. Jim, Judy and Plato escape to Griffith Observatory, where Plato's erratic behaviour results in his being shot and killed by police. Jim takes off his red jacket and lays it over his deceased friend – at last, peaceful and untroubled. At the film's close, Jim introduces Judy to his father, and the three walk away together. With the red jacket left behind, the restored relationship between father and son, and the accompanying optimistic music, Jim's rebellious days appear to be behind him.

As made clear in this outline, the film emphasises that Jim – in the spirit of Brando's Johnny Strabler – is a redeemable rebel, whose family has misunderstood him. Further, Jim's regeneration is a result of Inspector Fremick's efforts. For this reason, Peter Biskind argues that *Rebel*'s delinquents were sentimentalised to endorse the intervention of a wider network of teachers, social workers and psychiatrists; and show that the family was unable to contain the youth problem single-handedly.[5] Andrew Caine further asserts that *Rebel* continued, rather than disrupted, Hollywood's penchant for melodrama by including a conciliatory, happy ending.[6] Nonetheless, Warner Brothers' pressbook suggests that the director Nicholas Ray's original intention was to produce an unsentimental commentary on a serious issue. Promotional materials describe Ray's burgeoning interest in the topic after reading Robert M. Lindner's academic study of juvenile delinquency, *Rebel Without a Cause: The hypnoanalysis of a criminal psychopath* (1944). After drafting a story outline, Ray and his screenwriter, Stewart Stern, went on an 'eight-month nationwide' research project across the country that involved meeting highly regarded psychiatrists. In effect, Warner Brothers regarded their film as the outcome of a sustained scientific inquiry into a pertinent social issue.

American popular culture of the 1950s both informed and was influenced by *Rebel Without a Cause*. Thomas Doherty argues that it familiarised mainstream audiences with drag racing, and created a niche for 'hot rod' films directed at the youth market.[7] Claudia Springer's study demonstrates that new generations of American filmmakers have borrowed and adapted Dean's rebellious iconography.[8] Thus far, Dean's British fan base and influence on popular culture has not received any substantive academic attention. Reconstructing a wide range of responses to James Dean in Britain, then, provides an alternative history of his stardom.

British audiences encountered *Rebel* in highly unusual circumstances. By the end of September 1955, Dean had fulfilled his contractual obligations to Warner Brothers by completing his scenes for *Giant* (George Stevens, 1956). Always an avid speed enthusiast, Dean's prized possession was a Porsche Spyder that he nicknamed 'Little Bastard'. On 30 September 1955, Dean was en route to an organised racing event when he collided with another car in Cholame, California. Whilst the driver of the Ford Tudor Sedan sustained minor injuries, the 24-year-old actor was killed instantaneously. Cognizant that films starring recently deceased actors rarely enjoyed commercial success, Warner Brothers' executives debated whether to alter their advertising campaign.[9] The studio was spurred on by the (unexpectedly) enthusiastic responses of American fans; and within a short time, Hollywood publicists realised the commercial value of centring all promotion on Dean. The star's violent and sudden death appeared to have authenticated his rebellious screen character. As one British critic presciently observed: 'When James Dean slammed head on into another car, a legend was born.'[10]

British film censors and middle-class delinquents

The version of *Rebel Without a Cause* submitted to the BBFC for classification had already been modified by the Hollywood censors and received the PCA's seal of approval.[11] Censorship matters were not to prove so straightforward in Europe where widespread teenage hooliganism was attracting official and public condemnation. Daniel

Biltereyst contextualises the Belgian censors' officious attitudes to the film against the 'moral panic' surrounding emergent youth subcultures.[12] Similarly, in Britain, BBFC files and informal memoranda from the archives reconstruct a lengthy correspondence between the censors and Warner Brothers in which each party was determined to outmanoeuvre the other. Watkins, the BBFC Secretary, was a self-declared cineaste and a successful playwright, who described the ideal censor as someone who could project themselves 'out of our little eight-seater in Soho Square to a crowded Odeon on a Saturday night'.[13] Inevitably, screening juvenile delinquency resulted in the censors' intransigence and the Hollywood studio's compromise. More surprising, then, is Watkins' dismissal of the now-classic *Rebel* as 'rubbish.'

Given this negativity, it is useful to ask why Jim Stark aggravated concerns on the 'youth problem'. On a basic level, Jim's recalcitrant, obnoxious manner and sartorial flamboyance suggest that he is an American Teddy boy. Previous chapters have explored the British Teddy boy phenomenon. Dominic Sandbrook further argues that much of the 'moral outrage' against these working-class youths was their outlandish fashion choices and general extravagance.[14] Arthur Marwick contextualises the increase in juvenile crime as symptomatic of a more widespread hostility against authority by the working class men alienated from the apparent affluence of 'having it so good'.[15]

British media commentary on disorderly behaviour by Teddy youths – and the official responses to contain it – centred on cinemas, cafes (or milk bars) and other public spaces where young people had opportunities to congregate. In Brighton, coffee bars had become officially regulated for the 'menace' they posed by permitting working-class youth, in particular, to congregate 'outside official control and supervision.'[16] In Liverpool, cinema managers had decided to bar anyone wearing Teddy regalia to deter anti-social cinemagoing. In Northamptonshire, 'muscular' door attendants were employed to discourage gang fights at popular nightspots and ballrooms.[17] Chapter 1 contextualised the censors' reactions to films about juvenile delinquency against the notorious Craig-Bentley case (1952), which perpetuated a negative stereotype of the simple-minded adolescent fixated on Hollywood's gangsters. Further, John Beckley's murder (1953) by rival Teddy boys compounded the censors' worst concerns about the indiscriminate nature of violence between urban gangs. By reducing the attractiveness of screen violence, the BBFC believed it was fulfilling its function of protecting the 'impressionable' viewer from assuming the 'wrong' values from films.[18] To condone juvenile delinquency by glamorising screen rebels – constructed as sexually attractive and seemingly invincible – was entertaining for the discerning filmgoer but misleading for others. The British media frequently advocated these same restrictions. The screenwriter and *Daily Mail* critic, Fred Majdalany, disparaged Hollywood's latest trend of furnishing narratives around 'the Crazy, Mixed-Up Kid' whom he considered undesirable and potentially influential for 'bad' boys and girls in cinema audiences.[19]

Given their close ties to the Home Office, Watkins and his fellow examiners reflected official policy on initiatives to deter young people from juvenile delinquency. The Conservative government's appointment of the Committee on Maladjusted Children (1950) resulted in the Underwood Report (1955). The report outlined 97 recommendations for better coordination between schools and psychology units and increased training and resources to support 'maladjusted' children. With the introduction of the X certificate in 1951, the censors were doing their part in protecting those considered most vulnerable. The A certificate depended on the discretion of discerning parents to prevent children from seeing inappropriate films, but this concept conflicted with the habit of frequent cinemagoing. Hence, the X certificate was the surest means to prevent children from watching films that extenuated vice or crime or devalued the accepted standards of modern family life: those likeliest to impair public moral standards.[20] As mentioned earlier, the powerful lobbying of the Catholic League of Decency directed Hollywood films away from obvious licentiousness but resulted in a more lenient policy toward violent themes. To British censors, *Rebel Without a Cause* combined undesirable violence with a damning attack on the family. These themes resulted in the board's intractability with Warner Brothers to grant the film anything other than an X certificate. For British filmmakers the X certificate proved to be an insurmountable financial obstacle that nearly always proscribed mature themes on screen. However, no major Hollywood studio welcomed limited exhibition and reduced box office. John Wilcox in *Sight and Sound* argued against the protection offered by the X because it was 'the over-16 adolescent' who found the best opportunities for 'mischief'.[21]

As Secretary, Watkins was frequently called upon to explain the stringency of BBFC policy to the media.[22] Criticism was invariably deflected through recourse to the censors' mandate to protect children from cinema's harmful effects. By these means, Watkins conveyed information not only to the ordinary filmgoer but also to film producers. *Variety*, the oldest of the Hollywood trade papers, reported on Warner Brothers' unfavourable experiences in bringing *Rebel Without a Cause* to Britain. The article, which purportedly breached confidentiality issues, listed the numerous (and costly) deletions imposed by the British censors; and presumably provided a cautionary tale to Hollywood producers considering future films about juvenile delinquency.[23]

The juvenile delinquents brought to the screen in *The Wild One* and *Blackboard Jungle* were constructed as 'lost' boys from dysfunctional or abusive families who regained their sense of identity in gang life. The British censors recognised that *Rebel Without a Cause* was less violent but considered it inferior; they were equally perplexed by 'the accent on the sins of neglectful and quarrelling parents' for, what appeared to be, the 'recreational' mischief of affluent, middle class teenagers.[24] Judging films on their merits and not to a statutory code was the ostensible advantage that the British censors held over the PCA, their Hollywood counterparts. However, working to guidelines (formalised in 1917 and updated in 1926) allowed for their discretion but, equally, could be manipulated to exert their control over material.

As shown in the previous chapter, the British censors reduced idioms and slang used by American high school students in *Blackboard Jungle*: they were overdubbed or deleted wherever possible. Now their overriding concern was to dismantle James Dean's method acting, a signifier of excessive Americanness. That Dean's volatile dialogue and physical performance were considered a potential stimulant to the young and unsophisticated resulted in liberal changes to Inspector Fremick's first scene with Jim. Closer analysis of Dean's performance offers clues to why it was undesirable to those who placed highest importance on 'containing' the exuberant misbehaviours of (future) Teddy boys.

Figure 3.1 The dysfunctional American family: British censors were perplexed by James Dean's emotional register and his character's fiery confrontations with his parents (Ann Doran and Jim Backus) in *Rebel Without a Cause* (1955).

In the scene, Fremick permits – and invites – Jim to lash out as a cathartic expression of his disillusion with his parents. After his outburst, Jim has a fiery confrontation with his parents and grandmother. Here, Dean is privileged in close-ups that show his contorted, tear-stained face, and the camera accommodates his flailing arms, as he wails: 'You're tearing me apart! You [Mom] say one thing then straight away he [Dad] says another!' The British censors stipulated that all lashing out, and punching and kicking of the inspector's desk be removed. Ostensibly, the examiners' modifications conformed to O'Connor's guidelines because Jim's erratic behaviour may be cited as 'a drunken scene carried to excess' and constituted an action 'disparaging to public characters and institutions' [the police and the family].[25] However, this argument is weakened by Watkins' own admission that he considered the film to be 'rubbish'. Furthermore, the President of the BBFC, Sidney Harris is more precise in his estimation of the scene's potential to aggravate in his response to Watkins: 'I agree that it is rubbish for adults but poisonous stuff for the teddy-inclined adolescent.'[26]

Chapter 1 showed that censors believed that romanticised screen 'thugs' elicited the secret rapture of unsophisticated teenagers in the audience. As recalled, the virginal Kathie resists and then submits to Johnny's advances. Similarly, James Dean's delicate boyish looks and his tough-but-vulnerable duality made him very popular with teenagers. Dean's method acting and Jim's idiosyncratic sense of honour ennobled (what should have been presented as) bad behaviour; and attracted the 'morbid fascination' for 'young toughs' that greatly troubled the BBFC examiners. *Rebel*'s ingénue Judy, like Kathie in *The Wild One*, was to be 'protected' from any hints of promiscuity. For these reasons, the BBFC jettisoned any filmic moments or dialogue that conveyed that Judy lacked morals and thoroughly enjoyed being with 'the gang'. Particularly troublesome was Judy's ritualistic initiation of the 'chicken run': she stands between Buzz's and Jim's cars and starts the race with a waving of her necktie. Thus, the close-ups that conveyed Judy's 'unrestrained' and 'hysterical' elation were reduced because they conveyed her (potentially sexual) excitement at these proceedings.[27] The examiners were also concerned by how quickly she transferred her affections from the deceased Buzz to Jim because it made her appear immoral. To counter these notions, the censors shortened her screen kiss with Jim and deleted the word 'tramp' in Judy's dialogue: 'He calls me a dirty tramp – my own father!'[28]

Other censorship focused on the idioms used by teenagers and screen behaviours which conveyed the recreational element of crimes committed by real-life Teddy boys. In particular, the conversation between Buzz and Jim before their 'chicken run' was considered repugnant and, therefore, removed.[29] During this exchange, Buzz tells Jim that he likes him, which prompts Jim to ask: 'So, why do we do this?' Buzz shrugs his response: 'You've gotta do something'. Inevitably, the BBFC approached scenes that depicted knife crime – proscribed by guidelines as *modus operandi* – with heightened vigilance because of ongoing skirmishes between Teddy gangs. Therefore, a scene that showed Jim's car tyres being slashed and the dramatic switchblade fight between Buzz and Jim outside Griffith Observatory were heavily censored; and edits reduced the action but left the spectators' reactions intact to suggest what was going on.[30] The BBFC maintained that their deletions would not affect film continuity (nor detract from screen entertainment), but changes to the teenagers' knife fight were noticeable.[31]

Frequent media coverage located the worst incidences of high jinks or juvenile delinquency in and around venues that offered teenagers opportunities to congregate, whether at the local dance hall or amusement arcade. It was no surprise, then, that the BBFC objected to any scenes of 'organised hooliganism'; and found the 'chicken run' dare particularly objectionable for showing British teenagers exactly how this reckless stunt could be organised.[32] The BBFC's Memorandum to Film Producers (1949) forewarned them that depictions of violence and torture, including anguished facial expressions or cries of suffering in victims, would be censored.[33] For these reasons, the examiners' instructions reduced 'unpleasant' shots of Buzz's terrified realisation of his imminent crash and reduced his anguished screams of terror on impact as unnecessarily ghoulish.[34]

The BBFC's correspondence with the Warner Brothers executive, Arthur Abeles, and *Rebel*'s film editor, C. Wackett, shows that both concurred with satisfying all of the board's demands. Wackett duly reported that he had excised the 'terrifying and distasteful knife fight between two adolescents' but left intact Jim's 'praiseworthy' dialogue that foregrounded his heroism: 'Can't we meet someplace but not with those [knives]?' Changes to this scene reconfigured Buzz's death as an unfortunate accident rather than as a probable outcome to a pre-arranged gathering of hoodlums intent on doing harm.[35] In his account of the film's Hollywood censorship, Jerold Simmons illustrates how foreign rentals were essential – particularly in English-speaking Britain – in recovering the high production costs not met in the American domestic market alone.[36] An A certificate would have been the ideal outcome for Warner Brothers in this situation but Watkins considered *Rebel* far too violent for children, even if accompanied by a bona fide adult.[37] The A certificate was commended as a uniquely British and progressive extension of the BBFC ratings system by inviting parental discretion in their children's viewing habits.[38] However, the A certificate was also open to abuse. Parents did not always discriminate between films if it interfered with their regular patronage; and wily children had learned that they could petition any willing stranger to accompany them into the cinema.[39]

Earlier negotiations between British censors and Hollywood executives had rarely encountered problems with American films pre-approved by the PCA. Watkins, himself, regarded the X as 'heavy weather' for the re-edited version of *Rebel* that would be shown in British cinemas.[40] MGM had already failed to secure an A certificate for the re-edited version of *Blackboard Jungle* approved by the British censors. If Warner Brothers now expected leniency they were similarly disappointed: for an A certificate they would need to satisfy additional objections drawn up by the BBFC. For example, the examiners challenged the 'ridiculous' ineptitude of Jim's parents and wanted specific dialogue removed, such as Jim's line urging his father to 'knock [Mom] cold maybe then she'd be happy'. Jim's mimicking of a police siren – a now classic and iconic moment – was recommended for deletion. Duly targeted was Jim's 'unpleasant' reference to his school being a 'zoo' as was all American slang, including Mr Stark's innocuous reference to Jim's inebriated condition as being 'loaded'.[41] In muting the display of dysfunctional relationships, British censors had reiterated their mandate to remove material likely to impair moral standards and family values. Finally, Warner Brothers recognised the futility of the situation and politely refused to accommodate these additional recommendations for fear that their film would become entirely unrecognisable. In working to eradicate the inherent Americanness of the production, the BBFC invoked Maltby's useful assessment of censorship as a mechanism for protecting and elevating a host culture as different, distinct and superior to another.[42]

Selling Dean: a posthumous stardom

The evaluation of *Rebel*'s British censorship has demonstrated the challenges and obstacles that impeded its foreign distribution. This section analyses the promotional materials around the deceased James Dean to explore how Warner Brothers overcame and exploited these unusual circumstances. Their British publicity campaign retained sensational taglines that had sold the film to American audiences, such as: 'Jim Stark – from a 'good' family – what makes him tick like a bomb?' In the film trailer, in lobby cards and in other graphic materials, thrilling moments were isolated for audience consumption: Dean was presented as a contemporary action hero – the paradigmatic 'kid of 1955' – and romantic lead.

In developing audience anticipation for Dean's film, the Warner Brothers pressbook, replete with suggestions for exploitation, urged local exhibitors to follow the example of their West End cinema and transform their foyers into 'a picture gallery of teen-age violence'.[43] Biography items foregrounded Dean as a committed artist, who had trained at the Actors Studio in New York, and received excellent reviews for several performances on Broadway. Dean's co-star, Natalie Wood, who had been a child star, was now presented as the epitome of the fashionable 1950s teenager in her first prestigious 'adult' role. Furthermore, *Rebel*'s story 'promised' to unravel the conundrum of generational conflict while other features capitalised on Dean's sudden death.

Taglines drew attention to the film's temporal relevance, while Warners' pressbook exhorted their drama as the result of Lindner's prestigious scientific inquiry into juvenile delinquency. They emphasised how research had been informed by interviews with police officers, judges, youth leaders, juvenile welfare officers and the chief psychiatrist of criminology at the Nuremberg trials. According to these credentials, the film was intended to be consumed as social realism.

British reviewers and an American idiom

Whilst Warner Brothers capitalised on the timeliness of their social problem film, this did little to recommend the film to the majority of British critics. In the popular press and in some of the quality broadsheets, critics disapproved of Hollywood's tendency to indict American institutions – including the family – and portray an unappealing and pessimistic image of their nation for the sake of entertainment. Young men (aged 16–24) now outnumbered all other British cinemagoers (at 33.5 per cent of the audience) and Peter Evans in the *Daily Express* reasoned that this was why the 'crazy-mixed-up kid' and other unsavoury types had begun to appear on screens. Women who had traditionally made up the majority of film audiences were less inclined to enjoy gritty, realistic stories. 'At the pictures we should like a break', explained fellow reporter, Anne Edwards, who urged Hollywood to return to escapism and glamour. '[I]f I wanted to see a slut in a fish queue, or a couple of juvenile delinquents in the making, or a brawl in a pub, I should take a sixpenny tube down Elephant and Castle way', Edwards commented.[44] The long-serving film reviewer of the *Observer*, C. A. Lejeune, was just as perplexed with modern Hollywood for spoiling her childhood impressions by representing Americans as 'violent, maladjusted people unhappy in their home lives'.[45]

Genre was another topic that critics could not agree on. The *Sunday Times* critic Dilys Powell called the film 'wholly melodramatic'; and an unnamed *Manchester Guardian* critic decided, presumably because of these melodramatic undertones, that it could not match the *Dead End* tradition of realism. The *Daily Mail*'s critic, Fred Majdalany, was indignant at the film's sensationalising and distortion of the youth issue, whereas the *Evening News* critic, Jympson Harman, praised the realism of the production and urged every young marriageable couple to watch it for its relevant and truthful commentary.[46] In summary, then, *Rebel Without a Cause* appeared to occupy two generic camps in its melodramatic treatment of a social problem.

It would seem that *Rebel*'s idiosyncratic depiction of juvenile delinquency was the main reason it alienated film reviewers. Throughout the book, I have shown that the archetypal British Teddy boy was described as – and understood to be – an unsophisticated, semi-skilled working-class youth, motivated by privation and maladjustment. Unsurprisingly, then, the 'otherness' of the middle-class juvenile delinquency depicted in *Rebel* was its most remarkable (and unrealistic) feature. The reviewer in the *Daily Telegraph* described the material comforts and car ownership of the adolescent characters as 'phoney'. Similarly, the *Daily Worker*'s critic observed, with barely concealed bafflement, that '[t]hese California youngsters have money and cars but behave like gangsters'; while the *Financial Times* critic ascertained that it was 'a fascinating outré [sic] of Californian modes' that bore little resemblance to British life.[47]

The Underwood Report (1955) recognised that a supportive and structured school environment for maladjusted children was important in stemming the rise of juvenile delinquency. Based on this official discourse, it was no wonder that British critics struggled to identify a distinct adult authority figure in the film. The invisibility of the high school system within the narrative was a jarring obstacle to the film's plausibility and seemingly left Buzz and then Jim to organise school life as they wished. The *Evening Standard*'s critic suggested that what 'Mr [Nicholas] Ray's specimens' required was no more than a strict headmaster to regenerate them; and the *Times Educational*

Supplement reviewer commented on the 'appalling jaded precocity' of the 'barbarically young' Americans.[48]

Besides polarising opinions on the probable causes of delinquency, Nicholas Ray's drama of social realism and Dean's emotive performance mobilised critical discourses on method acting. Method actors were encouraged to use psychoanalytical techniques – and undergo therapeutic analysis, themselves – to enrich the credibility of their performance. The disparities between the British and American imaginary may be explained, then, by contrasting attitudes to Freudian theories. British critics were less convinced that audiences would enjoy Hollywood's current trend for depicting modern families as dysfunctional and neurotic. In addition, Milton Shulman, the *Sunday Express* critic, objected to fathers becoming 'the horrible example of every psychiatrist' and 'the necessary evil in the American family' because of his ignorance of Freud.[49]

Psychoanalysis was less widely familiar in Britain but had gained popularity and currency within post-war American society. Hollywood's contemporary stories mined this rich cultural landscape to explore familial relationships. Indeed, Stella Bruzzi argues that the Oedipus complex, narcissism and masculinity, and the development of sexuality were all explored through the Freudian father–child relationship that formed the basis of many American films of the 1950s.[50] *Rebel Without a Cause*, similarly, focuses on the Oedipal conflict between Jim, his overbearing mother and his weakened father; and between Judy and her father, who withdraws tactile affection from his daughter because of her burgeoning sexuality.

Dean's performance was generally praised for its sensitivity and earnestness. However, there were detractors of the solemnity of his method acting, which was to prove another obstacle to the meanings and implications critics took from the film. The *Manchester Guardian* reviewer, for example, allocated James Dean to Marlon Brando's territory of 'inarticulate muttering' and 'sudden bursts of violence', which he felt were 'difficult' for European audiences to 'access'.[51] Similarly, Vicky Graham in the *Spectator* believed that the 'Atlantic curtain comes down with a wallop' when she regarded the foreignness of Dean's teenage portrait as 'an incomprehensible, slightly alarming figure so far removed from our way of life he might be on another planet'.[52]

Proponents of the Method tended to be those industry professionals who wanted to assimilate fresh approaches into – and invigorate – the performing arts. Tony Richardson, then an experimental film-maker and stage director, challenged objections to method acting by explaining that it naturally accommodated the extrovert American psyche because it exteriorised inner psychic conflicts.[53] Others were concerned that the rigidness of British society would seriously hamper the development of mature and relevant cinema. The British actor Anthony Quayle brought attention to the 'flatness' of British drama that failed to recognise the importance of the inarticulate and underprivileged anti-heroes of modern American performance.[54] Similarly, the screenwriter and film critic Robert Muller urged national cinema to experiment with socially pertinent drama to produce 'its own James Deans'.[55] In contrast, *Picturegoer*'s Tom Hutchinson argued against a prospective method school of acting in London, and told readers that while the Method's emotional range suited American actors, it would prove an embarrassing debacle for British trainee actors and should not replace older acting traditions.[56]

Innovative American acting was accommodated and amplified by well-considered *mise en scène*. For example, Jim's row with his parents after Buzz's death is enhanced by a canted (or Dutch) camera angle that disorients the viewer and, therefore, better conveys the turbulent dysfunction within the family. Further, Dean's highly charged neurosis and Ray's experimental direction produced a new image of masculinity unfamiliar to audiences of the 1950s. Queer scholars have theorised on the gender fluidity central to all of Dean's on-screen masculinities. Judith Butler's well-known work, *Gender Trouble* (1990) has argued for the behavioural or performative aspects of gender rather than the pre-determined expression of inner essence. On this basis, Marie Carter considers Dean's adolescent portrait of Jim Stark to be a problematic and performative masculinity, sustained by the actor's own ambivalent sexuality, and strongly influenced by the butch women of the 1950s.[57] Indeed, elements of *mise en scène* such as the undefined nature of Plato's attachment to Jim sustain these arguments. Further, Nicholas Ray's playful blocking of Dean and Natalie Wood, where Dean is positioned as the 'feminised' object rather than the bearer of the gaze, deliberately undermines stable notions of heteronormative masculinity.

Figure 3.2 In love scenes with Natalie Wood, James Dean is 'feminised' by being positioned as the love object rather than the instigator of their kiss.

As described in Chapter 1, Brando displayed his 'looked-at-ness' through elaborate and revealing costuming. In *Rebel*, Dean's vulnerability and gentle beauty are privileged in close-ups, and emphasised in the love scenes between Jim and Judy. In these, the reclining Dean is positioned low in the frame while Wood is above him – elements that combine to show that Jim is the receiver rather the instigator of the kiss.

The most ebullient and consistent praise for *Rebel Without A Cause* came from the intellectual essayists who evaluated films for several prestigious cineaste journals. These critics responded to the graceful choreography of Dean's method acting and Ray's candid and realistic commentary on the American Dream. Gavin Lambert's reviews, for example, focused on Dean's rare talent for 'tormented' acting and on Ray's sharply angry and original observations on patterns in American family life.[58]

Derek Prouse described Dean's acting as the 'awkward grace of youth' and ascribed an iconic status to his performance as a genuinely poetic account of 'a modern misfit'.[59] These critics were exponents of the experimental Free Cinema movement – spearheaded by fellow Oxbridge graduate, Lindsay Anderson, whose manifesto promised: 'No Film Can Be Too Personal.'[60] Across their reviews was celebration – rather than discomfiture – of the exposé of the small, private world of individual stories from 'a rarely opened family album'.[61] These reviewers were less inspired by an imitative British production about a rebellious teenager. *My Teenage Daughter* (Herbert Wilcox, 1956) told the coming-of-age story of a middle-class teenager Jan (Sylvia Syms), who lives comfortably in Hampstead with her mother (Anna Neagle) and younger sister (Janet Carr). When Jan becomes involved with Tony (Kenneth Haigh), a petty criminal, she becomes estranged from her mother and spends much of her time drinking and dancing at nightclubs. Finally, Jan is persuaded to run away with Tony. Tony tries to coerce his elderly aunt into giving him money and when she refuses he pushes her and she suffers a fatal head wound. Tony decides not to tell Jan about this accidental killing and they go ahead with their plan to run away together. Eventually, Tony's car is spotted and he and Jan are chased down and arrested by the police. Exonerated from any involvement, Jan is collected from the police station and realises how misguided she has been. Mother and daughter lovingly agree to communicate with one another in future. The *Monthly Film Bulletin* review commended the film for attempting to comment on a topical issue but concluded that it was 'a very British, somewhat lukewarm *Rebel Without a Cause*, which skirts around its subject without ever convincing one that its authors are really anxious about the problem'.[62]

Hollywood films featured in the high–low art debates generated in the Americanisation discourses of the 1950s. Like the others in her set, Penelope Houston, the editor of *Sight and Sound*, balanced her passion for the medium against its commercial constraints: films had to temper realism with novelty to attract audiences. In this spirit, Houston emphasised that good cinema – dependent on experimental and socially pertinent narratives – had as much value to the culture of a society as highly regarded literature. Thus, she analogised Dean's superlative study of adolescence with J. D. Salinger's enduring outsider Holden Caulfield in *The Catcher in the Rye* (1951).[63] Literary critic and author Kenneth Allsop, however, could not draw such parallels and was discouraged by contemporary Hollywood cinema. Allsop distinguished the 'coffee-bar crowd's Deanish sullenness' from the 'dignified university group' who appropriated Holden Caulfield as their role model.[64] Although class differences between these groups were not made explicit, 'the coffee-bar crowd' and Richard Hoggart's 'juke-box boys' – working-class youth of conscription age – appear to be the same group of young people criticised for 'misspending' their leisure time.[65] Coffee bars increased concurrent with the healthy growth of post-war teenage consumerism and provided alternative leisure spaces for young people. The young journalist Shirley Lowe provides a useful commentary on her generation's avoidance of traditional pub culture:

> Who can expect a young generation brought up on the glamour of American films to spend the evening in a chipped brown bar when they can be in bright, fresh surroundings, with indoor plants creeping up the walls, bright red lamps casting a warm glow on the modern tables, clean bar, gay-coloured murals, comfortable bench-back chairs, music – and an appetising menu?[66]

British film fans and an American rebel

This section uses fan materials and media commentary to reconstruct the British stardom of the iconic James Dean. In his first screen role, Dean played Cal Trask in *East of Eden* (Elia Kazan, 1955). The film adapted the second half of John Steinbeck's epic novel, *East of Eden* (1952), and purported to tell a modern version of the Cain and Abel story. Cal lives with his father, Adam (Raymond Massey), a Californian farmer, and his gentle-natured brother Aron (Richard Davalos). Cal deeply resents Aron and clashes with his father, and soon develops feelings for Aron's girlfriend, Abra (Julie Harris). On discovering that his mother (Jo Van Fleet) is not deceased – as Adam had claimed – but is actually the madam of a brothel, the family begins to fragment. The distraught Aron leaves to enlist in the First World War, Adam suffers a stroke, and Cal and Abra remain to care for him.

Cast in another Freudian father–child relationship, Massey and Dean also shared a mutual animosity off-screen. 'The screen was alive with precisely what I wanted,' recalled the director, Elia Kazan, adding, 'they detested each other. Casting should tell the story of a film without words; this casting did.'[67] Dean's tortured performance as Cal was honoured posthumously: he was nominated for a Best Actor Academy Award and received a Golden Globe for Special Achievement as Best Dramatic Actor. Despite these accolades, British publicity around *Rebel Without a Cause* earmarked the little-known actor as another of 'the Brando Boys'.[68] Jympson Harman's rare assessment distinguished Dean as an individual whose childhood trauma – his mother's early death to cancer – sustained the credibility of his method acting and gave 'him bitter experience of youth's yearning for parental comfort and understanding.'[69] More typical was Peter Burnup's judgement. Unable to reconcile middle-class material comforts with delinquency, Burnup asked, 'I wonder what the ordinary movie-goer will make of this American Teddy-boy saga.'[70] By the end of 1956, cinema managers across Britain would include Dean's performance as Jim Stark on the prestigious list of 'best individual performances' in their trade journal, *Kinematograph Weekly*.[71]

If British critics could not anticipate the enduring cult status of *Rebel Without a Cause*, it proved immediately popular with the younger generation. As a precursor to the Angry Young Man, Dean was the first global star to articulate the teenage syndrome of rebellion and alienation from parental authority. British fans joined the ranks of a global fan base that became known as 'Deanagers'. The term 'Deanager' found its way into common vocabulary, and the label offered fans something of a separate identity from non-fans (and adults). Some of the British school leavers in Thelma Veness's sociological study identified as Deanagers.[72] Deanagers developed their own rituals and practices to show their adulation of the late actor.

Jackie Stacey has theorised on the wide range of behaviours that connect British fans to their favourite Hollywood stars of the 1930s and 1940s.[73] British Deanagers participated in these interactions by similar means. They copied the actor's appearance and mannerisms and identified strongly with the story of Jim Stark. In some extreme cases, fans imitated Dean in their own lives, by combining elements of Jim Stark with the 'real' Dean from polysemic accounts pieced together from publicity materials, posters and photographs, movie soundtracks, biography, gossip and interviews with those who knew him.

Adam Faith's enduring 'worship' of Dean provides a detailed account of this interactive fan behaviour. Faith, born Terry Nelhams, grew up in a council estate in Acton, West London, and was a regular filmgoer. He became fascinated by Dean when he saw his emotionally charged performance in *Rebel Without a Cause*, and found himself returning to watch the film repeatedly. Faith then spent many weeks sourcing as similar a red jacket to Jim Stark's as he could locate, and wore the prized item with pride in his daily life. Faith interpreted and assimilated Dean's rebellious persona as self-determinism to pursue a career in the performing arts – then considered a genteel profession for the upper middle classes – and hitherto achieved what he had believed to be an impossible 'dream'.[74]

British cinemagoers were responding to Dean's performance in *Rebel*, with the knowledge that he had been killed in circumstances not unlike those dramatised on screen. The immediate wave of public interest in a dead film star was soon compared to the cult that had enveloped the silent screen idol Rudolph Valentino in the 1920s. Valentino's premature death from peritonitis at the age of 31 was a major international news story that generated sensationalised accounts of his mobbed funeral procession, mass female hysteria and the reactive suicides of obsessive fans.[75] Now it was Dean's death cult that gained momentum. The British popular press speculated on the nature of Dean's death in a car crash, and reported ghoulish stories and insalubrious rumours, gossip and new theories by drawing on American news services or their overseas British news correspondents. One 'horrified' young British fan implored the *Daily Mail* to confirm whether Dean was actually alive but severely disfigured and living in seclusion.[76] The tabloid press anticipated the exposé magazines of the 1960s by concocting 'exclusives' from hearsay and recycled biographical information. *Weekend Mail*'s front page headline, for example, offered readers 'an amazing new theory' of Dean's death, and developed a story around his probable 'suicide' drawing on information that he had been rejected by his girlfriend, the actress Pier Angeli, and was distraught at her marriage to the singer, Vic Damone.[77]

Britain's most popular film fan magazine, *Picturegoer*, awarded prize money for letters published in its 'Focus' section. The age of contributors was not always provided but strong emotions indicate a teenage point of view. When Dean's role in *East of Eden* failed to win Best Actor Oscar of 1956 one British Deanager shared her indignance: 'I'll never again take the Oscars seriously. Ernest Borgnine [in *Marty* (Delbert Mann, 1955)] – was nowhere near the remarkable James Dean.'[78] In addition to individual letters, *Picturegoer*'s annual awards – that rated specific performances – reflected the subjective views of actual cinemagoers rather than those in the trade.[79] Dean's resounding popularity with *Picturegoer* readers was demonstrated when he won two successive *Picturegoer* Best Actor awards for *East of Eden* (1955) and *Rebel Without A Cause* (1956) and fans petitioned the magazine to award him for his third and final film role in *Giant*.[80]

Glossy portraits of Dean were soon available from the *Picturegoer Salon* stock of stills; and interviews with Dean's co-stars and friends continued throughout 1956 and 1957 and satisfied readers who wanted to know the 'real' Dean.[81] In her study of fandom, Samantha Barbas argues that both the 'inside scoop' and regular trivia from gossip columnists provided the principal means of connection between fans and their favourite stars.[82] No doubt, this interdependent relationship became intensified because Dean was dead and could never meet his fans in person.

News features continued to draw parallels between Dean's love of speed racing and Jim Stark's rebellion. This convergence – the actor and his character shared the same first name – collapsed the public persona and fictional characterisation into a single narrative of Dean's short life. The *Daily Express*, for example, referred to *Rebel Without a Cause* as 'Dean's last dare'.[83] In his feature-length fan essay, Robert Muller blurred the boundaries between fact and fiction, and fostered an image of the film as a retelling of Dean's actual life story.[84] For the most part, tragedy and manic depression, childlike vulnerability, personal torments and suicidal tendencies appear to have characterised the young actor in the British press. A rare exception to presenting Dean as the prototypical 'mixed-up kid' was an *Evening News* interview with Nicholas Ray. Here, Ray emphasised Dean's stage training and normalised his interest in speed racing as a typical leisure pursuit among young Californians.[85] Further, Natalie Wood and Nick Adams, another of *Rebel*'s cast members, described Dean for *Picture Post* as 'Jimmy the wit, Jimmy the ham, Jimmy the practical joker' and provided alternative, less tragic perspectives of the actor.[86]

Thousands of fan letters were sent to the Warner Brothers studio in Los Angeles on a weekly basis. It became obvious that youngsters from around the world wanted to share their strong feelings of grief and frustration about Dean's death, and typically asked, 'Why didn't someone stop him from driving so fast?'[87] Within several full-length analyses in the British media, American Deanagers were depicted as 'morbidly obsessive': the victims of ruthless commercialisation or the sexually precocious or homosexual admirers who placed Dean at the centre of their lurid fantasies. Unlike American Deanagers, British fans were said to have responded to the abject loneliness Dean projected and wished they could have been his friend. Whether Dean aroused homosexual desire in British teenagers was not a topic for debate. In the 1950s, homosexuality was still punishable by law. While the Wolfenden Report (1957) would recommend greater tolerance for gay men (lesbians were not part of the study) homosexuality was not decriminalised until the Sexual Offences Act (1967). Hence, the boys and young men who featured in British fan articles were described as sharing an intense identification with Dean and, therefore, felt compelled to write fan letters for the first time in their lives.[88]

These polarised views on American and British fans appear to have negotiated the increased interest in Dean's death cult and evoke the broader concerns of Hollywood films and Americanisation discourses. The 'spectacular' and 'frenzied' nature of America's Dean cult may well have been the logical outcome of a greater population of teenagers: there were reputedly 360 fan clubs across the USA.[89] Other than this, there is no conclusive evidence to validate the emotional, moral or sexual differences between fans. After all, the British media selected which American fan behaviour to report and which British activity to omit. It is fair to assume that a reiteration of these national differences in the media was most likely motivated by cultural protectionism. My own survey demonstrates that British Deanagers were as impassioned and unrestrained as their American equivalents. One news story verifies that British youngsters were capable of the reckless and 'hysterical' behaviour that purportedly characterised American fans. The *Daily Mail* reported that in north London, two Teddy girls had come across the injured victim of a car crash and 'mobbed' him in the belief that he was the 'living' James Dean.[90] Furthermore, although American fans were reported to have 'pestered' the Warner Brothers studio for items of Dean's clothing and schoolbooks, British fans asked them about the minutiae of Dean's physical appearance and expressed their desire to build a memorial to him in Britain.[91]

British fans were staunchly proactive and participated in a range of behaviours and rituals to celebrate Dean's stardom. In addition to writing fan letters, care of the Warner Brothers studio and to British fan magazines, they formed their own fan clubs. It was also reported that 'intelligent youngsters' rather than 'rock 'n' roll types' were requesting the *Rebel Without a Cause* soundtrack in the nation's record shops. This may have been because the record comprised classical music such as *Ride of the Valkyries* by Richard Wagner and original jazz such as *I'll String Along with You* by Harry Warren. These teenagers explained that they had bought the soundtrack because playing the record at home 'brings Dean closer'.[92]

The British tabloids had generated a pessimistic image of American youngsters, showing how easily they had been swept up in Dean's death cult. Once the cult gained momentum in Britain, contradictions and discrepancies appear in the media. On the one hand, Dean's cult attracted young readers – the increasingly important 'teenage consumer' – and, therefore, made excellent copy and sold papers. On the other, British journalists did not want to participate in inciting – and recreating – the unprecedented hysteria that had launched the Valentino cult. In his feature article for *Picture Post*, Gavin Lyall negotiated these concerns by distinguishing between American and British fans and also in selecting suitable candidates for his interviews. In so doing, Lyall proposed that Dean had 'tickled' the 'intellectual funnybone' of British teenagers. For example, an unnamed Cambridge undergraduate asked the express permission of a cinema manager before tape-recording the entire soundtrack of *East of Eden*. Further, Brian Hurst, an 18-year-old architecture undergraduate at Oxford University, penned an elegy, 'On the death of James Dean (1931–1955)', which was reprinted in full in *Picture Post* and is quoted here:

> Throughout the history of the world
> Great Souls have lived and died,
> And many have refused the mould,
> The world accepts as guide.

> One memory will never die,
> Much sweeter than the rose,
> Much brighter than the burning sky,
> When day comes to a close.
>
> Time only can expand his fame,
> May his dear soul find rest,
> And all remember his great name –
> JAMES DEAN – the boy, unblessed.

Lyall considered the poem 'mediocre' and agreed it would 'not win a Nobel Prize' but preferred it to the 'Jimmy, we love you' and 'something that is loved can never die' sentiments of American fan mail.[93] Other teenagers consciously dissociated themselves from the pessimistic generalisations about post-war youth. 'I admire James Dean', explained Lesley Shuckford of Cheshire, adding, 'I have written countless poems to him. But they are secret things, private and dear to me. Am I then a hooligan?[94] Fans expressed their satisfaction in writing poems; others wrote essays and plays.

Michael Hastings was employed as a tailor's apprentice earning £4 a week when he was inspired to write a play about the late actor. *Mixed-Up Youth* was described by the media as a play about 'a frustrated post-war youth of the James Dean variety' – it opened at a playhouse in London's Notting Hill in the summer of 1956. Evidently, Hastings, like Adam Faith, channelled Dean's rebellious persona to fuel his own success: he was interviewed by the prestigious BBC and the play had a successful run. Detractors of this new writing showed their generational differences. Cecil Wilson in the *Daily Mail*, for example, considered *Mixed-Up Youth* the tedious repetition of a Hollywood formula that told 'the all-too-familiar story of the mixed-up kid twisted into a nervous tangle by squalid upbringing: in his case a young Jew living on his own with a drunken father and a promiscuous stepmother'.[95]

These examples of fan worship illustrate how the British media negotiated the Dean cult by contrasting 'hysterical' American fans to equanimous British Deanagers. There was also evidence of a generational divide as British film critics reported on the cult but were unsympathetic to its motivations. To take at face value the representations of British fans in the press would certainly produce a distorted account. Even first-hand testimony of the 'frenzied' and 'ghoulish' Dean cult in America were likely to be reported by British correspondents based in New York or Los Angeles and were, therefore, skewed by their own prejudicial and foreign perspectives. The Warner Brothers studio endorsed none of this activity and accommodated fans but attempted to deter and contain irrational behaviour. Invariably, elements of the cult in the USA were morbidly fascinating and provided exotic and tantalising titbits for British readers. It was reported, for example, that American junk dealers were exploiting teenagers by selling 'improbable bits of metal' as souvenirs of 'the death car'; and American 'soothsayers, crackpots, phoney astrologers and fake psychiatrists' had materialised to profit from the interest in Dean's death and his spiritual afterlife.[96] The *Picturegoer* film critic Guy Austin expressed his disgust at the American 'craze' and incited shock from readers that Dean's smashed car was being displayed to American teenagers.[97] What was not made explicit to readers was that Dean's car wreck toured the USA as part of a nationwide safety initiative to reduce the tens of thousands of road fatalities.

The enduring interest in Dean among his British fans mobilised contradictory responses among British journalists, as eager to cater to young film fans as they were to express disdain about Dean's 'Americanness' and the odd behaviours of his American fans. Assured of attracting young readers in large numbers, months after the premiere of *Rebel Without a Cause*, the *Daily Herald*'s Douglas Warth exploited the residual interest in the film and its star by serialising the story in a three-part double-page spread under lurid and sensational headlines.[98] As a follow-up, Warth wrote a confrontational piece on Dean, ostensibly warning British parents about the 'macabre hold' that the reckless young actor had over their children.[99] This inevitably generated strong support from Dean's film fans, who wrote in their hundreds to 'defend' their hero and defy Warth's opinion. A self-proclaimed Deanager from Bethnal Green warned Warth: 'I have heard persons saying you should be killed for what you have said.' A 16-year-old teenager from Liverpool stated her preferences succinctly: 'As one of the "frantic generation of problem children", I prefer to worship this one dead man than 20,000 like you.'

By the same token, not all Deanagers were 'silly' youngsters to be disregarded by the older generation. A 22-year-old from Plymouth explained the effect that Dean had had on his life: 'I'm no teenager. I dress the same as him, I'm learning to drive a car, and hope to die the same way as he did.' Other respondents related their own life experiences to Dean's depiction of a 'mixed-up' teenager, and decided that his sympathetic portrayal would help British parents better understand their children.[100] Yet again, the wide range of these responses does not tidily conform to the measured reactions that the British media tended to project about British fans.

At the core of every news article was a desire to unravel Dean's mystique and understand why young British fans venerated him. The popular weekly magazine, *Picture Post*, targeted a broad family audience and published a series of features that concerned youth interests, attitudes and aspirations. It was, for example, one of the few publications to attempt to demystify and understand the Teddy culture.[101] When the news magazine offered British teenagers a serious and in-depth coverage of Dean's life story and the cult surrounding his death it met with high praise from young readers.[102] The more astute British journalists argued that British youngsters admired Dean's individuality, his dress code and his behaviour, and marvelled at how he had died 'in his own rebellion' driving the car 'forbidden' to him by the Warner Brothers studio.[103] David Lewin of the *Daily Express* opined that 'over-emotional youngsters' were intrigued by the duality of the late actor: 'James Byron Dean was casual and arrogant; incoherent but vocal; brash but in need of comfort. He perfected the art of playing the little boy lost in a great big world. The youth at the cinemas saw themselves just like that.'[104] Offering an informed perspective, a London schoolmaster argued that the younger post-war generation was looking for a new moral code by following Dean's example.[105]

As shown by Jackie Stacey's findings, film fans who form a stronger attachment to their favourite star take pleasure in extra-cinematic practices that permeate their daily life.[106] Danny Winter, a 22-year-old factory worker from Shepherd's Bush, London, changed his personality once co-workers began to notice his resemblance to Dean. In his private life, Winter adopted the moniker 'Jimmy', sported jeans, T-shirt and a leather jacket; and rode a motorbike recklessly – deliberately without a crash helmet – around London's bohemian nightlife area of Soho. Involved in what Stacey has called 'play-acting', Winter formed this alter-ego by adopting the aspects of Dean's style and mannerisms he had gleaned from the star's film appearances and publicity photos. Following the release of *Rebel Without a Cause*, Winter enjoyed a brief interlude of fame when he featured in several magazine interviews, made TV appearances, was given a 'singing test' for a recording company, attended the British film premiere of *Giant* and began to receive his own fan letters from fellow Deanagers. Winter, himself, disregarded his idolatry as a simple 'impersonation': he believed that he shared an affinity with the rebellious actor because he also understood the restless languor of his generation. 'Looking and living like the late actor has made its mark', reported Patrick Doncaster for the *Daily Mirror*, adding that the episode was 'just another astonishing aspect of the James Dean cult'.[107]

As Danny Winter's case demonstrates, intense identification with Dean outside normal cinemagoing was not confined to British teenagers. The case of middle-aged Douglas Goodall, a post office van driver from Catford, south-east London, illustrates the breadth of Dean's fan base and the dangers of identifying too closely with a star persona. Stacey usefully describes the complete self-absorption into a star's persona as an 'extra-cinematic transformation' driven by the desire to compensate for the ordinariness of one's daily life.[108] Thus, Goodall's obsessive attachment to Dean developed around *Rebel Without a Cause*, which he watched a reputed 400 times. His ritualistic practices began with impersonation; he wore a St Christopher Cross identical to Dean's and sourced a red jacket much like that of Jim Stark. Eventually, Goodhall sacrificed his individuality in his exuberance to emulate his idol. Telling his friends and family that Dean reminded him of his younger self, Goodall changed his name by deed poll to 'James Dean', gave up his job to take up speed racing and travelled to Dean's birthplace hoping to 'adopt' the late actor's parents. 'My destiny is no longer my own', Goodall explained to the press. 'I like all the things [Dean] likes. Of course I have lost a lot of friends.' Interestingly, Goodall's wife, Edith, retained her married name and chose not to 'judge' her husband's 'extraordinary' behaviour that extended to adopting an American accent and attempting to acquire American citizenship. Five years later, Goodall parked his car in the garage of his employers and died of carbon monoxide poisoning. The coroner reached a verdict of undetermined death because he could not decide whether it was an accident or the result of Goodall's intense desire to die 'like his idol'.[109]

Compounded by the media, Dean's gravesite in Fairmont, Indiana, had become a sacred space and inspired pilgrimages from thousands of his fans from all over the world. While the journey was accessible to any American fan with a car, the same pilgrimage for British Deanagers was expensive and required careful planning. The teenagers Janet Worger and Maureen Fawbert from Brighton described the pilgrimage as an ultimate show of respect for their idol. 'What's the difference between laying wreaths at the Cenotaph and honouring the memory of Jimmy Dean?' reasoned Janet. Both young women had decided to give up their jobs because they considered making the pilgrimage a rite of passage. 'It's something we must do before we settle down or we shall never be happy', Janet and Maureen agreed.[110]

Impersonation and play-acting brought immense pleasure and satisfaction to Dean's fans. British censors had also warned that *Rebel Without a Cause* would inspire dangerous re-enactments of the 'organised hooliganism' it dramatised. Few news items explicitly link the film to teenage misbehaviour and, therefore, suggest that such concerns were exaggerated. As the case of *Blackboard Jungle* demonstrates, the British media customarily appropriated motifs from the rebel films to concoct eye-catching headlines and lead-ins. Such stories invariably concern low-level mischief and appear to perpetuate negative stereotypes of young people. The *Daily Mail*, for example, linked a new Teddy boy 'challenge' to – what they referred to as – 'Deanism' because it adapted the 'chicken run' given prominence in *Rebel*. In this 'on-foot' version of the stunt, participants were required to step into busy roadways and defy drivers to knock them down. The police broke up the game and no one was injured.[111] In other stories, minor incidents, teenage pranks and tests of nerve were linked to Dean's rebellious persona. For example, Johnny Silver, a 20-year-old Londoner, was one of a 'trio of Teddy boys' dared to climb to the highest point of the Crystal Palace aerial as crowds of onlookers watched them. Following the success of a rival group several months earlier, Silver explained to reporters: 'We just had to do it ... we had to prove we were not "chicken"'.[112]

A far more serious incident linked to the film was a fatal car crash. Seemingly inspired by Buzz and Jim's daring chicken run, a crowd of teenagers congregated to watch a high-speed hot-rod style race in their small rural village that resulted in the death of one of the drivers.[113] These stories demonstrate that elements of the film inspired some acts of teenage rebellion, but more persuasive is that the media was eager to link the film to juvenile delinquency.

Conclusion

In his final screen role as Jett Rink in *Giant*, Dean played a ranch hand who becomes an oil tycoon. The epic film adapted Edna Ferber's eponymous bestseller (1952) and dramatised the changing fortunes of the Benedicts, a wealthy Texan family in the oil business, over the course of twenty-five years. Promotional posters and trailers offered equal billing to Dean and his co-stars, the enormously popular Rock Hudson and Elizabeth Taylor. Dean's memorable performance offered his fans the pleasures of watching his underdog character become as rich and powerful as his rival, Bick (Hudson); and his sensitive portrayal of unrequited love for Bick's wife, Leslie (Taylor). In addition, there were the aesthetic pleasures of Dean in cowboy clothing and an eerie depiction of how the older actor might have looked as Jett Rink ages from a teenager to a middle-aged man – an effect achieved through ageing makeup and special effects.

Dean's final film role earned him a second Academy Award nomination but British reviews were mixed. Critics alternately praised Dean's method acting or considered it jarring to the performance styles of Hudson and Taylor; they marvelled at Dean's ability to play an older character or considered it beyond his range and experience. Leonard Mosley's review in the *Daily Express* was particularly vituperative and disdained Hollywood's vulgar exploitation of their 'dead star', ridiculed Dean's caricatural portrait of the older Jett Rink, and branded *Giant* 'the sad epitaph to a gloriously promising career'.[114]

Subsequent chapters further develop the concept of teenage consumers as 'powerful' and examine how the youth market redirected cinema and popular culture. As this chapter has shown, British Deanagers participated in the posthumous stardom of James Dean. While *Giant* neared completion weeks before Dean's fateful crash, *The James Dean Story* (Robert Altman and George W. George, 1957) was made in direct response to the global phenomenon of Dean's death cult. This black and white documentary narrativised

Dean's early life through interviews with relatives, unseen footage and a montage of photos. The European premiere of *The James Dean Story* was held at the National Film Theatre in London in November 1957 but it was not a box office success. Backlash for commercialising Dean's legacy may have encouraged Hollywood to produce this low-key and modest film biography. Conveying Dean's fragile inner world through Martin Gabel's humourless voiceover – scripted by Stewart Stern – and a melancholy jazz soundtrack proffered fans an intimate portrait of their tragic hero. That this sombre production proved largely unsuccessful suggests that Dean's characterisation of Jim Stark, in vibrant Technicolor, forged an enduring and compelling portrait of adolescent rebellion for British teenagers. Harold Conway's commentary on *Rebel Without a Cause* usefully summarises these key points. 'Even in the cut version, this would be an appealing film for children to see', Conway reasoned, 'because Nicholas Ray's direction, the dialogue and the acting – with their brilliant insight into adolescent minds – insidiously persuade you into crediting the story against your reason. That kind of brilliance, in this kind of picture, can be dangerous.'[115]

The majority of British critics had lauded Dean for his sensitive acting but failed to recognise his enduring legacy to young cinemagoers. Dean's posthumous stardom illustrates the generational gap that separated parents from their adolescent children, and British critics from a younger generation of filmgoers. The novelist Ray Gosling provides a vivid and poignant description of Dean's influential persona in his remembrances of cinemagoing. Gosling was one of several boys in grammar school whose regular misbehaviour or 'barracking' in the auditorium was as entertaining as the main feature. When he and his friends first saw Dean's sensitive portrayal of Jim Stark, the knowledge that the actor was 'alive in the film, [but] dead in real life' conferred it a 'religious' meaning and an enduring status. '*Rebel Without a Cause* was a real film – and a lot of us said "Hush" when anyone tried to barrack it', Gosling recalled. 'It was watched in an unusual and rather disturbing embarrassment. I saw it three nights running and it had a lasting effect on me.'[116]

The mediocre box office of *The James Dean Story* demonstrated to the film industry that dead stars could generate only a limited interest for audiences. Trade and fan magazine editorial, which had catered to British Deanagers, now heralded Dean's successors to anticipate the end of what had been – to them – a strange and morbid cult. Emerging actors – neurotic, introspective and sensitive types – were promoted to 'replace' the late actor in the film industry's drive for young cinemagoers to form new allegiances. Dean had been contracted to portray the Italian boxer Rocky Graziano opposite Pier Angeli in the film *Somebody Up There Likes Me* (Robert Wise, 1956). When Paul Newman, another graduate of the Actors Studio, filled the role, he was unfamiliar to British audiences and required an introduction. 'In the film business, life and work go on, no matter what,' Margaret Hinxman explained to British Deanagers. 'So forget about what James Dean might have been. Let's honour instead what Newman – this exciting new star – IS!'[117] Similarly, Leonard Mosley tipped the wiry-framed and neurotic Anthony Perkins as likeliest to scourge Dean from the public imagination.[118] In *Fear Strikes Out* (Robert Mulligan, 1957), Perkins evoked Dean's persona in his depiction of Jim Piersall, an actual American baseball player, whose disciplinarian father (Karl Malden) caused him to suffer a complete mental collapse.

As a precursor to the Angry Young Men of the New Wave, Dean also influenced a rising generation of British actors. David McCallum was heralded as 'the first British James Dean' for his blondness and slender physique, and comparably nervous acting style; and British producers exploited this resemblance by dressing him in Dean's quintessential leather jacket, white T-shirt and blue jeans.[119] Albert Finney was later nominated as the young actor who 'spoke for teenagers' with the most authoritative voice 'since James Dean' when he made his screen debut as the rambunctious Arthur Seaton, in *Saturday Night and Sunday Morning* (Karel Reisz, 1960).[120]

British Deanagers had demonstrated the 'power' of the teenage consumer in perpetuating the unlikely career of a dead Hollywood film star. Douglas Warth's inquiry into the Dean phenomenon for the *Daily Herald* elicited hundreds of fan letters that testified to the depth of feeling the late actor had inspired. Against his better judgement, Warth concluded that Dean's on- and off-screen lives converged as a 'symbol of rebellion' against the boredom, frustration and restlessness of a rising post-war generation. Dean's unrestrained emotional register – his interpretation of method acting – in his role as the juvenile delinquent, Jim Stark, confronted (and affronted) the values of an older generation indoctrinated with the 'keep calm and carry on' mentality of wartime self-sacrifice, resilience and quiet endurance. Perhaps because it illustrated the generational divide between cinemagoers, Dean's enigma and mystique still have currency. His image as Jim Stark remains compelling and proliferates as an iconic and highly commercialised symbol of teenage rebellion of the 1950s. The theatrical poster for *Rebel Without a Cause* that shows Dean's defiant pose in a red jacket, white T-shirt and blue jeans was ranked second on Sotheby's bestseller list in 1980.[121]

This chapter has demonstrated that British cinema audiences responded to *Rebel Without a Cause* in complex and unexpected ways that did not answer the worst of the BBFC's concerns about screened juvenile delinquency. In 1985, when the Teddy boys were remembered with fond nostalgia, the British censor reclassified *Rebel Without a Cause* for video format as a PG and reiterated what Warner Brothers had originally intended: this was an edifying 'moral tale' that would encourage parents and children to share common difficulties.[122]

As sensational as it was, Dean's screen rebellion did not elicit the dangerous 'organised hooliganism' anticipated. Chapter 4 explores the reception of *Rock Around the Clock*, a banal film with a rock 'n' roll soundtrack that incited the cinema riots the British censors had thus far averted.

Notes

1 Arthur Watkins to President Sidney Harris, 21 November 1955 (*Rebel Without a Cause*, BBFC files).
2 Miss S. E. Manly, 'Remembered', *Picturegoer*, 31:1086, 25 February 1956, p. 3.
3 *Rebel Without a Cause* pressbook (Warner Brothers, 1955, BFI microfiche), p. 5.
4 Arthur Watkins to Arthur Abeles, 17 October 1955 (*Rebel Without a Cause*, BBFC Files).
5 Peter Biskind, *Seeing is Believing: Or How Hollywood Taught us to Stop Worrying and Love the '50s* (London: Bloomsbury, 2001), p. 201.
6 Andrew Caine, *Interpreting Rock Movies: The Pop Film and its Critics in Britain* (Manchester: Manchester University Press, 2005), p. 32.

7 Thomas Doherty, 'Dangerous youth', in *Teen Pics: The Juvenilization of American Movies* (Philadelphia: Temple University Press, 2002), pp. 83–114.
8 Claudia Springer, *James Dean Transfigured: The Many Faces of Rebel Iconography* (Austin, TX: The University of Texas, 2007).
9 'Death of James Dean, promising star of 24, not affecting "Rebel"', *Variety*, 200:5, 5 October 1955, p. 7.
10 David Griffiths, 'The James Dean legend', *TV Times*, 25 October 1957, pp. 16–17.
11 Jerold Simmons, 'The censoring of *Rebel Without A Cause*', *Journal of Popular Film & Television*, 23:2, 1 July 1995, pp. 57–63.
12 Daniel Biltereyst, 'Youth, moral panics, and the end of cinema: on the reception of *Rebel Without a Cause* in Europe', in David. J. Slocum (ed.), *Rebel Without a Cause: Approaches to a Maverick Masterpiece* (Albany: State University of New York Press, 2005), pp. 171–89.
13 Arthur Watkins quoted in Robert Muller, 'A seat beside the censor', *Picture Post*, Issue 13, 25 June 1955, p. 10.
14 Dominic Sandbrook, *Never Had it so Good: A History of Britain from Suez to the Beatles* (London: Abacus, 2006), pp. 443–4.
15 Arthur Marwick, *British Society Since 1945* (London: Penguin, 1996), pp. 148–9.
16 Bill Osgerby, '"Well, it's Saturday night an' I just got paid": youth, consumerism and hegemony in post-war Britain', *Contemporary Record*, 6:2 (Autumn 1992), pp. 287–305 (p. 297).
17 'International: Edwardian dress is out for Teddy boy juves at Liverpool filmhouses', *Variety*, 195:13, 1 September 1954, p. 25; 'Muscle men move in on hooligans', *Melody Maker*, 3 December 1955, p. 8.
18 John Trevelyan, 'Why are films censored before we see them?' in *Censored* (Southampton: The Millbrook Press Ltd, 1962).
19 Fred Majdalany, 'At the cinema: but does this do anyone any good?' *Daily Mail*, 20 January 1956 (*Rebel Without a* Cause, BFI microfiche); *Daily Mirror*, 25 March 1955, p. 10.
20 John Sampson, 'Stop film brutality – Britain tells US', *Daily Mirror*, 23 October 1950, p. 1; 'Report on the X', *Sight and Sound*, 23:3, 1 January 1954, p. 123.
21 John Wilcox, 'The small knife: studies in censorship', *Sight and Sound*, 25:4 (Spring 1956), pp. 206–10 (p. 210).
22 See for example Robert Muller, 'A seat beside the censor', *Picture Post*, 25 June 1955, pp. 10–11; Arthur Watkins, 'The censor speaks', *Picture Post*, Issue 13, 25 June 1955, p. 12; Catherine de la Roche, 'Don't shoot the censor', *Films and Filming*, 12 (April 1955), p. 12.

23 'Pictures: cuts ease way in Britain for "Rebel"', *Variety*, 200:5, 23 November 1955, p. 13.
24 Memorandum, 14 October 1955, President (SH), Secretary (AW), FNC and AOF (BBFC files).
25 Quoted in full in Sarah J. Smith, *Children, Cinema & Censorship: From Dracula to the Dead End Kids* (London: I. B. Tauris, 2005), Appendices, p. 179.
26 Internal memorandum between Arthur Watkins and Sidney Harris, 21 November 1955 (BBFC files).
27 Internal memorandum President to Watkins, 21 November 1955 (BBFC files).
28 Examiner's report, President, Secretary, FNC and AOF, 14 October 1955; and Note from Examiners, FNC, 16 November 1955 (BBFC files).
29 Arthur Watkins to Arthur Abeles, 17 October 1955 (BBFC files).
30 Letter of C. Wackett to Arthur Watkins, 25 October 1955 (BBFC files).
31 Gavin Lambert, 'Longer notices: *Rebel Without A Cause*', *Monthly Film Bulletin*, 23:264 (January 1956), p. 17.
32 Memorandum, 14 October 1955, President (SH), Secretary (AW), FNC and AOF (BBFC files).
33 Appendix BBFC Memorandum of 1951, printed in full in Sue Harper and Vincent Porter, *British Cinema in the 1950s: Decline of Deference* (Oxford: Oxford University Press, 2003), p. 242.
34 Internal Memorandum, Arthur Watkins to Sidney Harris, 21 November 1955 (BBFC files).
35 Arthur Watkins to Arthur Abeles, 17 October 1955; C. Wackett to A. T. L. Watkins, 25 October 1955; Arthur Abeles to Arthur Watkins, 4 November 1955 (BBFC files).
36 Simmons, 'The censoring of *Rebel Without A Cause*', p. 62.
37 Watkins to Abeles, 17 October 1955 (BBFC files).
38 De la Roche, 'Don't shoot the censor', p. 12.
39 Harper and Porter, *British Cinema in the 1950s*, p. 223; Smith, *Children, Cinema & Censorship*, p. 109.
40 Internal Memorandum, Arthur Watkins to Sidney Harris, 21 November 1955 (BBFC files).
41 Examiner's Note [FNC], 16 November 1955 (BBFC files).
42 Richard Maltby, 'D for disgusting: American culture and English criticism', in Geoffrey Nowell-Smith and Steven Ricci (eds), *Hollywood & Europe: Economics, Culture, National Identity* (London: BFI, 1998), pp. 104–15 (p. 109).
43 *Rebel Without a Cause* pressbook.

44 Peter Evans and Anne Edwards, 'More men than women going to films!' *Daily Express*, 24 January 1956, p. 2.
45 C. A. Lejeune, 'At the films: "Homes unblessed", *Observer*, 22 January 1956 (*Rebel Without a Cause*, BFI microfiche).
46 Dilys Powell, 'At the films', *Sunday Times*, 22 January 1956; 'Story of three "mixed-up" adolescents: a study in the American idiom', *Manchester Guardian*, 21 January 1956; Fred Majdalany, 'At the cinema: but does this do anyone any good?', *Daily Mail*, 20 January 1956; Jympson Harman, 'At the cinema: tribute to the late Mr Dean', *Evening News*, 19 January 1956 (*Rebel Without a Cause*, BFI microfiche).
47 Campbell Dixon, 'Film notes: more mixed-up kids', *Daily Telegraph*, 21 January 1956; Thomas Spencer, 'Films: delinquent parents', *Daily Worker*, 21 January 1956; Derek Granger, 'Crazy kids: middle class delinquents', *Financial Times*, 23 January 1956 (*Rebel Without a Cause*, BFI microfiche).
48 Alan Brien, 'Not even Brando could equal this: Mr Dean creates a portrait in three dimensions', *Evening Standard*, 19 January 1956; Special Correspondent, 'At the cinema: in search of causes', *Times Educational Supplement*, 10 February 1956 (*Rebel Without a Cause*, BFI microfiche).
49 Milton Shulman, 'Who would be an American father?' *Sunday Express*, 22 January 1956 (*Rebel Without a Cause*, BFI microfiche).
50 Stella Bruzzi, *Bringing up Daddy: Fatherhood and Masculinity in Post-war Hollywood* (London: BFI, 2005), p. xiv. Further discussion of Freud in 1950s Hollywood cinema may be found in Barbara Klinger, *Melodrama and Meaning: History, Culture, and the Films of Douglas Sirk* (Bloomington: Indiana University Press, 1994). Elaine Tyler May provides a social context in *Homeward Bound: American Families in the Cold War Era* (UK: Hachette, 2008).
51 *Manchester Guardian*, 'Story of three "mixed-up" adolescents: A study in the American idiom', 21 January 1956 (*Rebel Without a Cause*, BFI microfiche).
52 Vicky Graham, 'Fogbound', *The Spectator*, 20 January 1956, p. 82.
53 Tony Richardson, 'The Method and why: an account of the Actors Studio', *Sight and Sound*, 26:3 (Winter 1956), pp. 132–6. Tom Hutchinson insisted that the Method was a mismatch for British actors in 'Don't bring the Method here', *Picturegoer*, 32:111, 18 August 1956, p. 9.
54 Anthony Quayle, 'Society and the actor', *Films and Filming*, 3:10 (July 1957), pp. 6, 30.
55 Robert Muller, 'The strange world of James Dean', *Picture Post*, 7 January 1956, p. 19.

56 Hutchinson, 'Don't bring the Method here', p. 9.
57 Marie Carter, 'The butch woman inside James Dean or "What kind of person do you think a girl wants?"', *Sexualities* (2003), 6 (3–4), pp. 443–58.
58 Gavin Lambert, 'Review of *Rebel Without a Cause*', *Monthly Film Bulletin*, 23:264, 1 January 1956, p. 17.
59 Derek Prouse, '*Rebel Without a Cause*', *Sight and Sound*, 25:3 (Winter 1955), pp. 160–1 and 164.
60 For a clearer understanding of the spirit of the movement see Gavin Lambert, 'Free cinema', *Sight and Sound* (Spring 1956), pp. 173–7.
61 Prouse, '*Rebel Without a Cause*', p. 164.
62 J. W., 'My teenage daughter', *Monthly Film Bulletin*, 23:264, 1 January 1956, p. 86.
63 Penelope Houston, 'Rebels without causes', *Sight and Sound*, 25:4 (Spring 1956), pp. 179–81 and *The Contemporary Cinema* (Harmondsworth: Penguin, 1966), p. 72.
64 Kenneth Allsop, 'The catcher cult catches on', *Daily Mail*, 4 January 1958, p. 4.
65 Richard Hoggart, *The Uses of Literacy* (Harmondsworth: Penguin, 1957), pp. 246–8.
66 Shirley Lowe, 'I'll give you a cure for – the beer blues frankly', *Daily Express*, 21 July 1955, p. 4.
67 Elia Kazan, *Elia Kazan: A Life* (London: Andre Deutsch, 1988), pp. 535–6.
68 'This demon Dean', *Photoplay* [GB], 6:9 (September 1955), pp. 8–9, and 53. See also Robert Muller, 'The strange world of James Dean', *Picture Post*, Issue 1, 7 January 1956, pp. 18–19 (p. 18); Robert Muller, 'Brando or beefcake?', *Picture Post*, Issue 10, 4 June 1955, pp. 44, 47 and 50.
69 Jympson Harman, 'At the cinema: tribute to the late Mr Dean', *Evening News*, 19 January 1956 (*Rebel Without a Cause*, BFI microfiche).
70 Peter Burnup, 'Teddy boy from USA', *News of the World*, 22 January 1956 (*Rebel Without a Cause*, BFI microfiche).
71 'The year's best', *Kinematograph Weekly*, No: 2574, 13 December 1956, p. 6.
72 Thelma Veness, *School Leavers: Their Aspirations and Expectations* (London: Methuen, 1962), p. 10.
73 Jackie Stacey, *Star Gazing: Hollywood Cinema and Female Spectatorship* (London: Routledge, 1994).
74 Adam Faith, *Acts of Faith: The Autobiography of Adam Faith* (London: Bantam Books, 1996 [large print]), pp. 26–8.
75 Mark Glancy explores how the British media negotiated female fan culture around Valentino's death cult. See *Hollywood and the*

Americanization of Britain: From the 1920s to the Present (London: I. B. Tauris, 2014), pp. 42–77.

76 Cynthia, 'Live letters: deathless legend, conducted by the old codgers', *Daily Mirror*, 9 August 1956, p. 14.

77 Alec Thomas, 'Broken-hearted Dean wanted to die!', *Weekend Mail*, 6–10 December 1956, p. 8.

78 K. Dam, 'Oscar verdict', *Picturegoer*, 31:1098, 19 May 1956, p. 3.

79 Harper and Porter, *British Cinema in the 1950s*, p. 250.

80 L. Taylor (Miss), Fulham, London, Focus: 'Even the men cried', *Picturegoer*, 32:1108, 28 July 1956, p. 5.

81 For example, see Julie Harris, 'How I remember James Dean', *Picturegoer*, 16 June 1956, p. 10.

82 Samantha Barbas, *Movie Crazy: Fans, Stars and the Cult of Celebrity* (New York: Palgrave, 2001), p. 85.

83 'Dean's last dare', *Daily Express*, 20 January 1956 (*Rebel Without a Cause*, BFI microfiche).

84 Muller, 'The strange world of James Dean', p. 19.

85 Jympson Harman, 'At the cinema: tribute to the late Mr Dean'.

86 Charles Hamblett, 'The great Deanage rebellion', *Picture Post*, Issue 2, 15 October 1956, p. 27.

87 Hamblett, 'James Dean: the name goes marching on', *Picture Post*, Issue 1, 8 October 1956, pp. 19–25 (p. 19).

88 Gavin Lyall, 'Dean worship in Britain', *Picture Post*, 22 October 1956, pp. 35–8.

89 Peter John Dyer, 'Youth and the cinema 1: the teenage rave', *Sight and Sound*, 29:1 (Winter 1959/60), pp. 26–30 (p. 51).

90 'Teddy girls ("It's James Dean!") mob crash victim', *Daily Mail*, 22 July 1957, p. 5.

91 Lyall, 'Dean worship in Britain', p. 35.

92 *Ibid.*, p. 36.

93 *Ibid.*

94 Lesley Shuckford, Eastham, Cheshire, 'James Dean – the rebels fight back', *Daily Herald*, 12 October 1956 (*Rebel Without a Cause*, BFI microfiche).

95 Cecil Wilson, 'Mixed-up kid, by author aged 19', *Daily Mail*, 26 July 1956, p. 3.

96 Christopher Lucas, 'Jimmy Dean cult may beat Valentino', *Daily Mail*, 11 October 1956, p. 3; Hamblett, 'James Dean: the name goes marching on', *Picture Post*, pp. 19, 21.

97 Guy Austin, 'No thanks for this memory', *Picturegoer*, 31:1103, 23 June 1956, p. 14; and in response to Austin, June Bennet, 'Focus: stop this Dean publicity', *Picturegoer*, 32:1108, 28 July 1956, p. 3.

98 *Daily Herald*, 25 October 1956 (*Rebel Without a Cause*, BFI microfiche).

99 Douglas Warth, 'James Dean: symbol of an age, the ghost who is a god', *Daily Herald*, n.d (*Rebel Without a Cause*, BFI microfiche).
100 A. J. Hooper, Deanager, Bethnal Green, London; Miss B. Burke, 16, Liverpool; and Ed, Plymouth, 'James Dean – the rebels fight back', *Daily Herald*, 12 October 1956 and Miss Z. Gabler, 'Disgruntled 19-year-old, Sunderland', *Daily Herald*, 15 October 1956 (*Rebel Without a Cause*, BFI microfiche).
101 Hilde Marchant, 'The truth about Teddy boys', *Picture Post*, Issue 9, 29 May 1954, pp. 25–7.
102 Charles Hamblett, 'From a young star's coffin, a Hollywood legend is born', *Picture Post*, Issue 13, 1 October 1956, p. 35.
103 Hamblett, 'The Great Deanage rebellion', p. 21.
104 David Lewin, 'Sweeping through America – the most staggering story in show business', *Daily Express*, 14 August 1956.
105 Michael Croft interviewed in Lyall, 'Dean worship in Britain', p. 38.
106 See Stacey, *Star Gazing*, p. 163 for a discussion of how individuals reinterpret aspects of a star's performance.
107 Patrick Doncaster, 'The boy who looks like James Dean', *Daily Mirror*, 9 January 1957, p. 2.
108 Stacey, *Star Gazing*, p. 163.
109 Edward Goring, *Daily Mail*, 'A new James Dean heads west of Catford', 24 December 1957, p. 3; Gordon Sigsworth, "James Dean' dies at the wheel of a car', *Daily Mirror*, 16 March 1962, p. 11.
110 Janet Worger and Maureen Fawbert are quoted in 'The James Dean Story premiere', *Daily Herald*, 11 November 1957 (*James Dean*, BFI microfiche).
111 'Za! Za! The new Teddy boy game', *Daily Mail*, 16 August 1956, p. 5.
112 Timothy Aspinall, 'Johnny answers a James Dean taunt', *Daily Mail*, 2 June 1958, p. 5.
113 Michael Brown, 'Village daredevil killed for £1 bet', *Daily Mail*, 14 August 1957, p. 5.
114 Leonard Mosley, 'This final James Dean film dims the legend, *Daily Express*, 3 January 1957 (*Giant*, BFI microfiche).
115 Harold Conway, 'Hair-raiser shows James Dean at his greatest', *Daily Sketch*, 20 January 1956 (*Rebel Without a Cause*, BFI microfiche).
116 Ray Gosling, *Personal Copy: A Memoir of the Sixties* (London and Boston: Faber & Faber, 1980), pp. 31–2.
117 Margaret Hinxman, 'Stop mooning about Dean', *Picturegoer*, 32:1124, 17 November 1956, p. 7.
118 Leonard Mosley, 'Tip: This boy to help kill the James Dean cult', *Daily Express*, 24 May 1957, p. 8.

119 Peter Evans, 'They're making him the ghost of James Dean', *Picturegoer*, 5 September 1956, p. 11.
120 Bill Edwards, 'Finney – new voice of the teens', *Picturegoer*, 39:1296, 23 April 1960, p. 8.
121 Barry Baker, 'The wanted posters!' *Daily Mail*, 19 June 1980, p. 24.
122 Report from Sally Sampson/WGT to MHB/WGT, 1985 (BBFC files).

4

'A teenage revolution': Bill Haley and the rock 'n' roll cinema riots

> My own opinion is that if it hadn't been for *Blackboard Jungle* all this would never have happened.
>
> Anthony Carthew, *Daily Herald*, 20 July 1956[1]

> Our boys and girls are a grand generation, but, as always, they need discipline. There is nothing like the discipline of work and service to knock the Rock 'n' Roll out of these babies and to knock a bit of sense into them.
>
> 'Rock 'n' roll babies', *Daily Mail*, 5 September 1956[2]

On 5 February 1957, hundreds of British fans waited for Bill Haley to disembark from the *Queen Elizabeth* at Southampton docks. Among them were two 'attractive' girls who wanted to share a particularly special message for the rock 'n' roll singer: 17-year-old Sylvia Wakefield and 15-year-old Diane Thompson, who had spent the previous night embroidering their idol's name along the entire length of their blue jeans.[3] Making their way through the surging, screaming crowds, waving placards and jostling one another to get closer to their hero, the teenage girls were among the select few invited aboard Haley's specially chartered train bound for London's Waterloo station. The 31-year-old Haley – already a father to seven children – had brought his second wife along on the tour. Once the couple were safely aboard, the jubilant celebrations continued with fans singing and clapping and jiving up and down the aisles.[4]

Hundreds more fans waited for their idol in London in celebratory and riotous mood. In 'the Second Battle of Waterloo' – as the media called it – Haley disembarked to heaving crowds, who screamed, shouted and pushed one another for a closer glimpse of the rock 'n' roll singer. Police struggled to maintain control as fans lunged at the vehicle taking Haley and his wife to London's city centre; some overly exuberant youngsters were forcibly escorted out of the station.[5] Poised to begin a nationwide tour, Haley's diary entry described his amazement at the extraordinary reception of British fans: 'Docked at Southampton, England at 2 p.m. and all hell broke loose. 5000 people almost killed us.'[6]

Haley's nationwide tour of Britain came in response to the success of his hit record, *Rock Around the Clock*, which had featured as the soundtrack to *Blackboard Jungle* (Richard Brooks, 1955) examined in Chapter 2. Played over the opening titles and reprised during fight scenes, the song became indelibly associated with the teenage 'spirit' of the film. It was the first million-selling record in Britain and the bestselling record of the 1950s. Based on this phenomenal success, Haley and his Comets became the first rock 'n' roll artists to make the transition to Hollywood films. *Rock Around the Clock* (Fred F. Sears, 1956) and *Don't Knock the Rock* (Fred F. Sears, 1956) were released in British cinemas in April and December 1956, respectively. The song *Rock Around the Clock*, then, is the nexus between Hollywood's juvenile delinquency films and the rock 'n' roll films starring Haley and later Elvis Presley as a 'rock 'n' roll rebel'.

Chapter 2 showed that the British censors came close to denying a certificate to *Blackboard Jungle* because of its gritty and unremitting engagement with juvenile delinquency. As this chapter demonstrates, *Rock Around the Clock* encountered no censorship issues but incited the so-called rock 'n' roll cinema 'riots' of 1956. It is against this unusual background that I contextualise the film's reception and reconstruct Haley's stardom to illuminate this little-known episode in British youth culture.

The BBFC considered *Rock Around the Clock* as 'harmless' fun. The simple storyline centres on a big-band promoter, Steve Hollis (Johnny Johnston) and his business partner, Corny (Henry Slate). Both men have realised that band music has become passé. When they stop over at Strawberry Springs en route to New York, they chance upon Bill Haley and his Comets performing rock 'n' roll music in the town hall. The town hall is packed, and couples are jiving energetically on the dance floor. Intrigued, Steve wants to find out more about Haley and his band and define this new style of popular music having such a positive effect on the crowd.[7] Steve

Figure 4.1 Bill Haley (left) and the Comets were the first band to achieve a million-selling hit record in Britain. The phenomenon of the song *Rock Around the Clock*, featured as the soundtrack to *Blackboard Jungle*, boosted Haley's musical career and launched his Hollywood fame.

defines rock 'n' roll (for the mainstream cinema audience): 'It isn't boogie, it isn't jive, and it isn't swing. It's kind of all of them.'

A thinly derived subplot centres on the love triangle between Steve and Lisa Johns (Lisa Gaye) – the dancer in Haley's troupe who partners her brother Jimmy (Earl Barton) – and Corinne Talbot (Alix Talton), a powerful talent agent from New York. Spurned by Steve, Corinne sets out to impede the band's success. The narrative follows Haley's successful rise to fame, playing in 'small dives' and finally winning a spot on a Hollywood TV show.[8] In the finale,

Haley and the Comets perform *ABC Boogie*, in which they cavort with and swing their instruments, offering cinemagoers an experience of their 'live' concert appearances. The film also showcases music acts popular at the time such as The Platters, Freddie Bell and the Bellboys, and Tony Martinez and his Band. Alan Freed, the well-known American disc jockey who coined the phrase 'rock 'n' roll', takes a cameo role as the night club owner pivotal to Haley's success.[9]

'A very delightful film': the BBFC and rock 'n' roll riots

When the BBFC evaluated *Rock Around the Clock* in April 1956, they did not produce a detailed list of exceptions (deletions). They unanimously agreed that the musical film was 'pleasant' and suitable for the whole family. The examiner Newton K. Branch opined that the film was 'practically a documentary film about how this dance became popular in the states'.[10] Indeed, a U certificate was awarded once Columbia Pictures executives agreed to the BBFC's request for several minor adjustments to dialogue. The seemingly innocuous exchange between Corny and Steve, 'Have fun – you'd be amazed at the number of boys who don't want to get married' and Corinne's line to Steve, 'I have another male warming up in the bull-pen' were removed.[11] A lingering shot of Lisa's legs was edited out because of Steve's accompanying dialogue concerning his 'imagination' and his 'taking advantage' of her. This focus on the mildly suggestive dialogue considered morally objectionable to family values did not pertain to any of the musical dance numbers. No further alterations were recommended. My earlier arguments have contextualised the BBFC's heavy-handed censorship of Hollywood films about juvenile delinquency against wider social anxieties about Teddy boys and crime. The rock 'n' roll riots, which came in response to *Rock Around the Clock*, surely disprove the BBFC's theories on audience suggestibility and screen delinquency: in all, the events around this film were to prove a perplexing conundrum to the board's morale and professional judgement.

News items, frequently on the front pages of the *Daily Mail* and the *Daily Mirror*, had warned of the immoral effects of American popular culture on British teenagers.[12] Victor Thompson in the *Daily Herald* had used his diary to condemn the James Dean's death cult and 'the dangerous influences' of rock 'n' roll that had placed the nation 'in the grip of a teenage revolution'.[13] When *Rock Around the Clock* instigated a flagrant display of anti-social behaviour among Teddy boys and girls, media hyperbole gave full expression to the cynicism of an older generation. Perversely, once the riotous disturbances had begun to make headlines, hordes of curious onlookers congregated outside cinemas hoping to witness the 'riots' for themselves. When photographs of these artificially augmented crowds appeared in the local and national press, they inevitably distorted public perception of the disturbances. News reports include detailed accounts of occasions when local residents and teenagers from other boroughs gathered in excited anticipation of altercations between police and rock 'n' roll delinquents.[14]

The teenage disturbances in and around cinemas do not correlate with our modern understanding of the term 'riot'. Useful as media shorthand, in truth, the term covered a range of low-level crime. In Dagenham, Teddy boys booed and hissed at police and held up traffic on their departure from cinemas. In Romford, 'trouble-makers' had left the area 'quietly' and no arrests were made. In Chadwell Heath, one youth was arrested after dancing in the cinema aisles and damaging seats; and in West Ham, one arrest was made after couples refused to stop dancing in the gangways. Further afield in Twickenham, ten youths were arrested for 'insulting words and behaviour'.[15] In the Elephant and Castle area, labelled 'the heart of London's rock 'n' roll trouble', because of its notorious Teddy boy gangs, the Commissioner of Metropolitan Police assured the public that 'hooliganism' would be 'stamped out', with the result that three hundred uniformed and plain-clothes police were stationed around the Trocadero cinema. It was here that six 'rhythm-crazed teenagers' were arrested for jeering, shouting, setting off fireworks and throwing glass bottles.[16] In Peckham, although a crowd of seven to eight hundred people waited expectantly outside the Gaumont cinema to witness the riots, only one youth was seen to kick a police constable after being ejected for jiving in the cinema aisle. A more sensational account described the activities of several teenagers, who had 'terrorised pedestrians' by performing 'a snake dance in a crazed hypnotised fashion' over parked vehicles near the Cenotaph in St Peter's Square, Manchester. One of these youths reportedly shouted: 'The police can't touch us, there are too many of us!'[17]

Other news reports focused on the multiple arrests of those involved in causing significant damage to cinema venues. At the Gaiety cinema in Manchester's town centre, the cinema manager recounted that a gang of fifty youths – purportedly brought in by lorry from a nearby market – had 'started to riot' as soon as they were inside. Here youths threw electric light bulbs, sprayed parts of the cinema with the fire hose and flicked their cigarettes from the circle directly into the stalls. In Bootle, Lancashire, young Teddy boys threw fireworks during a late-night performance and couples started to dance in the aisles before the police were called in to disband them.[18] In nearby Burnley, 'excited young people' caused a reputed £150 worth of damage to a local cinema. After the incident, the manager, William Howarth, told reporters that he was 'surprised and a little shocked' that local youths were capable of such misbehaviour.[19]

Local authorities implemented their own preventative measures to tackle future disturbances. For example, South London councils continued its new 'get-tough' policy deploying plain-clothes police to intermingle with cinema audiences and 'quietly evict' troublemakers as necessary.[20] For instance, at the Lewisham Gaumont, a boy who began 'jiving in front of his seat' was immediately led away by a policeman who had appeared 'very quickly at the end of the row and pointed firmly at him'.[21] Given that many altercations between Teddy boys and police occurred after screenings, police were stationed outside cinemas and police dogs used to deter revellers from loitering.[22] Some local authorities took extreme measures, overruled the BBFC and banned the film as was the case in areas of Liverpool, Carlisle and Warrington.[23] Smaller boroughs, such as councils for Lewes and Blackburn – worried that the film would inflame further displays of Teddy boy 'retaliation' and 'public disorder' – also chose to ban it.[24] In like manner, the Belfast Police Committee intervened to prohibit cinemas from showing the film.[25]

Cinema managers, responsible for upholding their exhibitor's licence, were, inevitably, concerned about damage to equipment and upholstery. Once they had received directives from the corporate owners of the major chains, managers implemented their own methods to combat these unprecedented responses from audiences. In an era of limited TV programming and few leisure options for teenagers, film fans followed *Rock Around the Clock* from cinema to cinema and watched it multiple times. To avoid outright bans but continue to profit from the film's popularity, cinema managers adjusted their policies to suit their clientele. Some pre-empted problems by turning away any girls or boys making a disturbance in the queue and refusing tickets to known troublemakers when spotted at the box office.[26] In Swansea, managers immediately removed undesirable patrons from their cinemas in the city centre. At the Empire cinema in Burnley, the manager walked among queuing patrons and appealed directly to young people, asking them to guarantee 'quiet' behaviour and reminding them that his licence was at stake.[27] In Scotland, Aberdeen cinemas had been the worst damaged by riotous crowds. Cinema managers there took a different approach by showing the film without the soundtrack, which they considered the main stimulant to audiences.[28] Further, the Rank Organisation took the unilateral decision to remove *Rock Around the Clock* from all their Sunday programmes and restrict showings of the controversial film to weekdays only.[29]

The press duly covered the legal proceedings against young cinema revellers. A survey of individual testimony presented before magistrates illustrates the extent of delinquency encouraged by the film. Generally, exchanges between police and cinemagoers became heated when youngsters felt they were unfairly evicted from the auditorium for dancing, and were then denied a refund. Alternatively, they had left screenings exuberant and were reluctant to go directly home after performances. The majority of youths were charged with 'insulting behaviour', which included 'jeering', 'ranting' and 'raving' at police, and 'disturbing the peace' of local residents. Juveniles (those aged 15 or under) were discharged conditionally on a nominated period of good behaviour, while those with previous convictions were shown less leniency and fined accordingly. In Leyton, for example, of the hundred youths ejected from the Gaumont cinema, only three were convicted. The group comprised two teenagers still in school and an older youth with a previous conviction, who were fined 20 shillings and 40 shillings, respectively. They told the examining magistrate that they had become angry and insulted police when they were ejected from the venue, and demanded reimbursement for the price of admission instead of leaving the area quietly. In West Ham, one youth was fined £2 for being rowdy and jumping over flowerbeds as he fled from police. In Twickenham, three youths from Middlesex, who had sung rock 'n' roll songs along the main road, were bound over for £25 and ordered to be of good behaviour for twelve months.[30]

Throughout the media furore, the BBFC publicly defended their decision to grant *Rock Around the Clock* a U certificate. Behind the scenes, however, President Sidney Harris watched the entire film again to be certain that he had not missed any details. For the second time, Harris confirmed that this was 'a very delightful film'.[31] Nevertheless, given Hollywood's new trend for rock 'n' roll films and the media's interest in audience misbehaviour, the BBFC sought external advice from cinema managers to better prepare against future riots. The secretary of the BBFC, Arthur Watkins, contacted managers in London districts where troublemakers had been most numerous, namely Shepherd's Bush and Kensington. His main respondent, known only as 'Mr Wilkins', was the manager of Kensington Odeon; he requested anonymity before compiling a detailed list of audience guidelines that drew on his many years of experience. To deter rock 'n' roll film fans, Wilkins turned on the house lights 'at the first sign of trouble' to identify 'the mischief makers' and ban them from future performances. If this failed, he called the police. Such methods were common to most cinema managers. More helpful perhaps were Wilkins' observations on the equal culpability and involvement of Teddy girls, who tended to 'egg' on their boyfriends to create a spectacle; and that groups of Teddy teenagers 'followed' *Rock Around the Clock* from 'district to district'.[32]

As discussed in Chapter 1, the cinema watch committees in Maesteg (Wales), Cambridge, Belfast and Glasgow were the only local authorities to overturn the BBFC's decision to ban *The Wild One*. In an unlikely reversal of fortune, local authorities overruled the expert opinion of the BBFC and banned this 'harmless' and 'delightful' film in Berkshire, Belfast City, Birmingham, Bolton, Bournemouth, Brighton and Hove, Flint, Gloucestershire, Gravesend, Leicester, Liverpool, Oxford, Reading, Stockport and Wigan and many other districts.

Given that the BBFC was founded in 1912 to expressly avoid this type of interference from local authorities, it was now essential that the board quelled the many voices of opposition. At Arthur Watkins' behest, in October 1956, the Cinema Managers Association (CMA) produced a full-length report on the cinema riots. Statistics were collated from industry personnel from the major cinema circuits in London and the provinces, including Northern Ireland and Eire.

The report proved edifying to the BBFC because it illustrated that *Rock Around the Clock* had played in 432 cinemas (187 of them owned and operated by the CMA) and been successfully rebooked at 18 of these. In addition, 25 ABC cinemas had exhibited the film and rebooked it in 12 locations; and 24 Essoldo cinemas had played the film and rebooked it at 9 locations. According to other data, 149 local authorities in London and the Home Counties passed the film, 16 had banned it and a mere 4 incidents of 'trouble' were reported at Harrow Road, Elephant and Castle, Lewisham and Dagenham. In Leeds cinemas, a similar story unfolds: 45 passes were recorded, as were 3 bans and 3 incidents of trouble. The final total of the nationwide tally amounted to 435 passes, 77 bans and 20 'incidents' of trouble.[33]

This information sustains Watkins' claims that many of the bans enforced by local authorities were 'arbitrary' rather than commonsensical. Furthermore, with this mitigating evidence at hand, Watkins advised the Cinematograph Exhibitors Association that, because 'trouble' had not started 'during the shows' but outside cinemas, it was 'youngsters and rougher elements' who instigated altercations with police rather than actual film audiences.[34] My survey of news items demonstrates that this was not entirely true: Watkins omits the fact that many of the disturbances had begun *inside* cinemas and then spilled out onto the streets.

In the ongoing controversy caused by *Rock Around the Clock*, the BBFC were discredited for their lack of perspicuity. In response, the examiners found it expedient to blame the media for over-embellished accounts of the trouble in cinemas. As we have seen, the media generally supported the BBFC's decision to refuse *The Wild One* a certificate. In this case, the media provided a platform for prominent members of the establishment to contest their professional judgement. High-ranking members of the clergy regarded the rock 'n' roll riots to be emblematic of the social decline of the nation and took the opportunity to participate in a moral crusade against contemporary cinema. Among these objectors, the Venerable Charles Tonks, Archdeacon of Croydon, cautioned the BBFC to 'consider the music – if such it can be called – as well as the text of the screen-play' for any future rock 'n' roll films they encountered.[35] Tonks had already formed a poor opinion of Teddy boys. He had delivered the eulogy at Constable Miles's funeral – the police constable shot dead by the 16-year-old Christopher Craig – so the spectre of Teddy boys rioting in cinemas only served to reinforce his perception of ever-declining national standards and moral turpitude.[36] Bishop William Woolwich was another clergyman who shared his pessimism: he believed that British teenagers were imitating American youngsters in their fervent displays of fandom.[37] Having witnessed the 'rowdyism' for himself after a recent performance, Woolwich blamed *Rock Around the Clock* for causing a 'serious setback' to the resolution of the 'Teddy boy problem' in South London.[38]

The BBFC files demonstrate that the examiners shared the establishment's distaste for rock 'n' roll music but this did not form the basis of renewed negotiations on *Rock Around the Clock*.[39] The Bishop and the Archdeacon had blamed the 'hypnotic' music for the recent outbreaks of delinquency and berated the censors for not taking adequate measures against its stimulant effects.[40] Watkins rehearsed his standard response and called the disturbances 'deplorable' but reiterated that the film itself was 'clean and innocuous entertainment'.[41] To stem the rising tide of criticism from local authorities, Watkins corresponded directly with the Secretary of the County Councils Association. In these exchanges, Watkins reinstated previous arguments that laid blame on the irresolute youths of the inner cities for the rioting, and on the media for creating unnecessary controversy around the film.[42] When the northern branch of the Cinema Exhibitors Association met at Newcastle upon Tyne, its members vindicated Watkins' assertions. They believed that media sensation had 'challenged the Teddy boys' to misbehave. As a result, the association petitioned the local watch committees for North Shields, South Shields and Gateshead to overturn their recent bans.[43]

As a precautionary measure, the BBFC approached publicity materials for upcoming rock 'n' roll films with greater vigilance. Nonetheless, by the end of 1956, *Rock Pretty Baby* (Richard Bartlett, 1956), *The Girl Can't Help It* (Frank Tashlin, 1956) and *Don't Knock the Rock* were all granted U certificates. The board meted out a measure of responsibility directly to county councils and asked councillors to send advance information specifically to local authorities where 'over-exuberance' might flare up again. In like manner, the secretary of the Association of Municipal Corporations urged licensing authorities not to take 'drastic' measures – that is to enforce outright bans – unless absolutely necessary.[44]

The BBFC's prediction for future rock 'n' roll films – correct as it turned out – was that 'this form of rhythm and the excitement aroused' would subside as more films in the genre were released.[45] Indeed, once *Shake, Rattle and Rock* (Edward L. Cahn, 1956) had played in cinemas in April 1957 without incidence, Watkins requested that the Secretary of the County Councils Association take no further action on subsequent rock 'n' roll films.[46]

This episode proved to be an embarrassing miscalculation for the BBFC, and one that required all of Watkins' diplomacy and tact to resolve. The previous chapters have argued that censorship measures operated to limit the attractiveness of American screen violence. The fact that *Rock Around the Clock* incited the very juvenile delinquency that examiners had worked to avoid illustrates an ever-widening generational gap between them and young cinemagoers. The British censors had reduced several mild sexual innuendos to uphold their moral mandate to family audiences, whereas teenagers found their greatest pleasures in the music and dance scenes. In the privacy of their Soho offices, the examiners recognised their misjudgement and resolved to 'bear in mind that this kind of dance, if carried to excessive lengths on the screen can have an undesirable effect on certain types of audience'.[47]

Selling *Rock Around the Clock* in Britain

In view of the BBFC's assessment that the film was 'practically a documentary' of Haley's rise to fame, it bears examination why his image does not figure more prominently in Columbia's promotional materials. Posters are monopolised either by Lisa Gaye and Earl Barton performing rock 'n' roll steps or by the slim and dark-haired Frankie Brent, the guitarist of Freddie Bell and the Bellboys. In lobby cards, Haley was featured alongside his fellow band members in a blaze of energy and instrumental delirium. Similarly, the film trailer provides brief glimpses of Haley and his Comets in musical excerpts but focuses almost entirely on the romance between Lisa Gaye and Johnny Johnston and Gaye's energetic dance routines with Earl Barton. In contrast to materials promoting Elvis Presley in his delinquency films, invariably dominated by the young singer's image, the 'absence' of Haley raises questions about his star persona.

British film critics tended to criticise Haley's aesthetic and the excessive perspiration that accompanied his singing and dancing: in fact, they showed a propensity to ridicule the singer. Typical was Fred Majdalany's scathing assessment in the *Daily Mail*: 'Mr Haley is enjoyable in small doses. [But] he resembles a Neanderthal college boy who has just been rescued from drowning and is still suffering from having shipped a lot of water.'[48] Since *Rock Around the Clock* did not comment on juvenile delinquency, the BBFC's chief concern was whether the Columbia studio had orchestrated the riots in British cinemas as a publicity stunt.[49] Once Mike Frankovich, Columbia's chief executive, had reassured the board that they had had nothing to do with the public disturbances, the BBFC permitted the company to release a nationwide 'News Bulletin' that discouraged local authorities from banning upcoming rock 'n' roll films.[50] Nonetheless, Columbia producers renamed Haley's sequel *Don't Knock the Rock* (rather than retain its original title, *Rhythm and Blues*) to illustrate the widespread censure rock 'n' roll had caused. Significantly, Haley's image became central in publicity for this sequel presumably to promote his upcoming European tour with the Comets.

The BBFC did not ignore the stimulant effects of rock 'n' roll on young audiences but only exploitative films necessitated stricter censorship. *Mad at the World* (Robert Essex, 1955) and *Running Wild* (Abner Biberman, 1955) were two such films that were re-edited to obtain the BBFC's final approval.[51] *Mad at the World* was a cross-genre film that combined juvenile delinquency with a rock 'n' roll soundtrack. However, it contravened many of the BBFC's guidelines concerning the modus operandi of criminals and scenes of vigilantism. The narrative tells of the 'Wolf Pack', a teenage gang, who injure an infant when they discard an empty bottle of alcohol during a rock 'n' roll party, and are hunted down by the child's aggrieved father. The rock 'n' roll soundtrack underscores the wilder aspects of the gang's psychology rather than *Rock Around the Clock*'s invocation of youthful exuberance. *Running Wild* features Mamie Van Doren – a voluptuous, platinum-haired sex symbol in the mould of Marilyn Monroe – whose career was confined to exploitation films. The dance sequence that proved contentious to the BBFC shows Van Doren jiving excitedly with a male partner to *Razzle Dazzle*, another of Haley and the Comets' billboard hits. Dressed in a tight-fitting outfit, Van Doren's eroticised dancing in a cavernous 'dive bar' attracts a frenzied crowd of teenage onlookers and lascivious ogling from several middle-aged men, seated with their dour-looking spouses. Finally, Van Doren ends her dance in breathless ecstasy. The barely masked sexual connotations of the scene would only have escaped the most naive audiences. By way of contrast, *Rock Around the Clock*'s Lisa Gaye athleticism is accommodated in modest, balletic costumes and she demonstrates new steps on a well-lit soundstage with another expert dancer, Earl Barton.[52]

Rock Around the Clock and the British media

Impervious to the immediate pleasures of rock 'n' roll, the BBFC considered *Rock Around the Clock* a film specifically for 'devotees' of 'hot rhythm' because it lacked a verifiable plot.[53] Similarly, British critics in the popular dailies and quality broadsheets realised that 'normal terms of criticism' did not apply because the film did not conform to any recognisable genre.[54] Jympson Harman, in the *Evening News*, concluded that 'the simple plot' was intended to 'squeeze onto film as much as possible of [rock 'n' roll's] horrible sounds'. Elizabeth Frank of *News Chronicle* facetiously referenced Haley's collegiate 'hep' talk to convey her disinterest, asking, 'Has anyone got any ear plugs for this square?'[55] Those who praised the film's light-heartedness and lack of pretention did so under a thin veneer of condescension. Thus, Harold Conway, in the *Daily Sketch*, considered this a 'nice' film with 'jolly nice' characters including a 'jolly nice villain'.[56]

Denigrating press commentaries demonstrate the generational gap that divided critics from the average young cinemagoer. In the cineaste journal, *Monthly Film Bulletin*, *Rock Around the Clock* was described as a 'negligible' story featuring 'the contemporary brand of jive' suitable for American and British teenagers.[57] Astute reviewers acknowledged the fragmentation of the family audience with more grace. Fred Majdalany, in the *Daily Mail*, for example, proclaimed himself an old 'fogey' but recognised the film's appeal to adolescents; and the perspicacious Reg Whitley, in the *Daily Mirror*, recommended the film to 'youngsters' but understood that 'Mum and Dad' would interpret Haley's music as 'a deluge of discord'.[58]

In response to the rock 'n' roll riots, the British press widened their commentaries to evaluate the new musical phenomenon. Critics appeared to be as bemused by rock 'n' roll as were British parents. Some attempted to demystify the trend by describing its derivative origins and referred parents back to the jive and swing dance crazes of their own generation. In the *Daily Telegraph*, Patrick Gibbs remarked on the 'primitive style and energy' of America's latest dance craze.[59] In the *Sunday Times*, Dilys Powell, who had little comment for the film's 'insultingly silly' story and unprepossessing cast, considered the 'intoxicating' music the 1950s version of the Charleston.[60]

Wider commentaries showed concern for the alacrity with which rock 'n' roll had permeated British youth culture. Invoking prejudices on American Deanagers, conservative Patrick Doncaster warned *Daily Mirror* readers that American rock 'n' roll fans were involved in 'riot, rape and alcoholism' in the USA.[61] The commercial success of *Rock Around the Clock* was another acrimonious topic that activated discourses of Hollywood dominance and exploitation. Sam Katzman had produced *Rock* on a tiny budget of $200,000 and it returned $1.1 million at the US box office. In the *Manchester Guardian*, Thomas Spencer remarked on Katzman's 'winning formula' of taking advantage of teenage interests and 'raking in' enormous revenues.[62] Penelope Houston, the editor of *Sight and Sound*, derided the cycle of low budget rock 'n' roll films as 'specious' entertainment with no lasting cinematic value: these films exposed Hollywood's profit-making machinery.[63] There was official consensus that American popular culture undermined British traditions and post-war identity. The social historian Harry Hopkins disdained rock 'n' roll as another 'American habit' that diminished Britain's status to being 'merely one more offshore island' of the USA.[64] An older generation of journalists discredited the outlandish Americanised behaviour of British fans of rock 'n' roll. In *The Times*, British cinemagoers were exhorted to stop disturbing the peace and confine their appreciation of rock 'n' roll to dance halls and 'their own homes'.[65] Similarly, media coverage of Bill Haley's unprecedented reception at Southampton dockside and in London registered amazement and disdain in equal measure: these emotionally unrestrained crowds were distinctly un-British.[66] Haley, himself, noted the frenzy of those who welcomed him: 'This is the best reception I've had anywhere in the world. I thought those stories I read about rock 'n' roll riots in Britain were publicity stunts.'[67]

The import of rock 'n' roll and the subsequent cinema rioting encouraged many to call for a return to old traditions. According to the *Daily Mail*'s front page, 'rock 'n' roll babies' reiterated Britain's urgent need for hard work and a stint of extended National Service to 'make men' of Teddy boys.[68] The National Service Act of 1948 conscripted young men aged 17–21 to serve for an 18-month period but, in 1950, service was increased to two years. At this time, the majority of National Service recruits were working class and, by the end of 1958, were predominantly early school leavers.[69] To the conservative-minded, national security and prestige in the post-war period, both in Britain and in the Commonwealth, could be sustained through a rigid National Service for this precarious demographic.

The call on health and social care experts compounded the view that teenagers were impressionable and made poor value judgements. To interrogate the fanaticism around rock 'n' roll, the *Daily Mirror* enlisted the opinion of several experts from the fields of psychology and medicine.[70] According to this panel, rock 'n' roll was not the root cause of teenage gangs or riots, rather there existed a small percentage of deviant 'mischief makers' who would 'riot for Mickey Mouse'. Dr Josephine McAlister Brew, the consultant psychologist to the National Association of Mixed Clubs, drew on established prejudices when she blamed the riots on 'American rowdies' who provided an imitative model for attention-seeking British teenagers. Cyril Stapleton in the *Daily Express*, took a highly pessimistic view and argued that all teenagers were 'troublemakers' by nature and drawn to 'hooliganism'.[71]

'We want rock 'n' roll': British teenagers and *Rock Around the Clock*

Fan magazines ostensibly functioned to promote upcoming films and develop new stars. Nonetheless, *Picturegoer*, Britain's best-selling film fan magazine of the period, was slow to recognise the importance of the teenage consumer and resistant to accommodating the rock 'n' roll trend in cinema. Despite the enormous popularity of *Rock Around the Clock* with American audiences, *Picturegoer*'s Tony

Brown considered it a clichéd musical and gave it a decidedly poor two out of five stars. Brown credited Haley's 'zestful get-up-and-go' but penalised him for his substandard acting ability and not having the slightest 'ping' of charisma; he described the Comets' stage show as laughable and gimmicky. Further, he delineates apparent differences between American and British rock 'n' roll fans. In Chapter 3, I argued that cultural protectionism motivated the British media's differentiation between American and British Deanagers. In this case, Brown describes how the overzealous reaction of American teenagers to rock 'n' roll met with staunch protest from church groups, and he (wrongly) forecast that British youngsters would be unimpressed with *Rock Around the Clock*. 'We shan't need the riot squads', Brown predicted in his column. 'Haley's comets aren't going to reduce our picturegoers to gibbering maniacs [because] American teenagers boil up into mischief quicker than ours.'[72]

The interactions between young British audiences and *Rock Around the Clock* were unprecedented. To clarify why these interactions were highly undesirable in the public space of auditoriums requires a survey of other legitimate and tolerated audience behaviours. In-house chatter and commentary, clapping and occasional booing were all familiar to the average cinemagoer: such low-level interaction with films enhanced the pleasures of viewing without greatly affecting other spectators. Jeffrey Richards and Dorothy Sheridan have analysed Mass Observation records to investigate wartime cinemagoing. Their assessment of how audiences interacted with *The Lion Has Wings* (Adrian Brunel, Brian Desmond Hurst, Alexander Korda, Michael Powell, 1939), a British propaganda film, reveals that there have long been accepted codes and practices for conveying pleasure and disapproval.[73] Mixed audiences were shown to have clapped in agreement, laughed collectively, asked questions of screen characters and made other audible comments to one another. This analysis also demonstrated that coughing restlessly conveyed disagreement or boredom at particular moments.

The Mass Observation records have also been sourced to theorise on the emotional reactions of audiences to wartime films. Thomas Dixon's account of 'weeping' in the cinema examines these documents to historicise emotional in twentieth-century Britain.[74] In addition, Sue Harper and Vincent Porter theorise on the 'depth of response' from both men and women and argue that particularly poignant films 'permitted' both genders to 'weep' openly.[75] Findings such as these indicate the range of accepted codes and (public) practices, which enhanced the enjoyment and emotional engagement with cinema, and challenge the preconceptions of a post-war society bound by the 'stiff-upper lip' ethos. Why would 'weeping' – arguably a 'private' display of emotion – be tolerated in the 'public' space of the cinema? Julian Hanich argues that 'cinematic tears' or 'weeping' – rather than noisy crying – is tolerated by other spectators because it is done *for* oneself without impacting on other people's enjoyment, takes place in the dark and only lasts the duration of the film.[76]

In comparison, *Rock Around the Clock* elicited unconventional audience behaviours. The rituals of spectatorship described above were established and had, therefore, become acceptable. By the mid-1950s, the majority of British filmgoers were aged between 16 and 24 – they comprised 60 per cent by 1960 – and film production was steered to suit their interests.[77] Needless to say, a new generation of cinemagoers would also cultivate their own rituals and practices of viewing; and *Rock Around the Clock* had precipitated these. In London, the film was rather short-sightedly paired with *Doctor at Sea* (Ralph Thomas, 1955). Not only was the latter a benign British comedy, it meant that patrons attracted to such mainstream entertainment were less likely to respond with any genuine enthusiasm to a noisy American film with marginal appeal.

Regardless of the extent that accounts of the cinema riots were hyperbolic, a teenage narrative must also be reconstructed for a fuller understanding. One South London teenager explained his frustrated desires when brought before a local magistrate for his part in cinema rioting: 'I wish they would show [*Rock Around the Clock*] in dance halls, without seats; then we could really enjoy it.'[78] The disruption to normal cinemagoing had demonstrated that teenagers wanted to act on the immediacy and enthusiasm conveyed by Haley's musical performances as though they were watching the 'live' spectacle of a rock concert. Piecing together teenage commentaries from the daily newspapers reframes youngsters not as degenerates but rather as different from older patrons. Depending on performance times and the location of the cinema, *Rock Around the Clock* could also generate collective appreciation that did not aggravate anyone. One teenager from Salford, Greater Manchester, described his experience of 'quite normal' audience participation

Figure 4.2 Haley (centre) and the Comets in *Don't Knock the Rock*. Their stage act and catchphrases encouraged unprecedented audience interaction from British audiences.

that consisted of 'clapping and some feet stamping' but 'no larking about'. However, he was one of several teenagers who had left their youth club to congregate outside a cinema hoping to witness challenges being made to police for themselves. They came to 'see what was going on' and became embroiled in the 'trouble' involving departing patrons. When asked by the magistrate about hose-pipe battles, the accused boy refuted these reports and answered: 'No one in their right mind would behave like that.'[79]

These testimonies illustrate that *Rock Around the Clock* encouraged a shared, if unorthodox, camaraderie between young spectators. At times of restraint, teenage fans were content to sway and wriggle in their seats, shout out Haley's popular catchphrases, and clap and sing along with the rock 'n' roll songs. Media commentaries reveal that the film brought together all kinds of young people – not just Teddy boys and girls – but also National Service recruits and tourists, who enjoyed repeat showings and were captivated by the audacity of bolder spectators who left their seats to dance. 'I've seen it five times [and] I'm going every night this week', enthused a 19-year-old soldier from South London. He recalled the forbidden dancing in the aisles: 'You should have seen this place last night. Jiving on the stage they were, till the cops came.'[80] In effect, the simple story mattered less either because young cinemagoers had seen the film several times before or because their primary enjoyment was found in one another's company.

Eventually, jivers and dancing couples were chased around the auditorium and evicted; and gangs of friends would follow them out and gesticulate to cinema managers and police. Across the news commentaries, Anthony Sampson's piece for the *Observer* is the most reflective and progressive. Having sat among teenage fans in a South London cinema, Sampson interviewed many before reaching his verdict on the cinema riots. Sampson believed that expecting youngsters to sit motionless and watch a lively film 'seemed a bit like playing a military march to a waiting room, or tickling a man in a strait jacket'.[81] At the Prince of Wales Cinema in Westbourne Park, south-west London, dancing became so lively that the cinema manager, John Pound, was assaulted as he tried to evict revellers. One adolescent barely recalled the film but describes this spectacle of audience participation with fondness: 'Before you knew it the place was a dance hall and every space was utilised; including the 2 [*sic*] raised aisles either side'.[82]

Evidently, screened rock 'n' roll contrasted greatly to any previous cinematic experience yet offered to young British film fans. Mim Scala, a self-professed Teddy boy rebelling against his domineering Italian father, discovered rock 'n' roll in a first viewing of *Rock Around the Clock* at the Red Hall cinema in Fulham. 'Bill Haley and his Comets had indelibly stamped my soul', recalled Scala, 'because anyone who heard the song once immediately knew the first forty-three words.'[83] *Rock Around the Clock* had become emblematic to British teenagers, who found in rock 'n' roll music and in the exuberance of Haley's performative style, a viable articulation of the generational gap they were experiencing in adolescence. Several memoirs confirm this in impressionistic accounts that describe how the film inspired and affected them in their formative years.

Growing up in a middle-class home in north London, the teenage Andrew Oldham, later the manager of the Rolling Stones, wanted to experience rock 'n' roll pandemonium first hand. Unfortunately, Oldham did not brave the journey to South London, and saw *Rock Around the Clock* in the 'primly sterile' atmosphere of the Haverstock Hill Odeon with 'twenty or so uptight patrons who tutted and shifted in their seats'.[84] The 16-year-old John Lennon similarly took his seat in a Liverpool cinema expecting mayhem to ensue. 'Nobody was screaming and nobody was dancing in the aisles like I'd read', recalled the disappointed Lennon. 'I was all set to tear up the seats, too, but nobody joined in.'[85] In Greater Manchester, the young Ray Gosling watched the film with his grammar school friends in celebratory mood. As recalled, there were police and bouncers stationed at the entrances and back doors, but this did nothing to dispel the feeling that 'a whole generation stood in the cinema aisles, bawling back at the screen'.[86] The adolescent Harry Webb, later Cliff Richard, was transformed by the film, and truanted with a friend in order to secure a ticket for Haley's live appearance at the Rank cinema, Edmonton. Later, scolded by his schoolmasters and warned that his life was taking a 'wrong direction' he lost his prefect badge but relished rather than regretted his behaviour.[87]

The public disturbances incited by showings of *Rock Around the Clock* may well be regarded as low-level misbehaviours when refracted by modern perspectives. However, these events were luridly presented in the media and provided a morbid fascination for an older generation who believed that teenagers in the 1950s were decidedly less disciplined than their generation had been. The BBFC examiner Audrey Field recorded her antipathy to a group of Teddy boys in a cinema in Sutton: 'These little idiots are liable to hurt other people, including the hard-pressed police, who have enough to do without keeping an anxious watch on the crowds coming out of the local Gaumont or Odeon.'[88] In like manner, F. E. Bancroft Turner, a magistrate in Manchester, provides, in his closing statement to a juvenile offender, the establishment's view of the cinema riots:

> It really is organised hooliganism in which you have no respect for other people's feelings or other people's property. The result is that a large number of police officers have to be called away from duty elsewhere, otherwise owners would resent your messing about with their cars and you risk being very ill-used. This destruction of property, interfering with the free passage of roads, and damaging other people's motorcars just cannot be tolerated.[89]

The cinema disturbances demonstrated the disparity between young and old and a shift in attitudes to authority. Arguments and altercations between young people and police were triggered because youths challenged rather than complied with those in authority. Statistics on juvenile crime delivered to the House of Commons in a speech by the Home Secretary, R. A. Butler, provide further evidence that there were troubling elements of post-war youth culture. The number of convictions for violence against the person had risen from 9,307 in 1956 to 10,960 in 1957 with the 'most serious' proportionate increase in the 17–21 demographic. The increase was nearly as high in the 14- to 17-year-old category.[90]

In view of these figures, the spectacle of 'marauding' Teddy boys challenging police in and around the nation's cinemas, though few in reality, provided another tantalising example of Britain's social decline. The older generation, who had been young adults during the Second World War, saw self-restraint as a national characteristic to be proud of. For them, loudness and exuberance were associated with the USA (and the dreaded American GIs). Thomas Dixon argues that traditions of British sentimentality ended with the stiff-upper-lip attitudes that coincided with the First and Second World Wars.[91] Inevitably, then, an older British generation who had been expected to uphold a stiff upper lip came to distinguish themselves from Americans (and other nations). The rising generation of the post-war period took the opportunity to break free of wartime culture by appropriating motifs of rock 'n' roll (and the motifs of rebellious film idols) and must have appeared Americanised to their elders as a result. Frankie Vaughan, a widely travelled entertainer popular with young people, dismissed as 'nonsense' the negative attitudes expressed by 'muddle-headed armchair critics' who branded the cinema riots as 'typical' of the 'nation's youth.'[92] Nonetheless, less sophisticated observers took media hyperbole at face value and remained contemptuous about the young. A letter to the editor of *Picture Post* from an 'armchair critic' expresses the persistent cynicism around young people: 'I hope that Bill Haley and his Comets appear on television [so that] we shall then see if these Rock 'n' Roll hooligans run amok in their own homes and break up the fittings, as they did in so many of our cinemas where Haley was featured.'[93]

'Of art, there is little in the Comets' work': Bill Haley's stardom in Britain

Rock Around the Clock was a very low budget film that quickly became a top 'money-maker' of 1956.[94] Given Haley's negative reviews, it is worth mentioning that low production values were matched by an equally short shooting schedule. Haley and his troupe were given little chance to rehearse, and filming took place between 6 and 13 January 1956.[95] With no formal acting training, Haley was required to 'play himself' and to introduce audiences to the vernacular commonly used by jazz musicians and American college students.

Reconstructing Haley's stardom is difficult because his fame was relatively transitory. Indeed, as this section demonstrates, Haley's public persona began the teen interest in rock 'n' roll but could not sustain it: by 1959, only two years after Haley's popular British tour, the singer's records failed to reach the top ten.[96] Haley's star persona must account for this rapid descent into relative obscurity. As a film star, Haley was hampered by a plain face and a rotund appearance: he did not resemble the typical leading man admired by young cinemagoers. One scathing commentary described Haley as 'a boxer who retired too late'.[97] Other aspects of his persona made him appear conventional and ordinary: he was married, had a large brood of children and, therefore, had more in common with an older parental generation. Furthermore, he looked very much older than his years making identification with his young fans less straightforward.

In the British press, the singer was presented as a 'gentleman' (rather than a rebel), and, in a short time, his persona and his music were subsumed into mainstream culture. Indeed, the entertainer contributed a series of articles for the *Daily Mirror* – referred to as 'Bill Haley's column' – which may be appraised in two ways. According to the Readership Survey of the Institute of Practitioners in Advertising, the *Daily Mirror* was the most popular paper among British teenagers in this period.[98] Apportioning an entire column to Haley, then, served a promotional function by directly connecting him to his young fans, and keeping them updated about his nationwide tour. It also constructed another narrative by establishing him as an entirely respectable family man. Using the column to describe his early career struggles, Haley foregrounded the pleasures of his simple and unglamorous lifestyle with his wife, Barbara 'Cuppy' Cupchak. Significantly, he personally vetoed the 'riots' that his appearances encouraged, and insisted that young rock 'n' roll fans show respect and behave calmly around his family and other band members.[99]

Haley was never personally targeted in the discourses of Americanisation and rock 'n' roll. This is in stark contrast to the ferocity of criticism levelled against Elvis Presley (examined in Chapter 5). Nor can it have harmed Haley's public image that he looked like a serious and mature musician, and conducted himself in a courteous manner in personal interviews. Despite his association with a 'rebellious' form of music, he personified a stable, more conventional masculinity than any of the anti-heroes in the key films. Neither was Haley exotic: his mother, Maude Haley, was from Ulverston, Lancashire. The press fondly reported that Haley had visited his English relatives during the northern segment of his tour. In these respects, Haley remained safely within the parameters of the British establishment. The disturbances around his screen performances could, then, be easily blamed on the impressionable 'mischief-makers' and not on the singer himself.

Haley's stardom, which introduced rock 'n' roll to Britain, soon legitimised it. Of note, then, is that rock 'n' roll was highly controversial for the period when it appealed primarily to Teddy boys and girls, and working-class teenagers with marginalised tastes. In a short time, rock 'n' roll became associated with members of the royal family and the 'smart set'; and the press were less inclined to resort to earlier scaremongering rhetoric to warn of its dangerous influences. When Queen Elizabeth asked for a print of *Rock Around the Clock* to replace *The Caine Mutiny* (Edward Dmytryk, 1954) during her annual summer stay at Balmoral it made headlines.[100] Haley responded to this uncustomary royal interest, as did the British press, when he 'cabled' the Queen directly to offer to play for her in person.[101] Further kudos was conferred on Haley when the 'jazz-loving' Princess Margaret asked the Royal Marines band to play his songs (in place of Gilbert and Sullivan). Later, she also took a print of *Rock Around the Clock* to enjoy during the royal cruise around Mauritius.[102] Concurrent with this royal veneration, bandleaders reported that rock 'n' roll was 'creeping in' to replace jazz in exclusive London nightspots. At the Gargoyle Club in Soho, for example, a regular haunt for the English aristocracy, barons 'shed their ties' and debutantes and baronesses 'kicked off their shoes' to dance to rock 'n' roll in 'stockinged feet'.[103]

Haley's growing popularity and respectability did not temper the negative responses from the film or music critics, who saw little merit in his abilities. There were, however, other positive outcomes to the changing status of rock 'n' roll. For instance, one British bandleader thanked Haley for bringing young people back into dance halls.[104] Furthermore, following the success of Haley's six-week nationwide concerts in Rank cinemas, after 1957, cinema chains continued to stage rock concerts during the week and show films at weekends.[105]

Conclusion

Haley's film career was launched in *Rock Around the Clock* and *Don't Knock the Rock*. Although his career slumped at the end of the 1950s, Haley had introduced mainstream audiences to rock 'n' roll and his catchphrases – such as 'see you later alligator' – that demanded active in-cinema participation were quickly assimilated into British popular culture. Notwithstanding the 'harmless' chanting tolerated at local football matches, post-war teenagers had previously been given few opportunities to call-and-respond in public venues.[106] Among the official voices of concern, Harry Hopkins termed the teenage fanaticism around rock 'n' roll 'a children's uprising' that alarmed their parents and instigated a phenomenon.[107]

The unprecedented interaction of British teenagers with *Rock Around the Clock* redefined cinema spectatorship by disrupting earlier precepts of cinemagoing. These 'perverse' spectators – to borrow Janet Staiger's phrase – appropriated their own meanings and pleasures from Hollywood films regardless of the consensus of legitimate or acceptable in-house behaviours.[108] As mentioned, unmarried, working-class people in their mid-teens and early twenties were the nation's most frequent cinemagoers. Rock 'n' roll films exploited the discretionary teenage spending documented by Mark Abrams in his economic study. Including unmarried 25-year-olds in his survey, Abrams placed going to the cinema and buying records (and record players) highest in the habitual leisure spending for the demographic aged 15–24.[109] In these respects, then, Haley's 'British' stardom reiterates the 'power' of teenage consumerism: teenagers disregarded Haley's lack of acting experience and unprepossessing appearance and 'chose' him as their pop idol. Commensurate with the key films already examined, the niche appeal of rock 'n' roll cinema continued to disintegrate the family audience as teenagers began to steer leisure and popular culture in a new direction.

This chapter has shown the ways in which *Rock Around the Clock* was influential in beginning a rock 'n' roll film cycle and generated widespread enthusiasm among British audiences. Nonetheless, the film is not included in the canon of 1950s cinema. The lack of a distinctive style or camp sensibility and the absence of a charismatic star may account for the film being largely forgotten by all but the most ardent rockabilly fans. *Rock Around the Clock*'s legacy, then, is that it anticipated the cult followings and singalong screenings of *The Sound of Music* (Robert Wise, 1965), *The Rocky Horror Picture Show* (Jim Sharman, 1975), and *Grease* (Randall Kleiser, 1978). During these special 'cult' screenings, audiences have reconfigured cinema spectatorship and dress up to look like their favourite fictional characters and collectively chant a series of venerated catchphrases. Juxtaposed to these films, *Rock Around the Clock* is better understood as a 'fad' – as predicted by critics of the 1950s – rather than as a film that has inspired a cult following. Film scholars have been able to distinguish between cult and fad films: a fad film does not generate or sustain the 'substantive interest' or 'expressive rituals' of those films that achieve cult status.[110]

Rock Around the Clock was a phenomenal success but Haley's fame faded soon after his live concert appearances. As a visual medium, film has naturally privileged handsome and charismatic stars in the mould of Marlon Brando and James Dean. On this premise, Haley's physical appearance, which had already been derided by film critics, attracted mixed responses from those British fans who saw him perform live. For the young schoolboy, Cliff Richard, for example, watching Haley and the Comets perform live was a pivotal moment of his adolescence and encouraged him to pursue a music career. For Andrew Oldham, however, seeing Haley was an anti-climactic experience. Expecting to see a rock 'n' roll rebel he could idolise, the reality of the plump family man, who looked like 'an Oklahoma City short-order cook', redirected the young Oldham to other musical talents such as Little Richard.[111]

Aside from the homely appearance so often remarked upon, Haley's obscurity was partly the result of his own ambivalence to rock 'n' roll. Biographies have described his earliest aspirations to a career in country and western music and this may account for the inconsistencies and instabilities of a star persona built around rock 'n' roll meanings. Haley and the Comets became known for a stage show that included cavorting with and climbing atop their instruments – stage antics ridiculed and scorned by *Picturegoer*'s Tom Brown. In her academic reappraisal of the Comets' British tour, Gillian Mitchell argues that the band used humour and exaggeration to destigmatise rock 'n' roll to parental authority and show that they were not serious about rock 'n' roll, which they regarded as a passing fad.[112] The renewed interest in Haley's pop career was the unplanned result of *Blackboard Jungle* including the song *Rock Around the Clock* on its soundtrack. Furthermore, Haley's diary entries attest to his physical and nervous exhaustion, and missing his family, in meeting the demands of a busy touring schedule.[113]

Haley's star text was developed around his maturity and family values that proved useful in mainstreaming rock 'n' roll. In the absence of acting credibility and matinee idol looks, the meanings that gave Haley an aura of respectability simultaneously destabilised his identification with teenagers. Once Elvis Presley was introduced to British cinema audiences, John Lennon, like thousands of other British teenagers would focus their adulation on him. Chapter 5 examines Elvis Presley's transformation, from a little-known singer to the glamorous rock 'n' roll 'rebel' of Hollywood cinema. In his early juvenile delinquency roles, he combined, for British fans, the pleasures of rock 'n' roll music and a transgressive, anti-establishment mystique.

Notes

1 Anthony Carthew, *Daily Herald*, 20 July 1956 (*Rock Around the Clock*, BFI microfiche).
2 'Comment: Rock 'n' roll babies', *Daily Mail*, 5 September 1956, p. 1.
3 'Dig that dockside', *Daily Mirror*, 6 February 1957, pp. 10–11.
4 A British Pathé newsreel (February 1957) documents Bill Haley's arrival at Southampton and his train ride to London Waterloo. Available at: www.youtube.com/watch?v=9mandPUBbRs (last accessed 4 April 2018).
5 'The Rock rolls around the world', *Radio TV Mirror*, July 1957, pp. 54–5.

6 Bill Haley's diary entry 5 February 1957, reprinted in Otto Fuchs, *Bill Haley: The Father of Rock 'n' Roll* (Kornwestheim, Germany: Wagner Verlag, 2011), p. 423.
7 David E. James argues that because Steve is the love interest and drives the band's success he, rather than Haley, is the main protagonist of *Rock Around the Clock*. See *Rock 'n' Film: Cinema's Dance with Popular Music* (Oxford: Oxford University Press, 2016), pp. 41–2.
8 Thomas Doherty argues that TV popularised rock 'n' roll because of its centrality in young people's lives. See *Teenagers and Teenpics: The Juvenilization of American Movies in the 1950s* (Philadelphia: Temple University Press, 2002), p. 68.
9 Old Negro songs – the 'field hollers' – used 'rocking and rolling' as a euphemism for sexual intercourse in rhythm and blues or 'race' music of the 1920s and 1930s. See Fuchs, *Bill Haley: The Father of Rock 'n' Roll*, pp. 107–13. Alan Freed popularised the term 'rock 'n' roll' when he was a disc jockey based in Cleveland. See Hank Bordowitz, *Turning Points in Rock 'n' Roll* (New York: Citadel Press, 2004), p. 63.
10 Newton K. Branch, Examiner's Report, 19 October 1956. The same views were exchanged between GRS and FNC, 29 August 1956 (*Rock Around the Clock*, BBFC Files).
11 'Exceptions list [GRS]', 25 April 1956 (BBFC Files). On 3 May 1956, Audrey Field noted that the cut was not enforced, further suggesting the film was considered innocuous by the board.
12 Stuart Hanson suggests that Britain's status as 'junior partner' to the USA led to anti-Americanism in the media. See *From Silent Screen to Multi-screen: A History of Cinema Exhibition in Britain since 1896* (Manchester: Manchester University Press, 2007), p. 107.
13 Victor Thompson's diary, *Daily Herald*, 15 October 1956, p. 4.
14 'Magistrate: Pity police can't rock 'n' roll you: youths in courts of two cities', *Manchester Guardian*, 12 September 1956, p. 8; 'Rock 'n' roll scenes: press blamed', *Manchester Guardian*, 19 September 1956, p. 2; Anthony Sampson, 'Rock 'n' roll notebook: "dig that crazy jive, man!"', *Observer*, 16 September 1956, p. 11.
15 '14 held in rock 'n' roll riots', *Daily Mail*, 3 September 1956, p. 1.
16 '300 police rut rockers', *Daily Mail*, 13 September 1956, p. 1.
17 'Pity police can't rock 'n' roll you', p. 8.
18 'Rock 'n' roll disturbances: film halted in Manchester, police dogs disperse London crowd', *The Times*, 11 September 1956, p. 8.
19 'Rock and wreck in film frenzy: youths do £150 damage', *Manchester Guardian*, 4 September 1956, p. 12.
20 '5 Towns ban the rock', *Daily Mail*, 15 September 1956, p. 5.

21 Sampson, 'Rock 'n' roll notebook: "dig that crazy jive, man!"', p. 11.
22 See for example, 'Dogs patrol a cinema, rock 'n' roll warning, *Manchester Guardian*, 14 December 1956, p. 2; 'Rock 'n' roll disturbances: film halted in Manchester, police dogs disperse London crowd', p. 8.
23 Arthur Watkins remonstrated against the decision taken by the Liverpool Chief Constable. Letter to Ellis F. Pinkney, Secretary of the London Cinematograph Exhibitors Association, 21 November 1956 (BBFC Files).
24 'Lewes Council fearing Teddy boys ban film', *Sussex Agricultural Express*, 5 October 1956; 'Blackburn: likely to lead to public disorder', *Hartlepool Northern Daily Mail*, 11 September 1956, p. 12.
25 '20 ships wait', *Belfast News-Letter*, 14 September 1956, p. 5.
26 See as examples 'Dogs patrol a cinema, rock 'n' roll warning', p. 2; and 'Rock film off for a day: Sunday precaution', *Manchester Guardian*, 17 September 1956, p. 12.
27 'Rock devotees subdued: appeal at the pay-box', *Manchester Guardian*, 6 September 1956, p. 14.
28 'Scottish flavour', *The Stage*, 27 September 1956, p. 4.
29 'Rock Film Off for a Day', *Manchester Guardian*.
30 'Rock 'n' roll disturbances: cases in London courts', *The Times*, 4 September 1956, p. 5.
31 Sidney Harris is quoted in a letter from Mike Frankovich to Paul Lazarus, 3 October 1956 (BBFC Files).
32 Extracts of Mr. Wilkins' recommendations, 'Behaviour of Teddy boys at Odeon Kensington' appear in Newton K. Branch's Examiner's Report of 19 October 1956 (BBFC Files).
33 These statistics were fully compiled on 29 October 1956 and were made available to the town clerks on a request basis.
34 Arthur Watkins to Ellis F. Pinkney, Cinematograph Exhibitors Association, 21 November 1956 (BBFC Files).
35 Tonks to Watkins, 22 September 1956 (BBFC Files). Watkins to The Venerable C. F. Tonks (BBFC Files).
36 The eulogy is quoted in Clive Emsley, *Hard Men: The English and Violence Since 1750* (London: Hambledon & London Publishers, 2005), p. 148.
37 'Opinion piece: stimulus behind "rock 'n' roll" disturbances', *The Times*, 15 September 1956, p. 4. Global opposition to rock 'n' roll music is given in Linda Martin and Kerry Segrave, *Anti-Rock: The Opposition to Rock 'n' Roll* (Hamden, CT: Archon, 1988).
38 This incident took place at the Gaumont cinema in Lewisham. 'Rock 'n' roll disturbances: film halted in Manchester, police dogs disperse London crowd', p. 8.

39 GRS and FNC, 29 August 1956 (BBFC Files).
40 Bishop William Woolwich, Blackheath, 'Rock 'n' Roll', *The Times*, 14 September 1956, p. 9.
41 AW replies to the Venerable C. F. Tonks, Archdeacon of Croydon, 24 September 1956 (BBFC Files).
42 Watkins to W. L. Dacey, County Councils Association, 29 November 1956 (BBFC Files).
43 'Rock 'n' roll scenes: press blamed', *Manchester Guardian*, 19 September 1956, p. 2.
44 Watkins to W. L. Dacey, County Councils Association, Westminster, 29 November 1956 (BBFC Files). These recommendations were reinstated in the letter sent to town clerks of boroughs responsible for licensing films for public viewing from the Association of Municipal Corporations, 30 November 1956 (HO 300/6).
45 G. H. Banwell, Association of Municipal Corporations to Town Clerks, 30 November 1956 (HO 300/6, National Archive). The letter was distributed to all boroughs which functioned as licensing authorities for cinematograph performances.
46 Watkins to W. L. Dacey, 10 January 1957 (BBFC Files).
47 Internal memorandum GRS to Arthur Watkins, 30 August 1956 (BBFC Files).
48 Fred Majdalany, 'At the new films: the king of rock rolls up again', *Daily Mail*, 18 January 1957, p. 4.
49 Watkins recorded his discussion with Frankovich in an internal memorandum addressed to President Sidney Harris, 28 September 1956 (BBFC Files).
50 The meeting took place on 13 November 1956 (and reported on 16 November 1956). The Board had already forewarned local authorities in the London County Council, Essex, Middlesex and Surrey about the upcoming rock films.
51 Newton K. Branch's comments regarding *Running Wild* (1955) and *Mad at The World* (1955) were recorded in a letter between GRS and FNC, 29 August 1956 (BBFC Files).
52 Patrick Gibbs noted Gaye's and Barton's advanced dance steps in 'Film notes: band parade', *Daily Telegraph*, 21 July 1956, p. 8.
53 GRS letter to FNC, 29 August 1956 (BBFC Files).
54 '*Rock Around the Clock*', *The Times*, 23 July 1956, p. 12.
55 Jympson Harman, '*Rock Around the Clock*', *Evening News*, 19 July 1956; Elizabeth Frank, '*Rock Around the Clock*', *News Chronicle*, 20 July 1956 (*Rock Around the Clock*, BFI Microfiche).
56 Harold Conway, 'The birth of the rock', *Daily Sketch*, 20 July 1956 (*Rock Around the Clock*, BFI microfiche).

57 '*Rock Around The Clock*', *Monthly Film Bulletin*, 23:264, 1 January 1956, p. 107.
58 Fred Majdalany, 'Save me from messages', *Daily Mail*, 20 July 1956, p. 6; Reg Whitley, 'This will rock the teenagers', *Daily Mirror*, 20 July 1956.
59 Patrick Gibbs, 'Film notes: band parade', *Daily Telegraph*, 21 July 1956, p. 8.
60 Dilys Powell, 'Mass-Music', *Sunday Times*, 22 July 1956, p. 4.
61 Patrick Doncaster, 'Do we want this shockin' rockin'?', *Daily Mirror*, 16 August 1956, p. 12.
62 'The top box-office hits of 1956', *Variety Weekly*, 205:5, 2 January 1957, p. 3. Thomas Spencer, 'Mr Katzman's winning formula: there's money in "Rock 'n' Roll"', *Manchester Guardian*, 15 September 1956, p. 1.
63 Penelope Houston, *The Contemporary Cinema* (Harmondsworth: Penguin, 1966), pp. 174–5; 'Hollywood in the age of television', *Sight and Sound*, 26:4 (Spring 1957), pp. 175–8 (p. 177); Walter Lassally, 'The cynical audience', *Sight and Sound*, 26:1 (Summer 1956), pp. 12–15.
64 Harry Hopkins, *The New Look: A Social History of Britain in the Forties and Fifties* (London: Secker & Warburg, 1963), p. 454.
65 'Opinion piece: stimulus behind "Rock 'n' Roll" Disturbances', *The Times*, 15 September 1956, p. 4.
66 'Minor battle of Waterloo: king of rock 'n' roll arrives', *The Times*, 6 February 1957, p. 4.
67 Bill Haley quoted in Marshall Pugh, 'The headline hunter', *The Times*, 7 February 1957, p. 4.
68 'Comment: rock 'n' roll babies', *Daily Mail*, 5 September 1956, p. 1.
69 Richard Niven, *National Service: Britain in Uniform 1946–1963* (London: Allen Lane, 2014), p. 78.
70 Ronald Bedford, 'Rock 'n' roll film ban in 2 towns: what is behind the riots?', *Daily Mirror*, 12 September 1956, p. 7.
71 Cyril Stapleton, 'Don't blame the music', *Daily Express*, 5 September 1956, p. 3.
72 Tony Brown, 'What's popping? We won't need riot squads', *Picturegoer*, 32:1111, 18 August 1956, pp. 18, 32.
73 Jeffrey Richards and Dorothy Sheridan (eds), *Mass-Observation at the Movies* (London and New York: Routledge & Kegan Paul, 1987), pp. 299–330.
74 Thomas Dixon compares *Brief Encounter* (David Lean, 1939) with *The Blue Lamp* (Basil Dearden, 1950) in *Weeping Britannia: Portrait*

of a Nation in Tears (Oxford: Oxford University Press, 2015), pp. 240–2, 391.

75 Sue Harper and Vincent Porter discuss *The Blue Lamp*. See *British Cinema in the 1950s: Decline of Deference* (Oxford: Oxford University Press, 2003), pp. 247–8.

76 Julian Hanich, 'A weep in the dark: tears and the cinematic experience', in Ralph J. Poole and Ilka Saal (eds), *Passionate Politics: The Cultural Work of the American Melodrama from the Early Republic to the Present* (Cambridge: Cambridge Scholar Publishing, 2008), pp. 27–45.

77 Houston, *The Contemporary Cinema*, pp. 174–5; 'Hollywood in the age of television', *Sight and Sound*, 26:4 (Spring 1957), pp. 175–8 (p. 177); Lassally, 'The Cynical Audience', pp. 12–15.

78 'Opinion piece: stimulus behind 'rock 'n' roll' disturbances, *The Times*, 15 September 1956, p. 4.

79 'More scuffles with police after rock 'n' roll film, ejections from cinema taken unkindly', *Manchester Guardian*, 11 September 1956, p. 16.

80 Sampson, 'Rock 'n' roll notebook, p. 11.

81 Anthony Sampson, 'Don't knock the rock', *Observer*, 10 February 1957, p. 10.

82 Pound's assault is mentioned in 'Rock 'n' roll film riot', *Daily Mail*, 29 August 1956, p. 1. Colgriffs shares his adolescent memories of the film performance at the Prince of Wales theatre. Available at: http://cinematreasures.org/theaters/15744 (last accessed 1 July 2017).

83 Mim Scala, *Diary of a Teddy Boy: A Memoir of the Long Sixties* (Ireland: Sitric Books, 2000), p. 28.

84 Loog Oldham, *Stoned* (London: Vintage, 2001), p. 29.

85 John Lennon is quoted in Philip Norman, *John Lennon: The Life* (London: HarperCollins Publishers, 2008), p. 78.

86 Ray Gosling, *Personal Copy: A Memoir of the Sixties* (London and Boston: Faber & Faber, 1980), p. 35.

87 See Cliff Richard's foreword in Fuchs, *Bill Haley: The Father of Rock 'n' Roll*, p. 15.

88 Audrey O. Field, 'Examiner's report: Gaumont, Sutton, Friday 14 September 1956, 7:25pm' (*Rock Around the Clock*, BBFC Files).

89 'Rock 'n' roll scenes: press blamed', *Manchester Guardian*, 19 September 1956, p. 2.

90 'Crime last year: serious increase among youth, R. A. Butler, Home Secretary', *The Times*, 1 August 1958, p. 4.

91 Thomas Dixon, *Weeping Britannia: Portrait of a Nation in Tears* (Oxford: Oxford University Press, 2015), pp. 325–7 (p. 325).

92 'Bon Droit', *Lancaster Guardian*, 12 October 1956, p. 8.

93 D. A. Sellars, Hyde, Cheshire, 'Why parents leave home', *Picture Post*, Issue 8, 25 February1957, p. 44.

94 'Other money-makers of the year', *Kinematograph Weekly*, 13 December 1956, p. 7.

95 As recalled by Rudy Pompeii, the saxophonist in the Comets. See Fuchs, *Bill Haley*, p. 208.

96 John Rockwell, 'Bill Haley', in H. Wiley Hitchcock and Stanley Sadie (eds), *New Grove Dictionary of American Music Vol. II* (Oxford: Oxford University Press, 1986), p. 308.

97 Anthony Carthew, 'Rock around the clock', *Daily Herald*, 20 July 1956 (*Rock Around the Clock*, BFI microfiche).

98 As illustrated by statistics for the 12-month period ending December 1958. See also, Mark Abrams, *The Teenage Consumer* (London: London Press Exchange: 1959), pp. 15–16 for a fuller analysis of readership tastes.

99 'Bill Haley's column', *Daily Mirror*, 31 January 1957, p. 9; 'Bill Haley's column: take it easy!' *Daily Mirror*, 7 February 1957, p. 2.

100 'The Queen wants to see that rock film', *Daily Mirror*, 18 September 1956 (*Rock Around the Clock*, BFI microfiche).

101 'Bill (Rock 'n' Roll) Haley cables the Queen', *Daily Mirror*, 20 September 1956, p. 5.

102 David Wynne-Morgan, 'Diary of a gay princess: she asked the marines for rock 'n' roll', *Daily Express*, 1 October 1956, p. 1.

103 'Tanfield's Diary: Now the bluebloods start to rock around the clock', *Daily Mail*, 27 September 1956, p. 14.

104 Nat Gonella, 'It's old stuff – this rock 'n' roll', *Picturegoer*, 32:1119, 13 October 1956, p. 18.

105 Colin Hanmer, 'A revolution in the cinemas', *Picturegoer*, 33:1140, 9 March 1957, p. 7.

106 Gosling, *Personal Copy*, p. 35.

107 Hopkins, *The New Look*, p. 433.

108 Janet Staiger, *The Perversity of Spectators: The Practices of Film Spectatorship* (New York and London: New York University Press, 2000), p. 37.

109 Abrams, *The Teenage Consumer*, pp. 9–10. Harry Hopkins also described this spending trend in *The New Look*, p. 432.

110 For a discussion of cult practices around specific films see Jonathan Rosenbaum, 'The *Rocky Horror Picture* Cult', *Monthly Film Bulletin*, 49:2 (Spring 1980), pp. 78–9 and Janet Staiger, *The Perversity of Spectators: Film Practices in American Cinema*, pp. 45–6, 108. For an exploration of the differences between cult and fad films see Patrick T. Kinkade and Michael Katovich, 'Toward a sociology of cult films:

reading "Rocky Horror"', *A Sociological Quarterly*, 33:2 (Summer 1992), pp. 191–209.

111 Oldham, *Stoned*, p. 29.

112 Gillian A. M. Mitchell, 'Reassessing "the Generation Gap": Bill Haley's 1957 tour of Britain, inter-generational relations and attitudes to rock 'n' roll in the late 1950s', *Twentieth Century British History*, 24:4 (2013), pp. 573–605 (p. 576).

113 Diary entries from Fuchs, *Bill Haley*, pp. 389–90.

5

'All-singing, all-fighting man': Elvis Presley as a rock 'n' roll rebel

> If I thought for one minute I was contributing to juvenile delinquency I'd go back to driving a truck.
>
> Elvis Presley, 'Why do they Criticise me?' (1957)[1]

> When [Elvis Presley] fixes me listlessly with those cold eyes, curls those insolent baby lips and, in a palsied paroxysm, sings 'Treat Me Nice', I yearn to treat him very nasty indeed.
>
> Cecil Wilson, *Daily Mail* (1958)[2]

In the early hours of 3 March 1960, on the completion of his army service in Germany, Sergeant Elvis Presley touched down in the little-known Scottish airport of Prestwick. Among the few hundred local fans clamouring to see the performer was Ann Murphy, a 16-year-old schoolgirl who, as the regular babysitter for an American officer's children, had been told of Presley's clandestine arrival. Ann told her best friend, Muriel, who was another fervent rock 'n' roll fan. Buoyed by the excitement of meeting their idol in person, the girls had changed into their American-style jeans and lumberjack jackets, before 'skipping' the three miles from town to the air field. In recollection of that fateful meeting, Ann remembered: 'Elvis was so handsome in his uniform. He waved and we started screaming. He shouted: "Where am I?" and people shouted back: "Prestwick" – but I was shouting: "I love you."'[3]

Moments before Presley's departure, Muriel leapt over a barrier to 'touch' Presley before she was 'scraped off' by military personnel. Later that day, the girls recounted their experiences to their friends, who remained unconvinced until Presley's visit made the front pages of the local paper. For Ann, the meeting was to have a profound and lasting effect. Eventually, she married Andy, crowned 'the

Prestwick Elvis' of a local talent show; and, after the couple made a football coupon win, they fulfilled their lifelong ambition to visit Graceland. This brief and unexpected visit to Scotland proved particularly significant for another reason: Presley would never again visit Britain. As a result, the town of Prestwick continues to celebrate its association with the performer through the commemorative celebrations organised by 'The Elvis Touch', the Glasgow Branch of The Elvis Presley Fan Club of Great Britain.[4]

In death, Presley has, for many, undergone an apotheosis. Fans from around the world make 'pilgrimages' to his childhood home in Tupelo and Graceland, situated on Elvis Presley Boulevard. Such extraordinary levels of idolatry have prompted one scholar to investigate Presley as a religious phenomenon.[5] The broadcaster David Frost accompanied 350 members of the Elvis Presley Fan Club of Great Britain (there were fifty branches in 1980) on a pilgrimage to commemorate the third anniversary of Presley's death.[6] One, a retired woman from London claimed to 'love' Elvis 'more than my husband', while a middle-aged man from Yorkshire believed that Presley was 'what every chap wants to look like in real life and what every woman wants for her husband.' Indeed, Frost acknowledged that these fans challenged stereotypes: they showed an intense hero-worship and high levels of identification with Presley, regardless of their age, gender or marital status.

To his music fans worldwide, Presley has been 'the King of rock 'n' roll' for several decades. But what of his acting? In the latter part of his Hollywood career, Presley appeared in a series of mundane formulaic vehicles geared towards selling his movie soundtracks. Yet my analysis of studio pressbooks and fan materials demonstrates that in his early roles as a juvenile delinquent he was presented as a credible actor-singer in Britain, and the natural successor to Marlon Brando and James Dean. This chapter focuses on *Jailhouse Rock* (Richard Thorpe, 1957) and *King Creole* (Michael Curtiz, 1958) to show that Presley's juvenile delinquency roles are the nexus between Hollywood's rebel films and the rock 'n' roll genre.

The British reception of Presley's early films reconfigures his Hollywood stardom. Andrew Caine's examination of Presley's British promotion at the time of *King Creole* reveals the fierce rivalry between *Melody Maker* and *New Musical Express* for acquiring teenage readers.[7] In other work on the evolution of rock 'n' roll music,

David E. James focused on how Presley's stardom negotiated many aspects of the prevailing American cultural discourses of the era, such as the generational gap, issues of class and racial exchange, and sexual politics.[8]

Fan discourses around Presley are characterised by images of unruly, screaming American teenage girls who watched his first live concerts. The majority of his British fans could only interact with these 'live' performances through the medium of film. Therefore, my analysis examines the extent to which Presley offered a foreign and alternative masculine type for young cinema fans (of both genders) growing up in post-war Britain. With unintelligible lyrics and a risqué dance style, Presley was antithetical to the conservative values of the establishment, which helps to explain the critical backlash surrounding his breakout film roles. Hence, my work also demonstrates that Presley was fortunate in making the crossover from music to cinema during a period of unprecedented teenage consumerism. The number of young cinemagoers (aged 16–24) almost doubled between 1945 and 1960.[9] In addition, the expanding youth market led to significant developments, which catered to their tastes, from TV programming to teen-interest magazines.[10]

In addition to his innovative musical sound, Presley's fascination for teenagers lay in his material wealth, which coincided with the 'having it so good' experience (or aspirations) of the average working-class teenager. In sharp contrast to the interwar years, the establishment of social security and the welfare state, full employment, rising wages, and low inflation meant that the working class of the 1950s prospered and thrived in ways not known before.[11] The teenage consumer with disposable income was central to this affluence discourse, and many working-class and lower-middle-class teenagers found parallels in Presley's biography. Hence, the Cinderella aspects of Presley's early life appealed more directly to the sensibilities of ordinary fans than to the British media.

Boys who wanted to grow up to 'be like Elvis' or 'sound like Elvis' took their own pleasures from the screen. In view of Presley not touring in person, fans made a study of their American idol in the dark of the local cinema. Magazines catered to Presley's fans by featuring a series of glossy colour photos that they could cut out and cherish. The Hollywood publicity machine exhorted British exhibitors to lavish their foyers with large, striking portraits of the star; and cinema managers regularly complained about the theft of such paraphernalia from their foyers. This coveting of Presley fan materials was not, as might be assumed, simply the predilection of teenage girls. For example, a 17-year-old youth was fined £2 for tearing down a film poster of *Love Me Tender* in the Wolverhampton area. 'I am a Presley fan', he told the examining magistrate, adding, 'I wanted his picture.'[12]

Rebel of Song: selling Elvis Presley in Britain

Presley's stardom can be reconstructed through an analysis of studio promotional materials and a survey of British trade journals. Despite the singer's enormous appeal to young rock 'n' roll fans, it was only after the success of *Love Me Tender* (Robert D. Webb, 1956), a western set during the American Civil War, that Hollywood began to formulate the Presley vehicle. Hence, his second film, *Loving You* (Hal Kanter, 1957) drew parallels with Presley's early biography. As such, this was a contemporary story of an amateur singer, who drives a truck for a living and is helped to stardom after a chance meeting with a talent agent (Lizabeth Scott). This lush colour film was fine-tuned to accommodate music fans' expectations and included many live performances of rock 'n' roll. With an insistence on Presley's romantic and rebellious readings, the narrative demonstrates the essential tough-tender duality of the anti-hero popularised by Marlon Brando and James Dean: Presley is a lover, who sings tender ballads, and a fighter, who throws punches when necessary.

To promote Presley's next film, *Jailhouse Rock*, MGM built upon taglines and imagery that had by now become familiar to his audiences. A short synopsis of the film demonstrates how the Presley vehicle incorporated his biography and offered varied contexts for his musical performances. The construction worker Vince Everett (Presley) accidentally kills an abusive drunk during a brawl in a bar. Convicted of manslaughter, Vince is sentenced to a stretch in jail. While serving time, he is mentored by his cellmate Hunk Houghton (Mickey Shaughnessy), a former country singer, who recognises his talent and encourages Vince to pursue a singing career. On release, Vince takes Hunk's advice and finds singing work in a nightclub. Soon, Vince meets Peggy Van Alden (Judy Tyler), a young talent scout for a record company, who recognises Vince's talent (and observes his volatile temper). Hunk becomes Vince's manager when he is released from jail. However, as Vince's career soars so does his arrogance, and eventually his attitude distances him from his closest confidantes, Hunk and Peggy. After hurting Peggy's feelings, Hunk and Vince share a heated exchange that turns physical; Vince's throat is injured so that he temporarily loses his voice. Whilst recuperating, the singer realises that he wants to make amends with Hunk. He reflects on his relationship with Peggy and realises that she is the one he loves.

The pressbook for *Jailhouse Rock* and the trade paper *Kinematograph Weekly*, offered exhibitors a plot summary and the strongest selling points for their foyer and lobby campaigns. Presley's phenomenal record sales and previous film successes meant that he was now repackaged as '[a]n exciting dramatic personality for all-age crowds as well as a rock 'n' roll riot for his teenage multitudes' in a campaign that aimed at a wider demographic.[13] Hollywood's success in film promotion lay in setting up audience expectations through intertextual references and stories that revisited popular or topical themes. Presley's popularity with rock 'n' roll fans was fundamental to the success of *Jailhouse Rock* in Britain. To guarantee Presley's trademark dance sequences, the film interlaced several songs with a contemporary storyline to attract cinemagoers. *Jailhouse Rock* was an original story by Ned Young, which meant that motifs and themes that had already proven popular could be incorporated into the narrative. As a result, *Jailhouse Rock* shares similarities with *The Wild One*, arguably to sustain the studio's promotion of Presley as 'the new Marlon Brando'. The freewheeling Johnny Strabler and the jailbird Vince Everett strike the viewer as equally reckless and headstrong. Johnny is the charismatic leader of a biker gang, and Vince orchestrates much of his own success in a film and music career. Both characters are fiercely independent and live on their streetwise machismo.

As recalled, Brando's publicity persistently referred audiences back to the brutish Stanley Kowalski; and Presley's screen persona assimilated the exuberant dancing and guitar-swaying of his live concerts. As actors, Brando and Presley conveyed an eroticism that departed from the conventional masculinities of the era. They forged images of men with sexual confidence and raw magnetism whose 'animal' instincts frequently overwhelmed their civilised exterior. For example, Johnny unceremoniously disentangles himself from his former girlfriend, Britches, and roughly seizes Kathie when he tries to seduce her. With a similar insouciance, Vince forces Peggy into an embrace and impulsively kisses her. Peggy, now furious, tells him: 'How dare you think such cheap tactics would work with me!' Vince's riposte is: 'That ain't tactics honey, that's just the beast in me.' According to the strictures of the Hollywood censor board, the PCA, which scrutinised sexual content, this passionate encounter would have been tantamount to attempted rape.[14]

The rebellious trope in Hollywood films would not have elicited sympathy or admiration with young audiences if he were not also capable of other emotional responses. Narrative codes ensure that we recognise that Johnny and Vince use aggression as a means of self-preservation – they are tender and vulnerable when given the right circumstances. Respective backstories establish that Johnny and Vince have each had troubled childhoods but are capable of falling in love with the 'right girl'. Johnny leaves his prized trophy with Kathie before leaving town; Vince sings tender love ballads to Peggy (and all the 'good' girls in the audience). The most obvious commonality is that both characters are the unwitting culprits of manslaughter. As we know, Johnny is knocked off his motorbike by a vigilante and the riderless vehicle kills an elderly man. In *Jailhouse Rock*, Vince punches an abusive drunk because he is being offensive to a woman in the bar only to be told that the man had a fatal heart condition.

MGM's marketing strategy sought to rebrand Presley as a serious dramatic actor. Publicity evoked James Dean in *Rebel Without a Cause* by using the tagline 'Elvis Presley, rebel of song' throughout all promotional materials.

Intertextual links to the other Hollywood rebel films originated in the studio pressbook.[15] In addition to foregrounding his early rock 'n' roll meanings, Presley is bestowed with romantic leading man status in publicity shots and lobby cards that demonstrate that Sherry (Jennifer Holden), the blonde Hollywood starlet, and Judy Tyler, the brunette 'girl next door', find him equally attractive. The *mise en scène* of Presley's love scenes also evokes the blocking of James Dean's love scene with Natalie Wood in *Rebel Without a Cause*, which placed Wood higher in the frame to enhance Dean's

Figure 5.1 American Teddy boy: Elvis Presley played an ex-convict in *Jailhouse Rock* (1957); he was promoted in Britain as James Dean's natural successor. Erotic dance sequences pleased his British fans but dismayed the film critics.

boyish and vulnerable qualities. By similar means, Presley invites the 'gaze' of an adoring Judy Tyler by being blocked lower in their close-ups to position him as the desirable 'object'.

In my earlier analysis of Bill Haley, I argued that his maturity and unremarkable features worked against his romantic readings for a teenage audience. As a result, Haley was rarely photographed without the Comets in film-related advertising. Contrary to this, Presley was central to all marketing materials connected to *Jailhouse Rock*. Furthermore, MGM urged British cinema exhibitors to select the largest format of colour photos and lobby cards available in their promotional foyer displays.[16]

The *Jailhouse Rock* trailer makes unambiguous references to earlier films about juvenile delinquency to broaden Presley's appeal beyond his original rock 'n' roll meanings. Hence, filmic moments such as Presley's part in a prison riot are carefully selected to reinforce Presley as an action-hero. Passionate embraces with Peggy and Sherry furnish his romantic readings and hint at a love triangle. The voiceover reiterates that here is 'an Elvis Presley you've never seen before' and promises 'his first big dramatic singing role'. Intertextual referencing to earlier films rebranded the singer as a credible actor. Thus, Presley was presented as 'a tough *Blackboard Jungle* kid' and 'the rebel with a voice'. To negotiate the tender-tough duality of his screen rebel, themes of violence and sexual impropriety are mollified by the film's close, with the final fade-out on Presley singing the ballad, *Young and Beautiful*, to Peggy.

Presley's second role as a young rebel was in the Paramount film, *King Creole*. A plot summary emphasises how *King Creole* was another Presley vehicle but also included iconography of earlier films about juvenile delinquents. Danny Fisher (Presley) is a failing high school student, who is burdened with financially supporting his father (Dean Jagger), an unemployed pharmacist, and his older sister (Jan Shepard). Danny falls in with Shark (Vic Morrow) whose gang works the protection racket for local crime boss and nightclub owner Maxie (Walter Matthau). Persuaded that petty crime has its benefits, Danny decides to help the gang rob a local store; he sings and plays his guitar to distract customers while Shark's gang empties the cash register. A local shop girl, Nellie (Dolores Hart), who has watched the proceedings, decides not to tell the police because she likes Danny, and they arrange a date. Danny plans to seduce Nellie by taking her to a local hotel on the pretext that there is a party going on in one of the rooms but he changes his mind.

To make ends meet, Danny waits tables in Maxie's club but when he sings for Maxie's girlfriend, Ronnie (Carolyn Jones), he is given a regular singing spot. Eventually, Danny becomes unhappy with working at Maxie's club and accepts the offer of work from a rival nightclub owner, Charlie (Paul Stewart). Maxie knows of the Fishers' financial problems and schemes to lure Danny back. On Maxie's instructions, the gang involves Danny in robbing the owner of the pharmacy where Mr Fisher fills prescriptions. While Danny keeps a look-out, he watches Shark and an accomplice cosh an old man in a dark alley. In fact, unbeknown to Danny, the victim is his father, who suffers brain damage after the attack. Maxie pays a top surgeon to tend to Mr Fisher and then uses this as leverage over Danny. To firm up arrangements, Danny visits Maxie's hideout where Ronnie has been instructed to seduce him. As planned, Maxie comes in to compromise Danny but instead the two men fight and Danny flees. Maxie sets his gang upon him and when Shark catches up with Danny, they tussle and Shark is accidentally killed with his own knife. Fearing repercussions, Danny hides out with Ronnie at a desolate spot near the Bayou River. When Maxie finds them, he is armed with a gun, and in a final shootout between Danny and Maxie, it is Ronnie who is accidentally shot and killed. When Danny and Maxie fight over possession of the gun Maxie is inadvertently shot dead. Exonerated by the police, Danny resumes his singing career at Charlie's nightclub and (the implication is that) he will marry Nellie.

The studio pressbook and film trailer promoted *King Creole* as Presley's 'finest acting' role in a highly prestigious production. Much was made of the strong supporting cast, which included the stage-trained actors Walter Matthau and Dean Jagger. It was also Presley's first pairing with Hal Wallis, the producer who had arranged his first Hollywood screen test, and would produce nine more of his films. In key publicity, Wallis emphasised Presley's commitment to learning new techniques to build upon his 'natural approach' to acting (as the nearest substitute to method training). Thus, Paramount's marketing includes photographs of a serious Presley in conference with Michael Curtiz, the director of many box office successes such as *The Adventures of Robin Hood* (1938) and *Casablanca* (1942).

King Creole was adapted from Harold Robbins' bestseller, *A Stone for Danny Fisher* (1952). The book concerns a Jewish boxer in Depression-era Brooklyn, who is eventually killed by racketeers. The reformulation of the novel indicates Presley's box office popularity and furthers Wallis's contention that, if skilfully handled, his protégé could become the 'singing James Dean'. Tailoring the story to showcase Presley's repertoire, the action is shifted to the underworld of New Orleans and evokes *Rebel Without a Cause*'s Freudian child–father relationship where a weak father creates juvenile delinquency in his son. Significantly, Vic Morrow, who had played Glenn Ford's nemesis Artie Shaw in *Blackboard Jungle*, reprised his role as a teenage gang leader, which set up an immediate association with the well-known film.[17]

Presley's persona was subsumed into mainstream culture by marketing him to a wider family audience. Tactically, the inclusion of a filmic love triangle met the expectations of Presley's rock 'n' roll fans while regular filmgoers would recognise the familiar motifs of Hollywood cinema. By positioning Presley between the 'bad' girl – the fallen woman trope – and the 'good' girl – the virginal ingénue trope – his star persona played out the essential duality required of Hollywood's new rebel male. In *Jailhouse Rock*, Presley's transgressive rock 'n' roll meanings would arguably have been satisfied by his involvement with Sherry, the glamorous platinum blonde actress who has been oversexualised by Hollywood. Peggy, on the other hand, is a conservative brunette from a good family – an earnest, hard-working record promoter who conforms to the feminine standard of 1950s proprieties. In *King Creole*, Presley is positioned between Ronnie, the gangster's moll, and Nellie, the unsophisticated shop girl, who resists seduction in the hope of marriage. Importantly, Nellie's character has been oversimplified in the screen adaptation of Robbins' novel in which she has Danny's child out of wedlock.

For Hollywood producers, selling *King Creole* – Presley's final film before army service – on the premise of his fine, solid acting was a means of safeguarding his future career in films. In an unpredictable industry, had Presley appealed solely to teenagers, his two-year career hiatus would most likely have led to rapid obscurity. By widening his fan base, Wallis hoped to ensure that Presley would continue to generate profits whilst in service and successfully resume his film career. Hence, the role of Danny Fisher was promoted as 'a role originally intended for someone like Marlon Brando or Paul Newman'; and his ability to 'sing Dixieland with a brass background, as well as rock 'n' roll ballads' demonstrated his musical versatility. Presley's varied costuming and shorter hair were duly emphasised as part of his commitment to subsume his real-life identity into his screen character. Thus, Presley's willingness to 'cut his sideburns' was highlighted and presented as a declaration of his serious intentions to become an actor of merit: 'For the first time in my screen career, I'm playing somebody other than [myself]. I didn't think the boy in this story would wear long sideburns.'[18]

Despite these efforts to add nuance to Presley's star image and extend his fan base, Hollywood publicity materials appear contradictory. On the one hand, Wallis promoted Presley as a method type actor; on the other, publicity stills and lobby cards foregrounded his status as a teenage idol. Contrary to studio hype that he was an all-round family entertainer, he was generally pictured surrounded by a bevy of beautiful and adoring co-stars. It was contradictions such as these that alienated the British media and undermined his status as a believable actor.

In the *King Creole* trailer, the same contradictions operate to sustain Presley's teenage fan base but widen his cinematic appeal. Celebratory taglines such as 'They've crowned a new king!' and '[Presley] is at the top of his amazing career!' were supplemented by assurances that the singer was making a transition from rock 'n' roll to New Orleans jazz. Less desirable filmic moments of juvenile delinquency were omitted. For this reason, there is no indication of Danny's shady involvement with Shark's gang. Instead, the voiceover contextualises Danny's rebellion as the driving force behind his rise 'from the gutter' to celebrity. Danny is recast as a 'rebel with a cause' – his cause being self-preservation – with carefully selected dialogue such as: 'I'm not a hoodlum, but I am a hustler – I've had to be for a very simple reason.'

In addition to publicity stills, other aspects of Paramount's marketing contradicted Presley's reformulation as a serious actor. As described earlier, *The Wild One* and *Rebel Without a Cause* were promoted as social realism and endorsed by James Dean's and Marlon Brando's acting pedigree. While Presley's films commented on juvenile delinquency, British exhibitors were encouraged to pander to the whimsy of his teenage fans. Fan club members were exhorted to enter Elvis lookalike contests and carry promotional film banners in street parades. Similarly, they could also be drawn into cinema foyers by 'Elvis jukeboxes', and even encouraged to buy fruit based on Liliane Montevecchi's (one of *King Creole*'s exotic nightclub dancers) appearance in a banana-clad bikini. Such indiscriminate and unscrupulous methods largely reflect those of Presley's manager,

Tom Parker, who wielded enormous influence and systematically commodified every aspect of his client's fame.

The BBFC's classification of *Jailhouse Rock* and *King Creole*

The BBFC decided that *Jailhouse Rock* and *King Creole* should be classified with an A certificates, which permitted children accompanied by a parent or a bona fide adult to watch them. This being so, the classification did not meet with universal approval. *Kinematograph Weekly*, the reliable trade paper for British exhibitors, considered the A certificate 'ill-merited' for *Jailhouse Rock* because the story had the 'mass appeal' of a musical and conformed to a moral story.[19] On the other hand, there was general agreement that the shady gangsters and disreputable nightclubs of *King Creole* made it identifiably 'an A' for its seamy 'adult fare' unsuited to 'bobby-soxers'.[20]

Presley's earliest star persona was formulated on the transgressive rock 'n' roll meanings he generated in the USA. Thus his British reception was founded on mediated reports of the parental and religious censure provoked by Presley's 'shocking' stage act and salacious TV appearances; and that American delinquents had appropriated his style as their own.[21] In the crossover to Britain, Presley wanted to reassure older audiences that he was not a juvenile delinquent and countered accusations that his music and style were a force for the corruption of youth. Rebranded as a carefree but well-meaning bachelor, Presley explained: 'I have as much fun as I can', and further asserted, 'I can only tell [my critics] they must remember doing similar things when they were young.'[22]

Given this background, it is surprising that Presley's eroticised film performances did not incite anything like the 'riotous' behaviour that accompanied *Rock Around the Clock*'s first showings. Further, Presley's juvenile delinquent films did not warrant an X certificate despite their sexual themes, a number of killings and a charismatic young performer in the lead. Questions must then be raised regarding the British censors' policy on musicals and their attitudes to Presley as a credible actor. Chapter 3 mentioned Mamie Van Doren's lewd dance scene in *Running Wild* that proved a rare exception to the censor's leniency with musicals. These facts aside, Presley's delinquent films were not entirely faultless or they would have been placed in the U category. Previously, his American Civil War western, *Love Me Tender*, secured a U certificate from the censor but only after six minutes of violence were removed.[23] Furthermore, when *Love Me Tender* was paired with an A certificate film unaccompanied children were duly barred.

The BBFC considered their unique A certificate 'a typical British compromise' that conferred a measure of responsibility to parents.[24] As noted in previous chapters, however, parental discretion was impossible to enforce and was rarely exercised. 'The great majority of parents drag their children to the cinema because they want to see a film with a total disregard for the effect it might have on the child', observed one filmgoer from Surrey.[25] Furthermore, wily children had their own methods of subverting the censor's recommendations: they could petition an unknown adult to accompany them into the auditorium. The film historian Tony Sloman, who grew up in South London, wanted to see Presley's films but, unlike his bolder friends, could never summon up the courage to ask a stranger to buy his ticket for him. As a result, he had to wait until Presley's films were shown in their second-runs at his local cinema.[26]

There were other reasons why Presley's films were not hampered by the restrictive X certificate. Pandro S. Berman, who produced *Jailhouse Rock* had obtained a satisfactory 'pass' for *Blackboard* Jungle around the same time that *The Wild One* was banned. No doubt, cordial relations between examiners and Hollywood producers were advantageous when Presley's delinquent films were submitted to the BBFC. Yet this is not an entirely satisfactory explanation. This study has now demonstrated that the BBFC did not reclassify films they considered unsuitable for children even after multiple cuts had been made. Therefore, other aspects of Presley's stardom are worth considering. Chapter 4 illustrated that British censors, like the majority of older cinemagoers, were impervious to the pleasures of America's latest musical trend: rock 'n' roll. It is just as likely that they regarded Presley as a gimmicky singer who appealed mainly to teenage girls rather than Teddy boys. Their actions suggest that they did not imbue him with the kudos of a Brando or a Dean. Furthermore, as musicals, neither *Jailhouse Rock* nor *King Creole* carried the gravitas of social realism.

As is often the case in archival research, there are inevitable frustrations. When the BBFC destroyed their original censorship files pertaining to *Jailhouse Rock* and *King Creole* it was a simple matter of reclaiming office space. Equally, American trade papers such as *Variety* and *Hollywood Reporter* offer no mention of any censorship problems these films encountered (as they did for *The Wild One*, *Blackboard Jungle* and *Rebel Without a Cause*). The fact that the BBFC did not preserve these files is further evidence that the films encountered no serious issues from the board. This study has now demonstrated that American screen violence and sexual themes that degraded women or sullied their reputations were the red flags to British censors. There are also many examples in the press in which Secretary Arthur Watkins reiterates the BBFC's moral protection of young people and children from violence and 'false values'.[27]

A case study of *Serious Charge* (Terence Young, 1959), a British film about juvenile delinquency that incorporated a rock 'n' roll soundtrack is useful in reconstructing the (missing) censorship around Presley's early films. *Serious Charge* reworked many aspects of *Jailhouse Rock* and *King Creole* and introduced audiences to Cliff Richard, a British singer who looked and sounded much like Presley. The story concerns an unmarried vicar, the Reverend Howard Phillips (Anthony Quayle), who takes up residence at a new parish with his mother (Irene Brown). Hester Peters (Sarah Churchill), the daughter of the retiring parish priest, becomes infatuated with Phillips but is reticent in sharing her feelings. As part of his pastoral duties, Phillips runs a weekly youth club and this brings him into contact with local teenagers. When a naive parishioner, Mary Williams (Leigh Madison), becomes pregnant by the local Lothario, Larry Thompson (Andrew Ray), she decides to confide in the vicar. Soon after, Mary spies Larry with his new girlfriend, Michelle (Lilliane Brousse), a seductive French teenager employed as a maid. Mary becomes so distressed that she runs into the road and is killed by a car. Alarmed by news of Mary's death, the vicar asks Larry to his home so that he can confront him: Phillips demands that Larry face up to his responsibilities or he will be forced to tell all of Larry's friends and his younger brother Curly (Cliff Richard) that he abandoned the pregnant Mary. Feeling cornered, Larry concocts a plan to punish Phillips for his meddling: he fakes a violent struggle, breaks furniture and tears at his own clothes. When Hester arrives on the scene, Larry tells her that Phillips has 'interfered' with him.

Unbeknown to the vicar, Hester is harbouring a grudge because she saw him meet up with Mary, and has misinterpreted their interaction as a romantic encounter. Consequently, Hester chooses to believe Larry's account and does nothing to stop vicious rumours about the vicar from escalating. As a result, Phillips is victimised and ostracised by the community he has been trying to help. The situation is only resolved when his mother persuades Hester to accept that he is innocent and stop spreading rumours about him; and Larry is beaten by his father for spreading vicious lies.

Serious Charge was adapted for the screen from Philip King's play of 1955, which meant that, as with all plays, it had been censored and approved by the Lord Chamberlain's Office before the public saw it. During early pre-production stages, Arthur Watkins watched the original play at London's Garrick Theatre for an initial evaluation of its suitability for the screen. Watkins deemed an A certificate 'intolerable' but worried that its homosexual undertones made it unsuitable for 'the mixed and immature provincial cinema audience which would see an X film'.[28] *Serious Charge* confronted the censors not only with the unsavoury – but by now familiar – depictions of juvenile delinquency but rather the controversial subject matter of male homosexuality. In the 1950s, homosexuality was still considered a criminal offence – misunderstood and shrouded in an aura of abnormality and degeneracy. Gay and bisexual men often became the victims of blackmail and intimidation in an era of witch-hunts.[29] Those prosecuted were socially stigmatised and professionally ruined. For example, the tabloids sensationalised the court cases against Alan Turing, convicted of 'gross indecency' in 1952, and Lord Montagu of Beaulieu, one of several men imprisoned for homosexual acts in 1954. Although Lord Wolfenden's report (1957) began the process of decriminalisation (recommending that adult males should not be prosecuted for consensual sex in private) substantive changes to the law did not occur until 1967.

For its association with homosexuality, then, *Serious Charge* underwent rigorous changes throughout its pre- and post-production stages. Between mid-1955 and 1959, the censors and the producers at Romulus Films worked towards making the necessary changes to warrant an X certificate. Eventually it was agreed that any dialogue that hinted at homosexuality or undermined the 'manliness' of the falsely accused clergyman – lest he should be coded as homosexual – was removed or overdubbed in the final version. Motifs borrowed from earlier teen-oriented Hollywood films were similarly censored. Scenes in which the teenagers misbehave were scrutinised.

This 'organised hooliganism' – by now familiar to audiences and to the BBFC – such as shots of teenagers brandishing bicycle chains and flick knives, were either reduced in length or excised altogether. *Serious Charge* also reworked *Rock Around the Clock*'s dance scenes and offered Cliff Richard the opportunity to imitate Presley's distinctive vocal style and stage mannerisms when he performed the hit rock 'n' roll song, *Living Doll*. For these reasons, *Serious Charge* is an excellent example of how quickly British films had assimilated American iconography. Significantly, it was rock 'n' roll that conveyed the wilder instincts of the film's teenage characters. In the youth club, Larry and his Teddy boy group disrupt the vicar's other activities by playing a rock 'n' roll record. Reverend Phillips watches in mounting dismay as jiving between teenage couples becomes more frenzied; he finally turns off the record player to disperse the crowd. Closer analysis of *mise en scène* demonstrates how this scene is derivative of *Rock Around the Clock*. The low-angle camerawork that had perfectly captured the energetic acrobatic jiving of Bill Haley's dancing couples is replicated in the British film.

In other ways, *Serious Charge* conforms to earlier British cinema commentaries on juvenile delinquency. Indeed, Larry displays the pathological and psychosexual dynamics of Tom Riley (*The Blue Lamp*) and Roy Walsh (*Cosh Boy*). Larry's egocentric and vindictive behaviour frames him as the unsympathetic juvenile delinquent already familiar to audiences. Like Tom Riley, who sadistically intimidates Peggy, Larry takes his greatest pleasure in hurting others, for example, when he attempts to sexually assault Hester (quite obviously coded as a virginal spinster). Evocative of Roy Walsh's seduction and abandonment of Rene, the promiscuous Larry callously breaks off relations with Mary when she becomes pregnant and seduces Michelle. Larry was a standard delinquent character that conformed to an archetype, a superficially attractive but unlikeable degenerate. Ultimately, Larry is denied the sexual charisma afforded to rebel characters portrayed by Marlon Brando and James Dean. Casting the dark-haired Cliff Richard in his screen debut as Curly exploited his uncanny resemblance to Elvis Presley. Although Curly was a small role, largely providing musical diversion, he importantly offers audiences a portrait of the redeemable delinquent type. '[Larry's] quite a scoundrel. I'm half-and-half', Cliff Richard surmised. 'I do what the other boys do – mainly because I'm in a gang – though I turn out to be rather a good lad in the end.'[30]

It was the 'problem' of male homosexuality that distinguished *Serious Charge* from Presley's films and from *The Blue Lamp* and *Cosh Boy*. Sophisticated audiences might have recognised the sexual ambivalence of the Reverend Phillips, despite the changes to the script that foregrounded his irreproachable heterosexuality. He was a bachelor living with his mother, who rebuffed Hester even though she was a marriageable Christian woman of his own age. It was these lingering hints of homosexuality that appear to have concerned the BBFC far more than the eroticised rock 'n' roll dance sequences. The board's recommendations worked to present the friendly Phillips as an irreprehensible and falsely maligned individual. On the other hand, Larry is reduced to a snivelling and cowardly liar and is fittingly punished when he gets a beating from his father.

Familiar Hollywood motifs were recycled in the trailer for *Serious Charge*. Reminiscent of *Blackboard Jungle*, a standard American voiceover offered British audiences a story 'as tough as today's headlines' and graphics promised them 'drama' and 'controversy'. Posters similarly capitalised on Larry's passionate kiss with Michelle, his attempt to assault Hester, Teddy boys and rock 'n' roll dancers. Such elements indicate that the British censors had modernised their outlook and relaxed their policies – under its new secretary, John Trevelyan – to permit British cinema to viably tackle adult material. One of the examiners at the BBFC acceded that *Serious Charge* was replete with the 'dangerous stuff' of 'cheap American films' characteristic of youth-oriented cinema: 'The vulgarisation of motion pictures intended for older teen-agers [*sic*] has proceeded so far in the past 3 years that it does not seem anything out of the way now.'[31]

With its commentary on male homosexuality in a period of censure, *Serious Charge* had pushed the boundaries of acceptable themes. In the 1980s, when the film was re-evaluated by the BBFC for VHS format, the sensitive subject matter continued to divide opinion for slightly different reasons. For one examiner, 'pederasty' and 'sexual molestation' involving a local parish priest proved an initial stumbling block to straightforwardly granting the film a PG certificate.[32]

Unlike *Serious Charge*, *Jailhouse Rock* conformed to a standard narrative of reformation and rehabilitation of an unruly (but redeemable) delinquent hero. The story did not condone the 'recreational' violence (the 'kicks' and 'giggles') associated with Teddy boy delinquency and given narrative space in *The Wild One*. Vince regains his sense of values and – de rigueur for the British censors of the 1950s – he is suitably punished and 'learns his lesson'. Indeed, regeneration appears to be the cohesive theme of *Jailhouse Rock*. Presley's transformation is conveyed through his transition in musical numbers that mutate from raucous rock to melodious ballads. Furthermore, in early scenes, Presley wears his trademark flamboyant pleated trousers and Cuban collar shirts, but later scenes show him in sophisticated menswear. This wardrobe faux pas was noticed by one of his female fans in Cornwall, who awarded Presley 'a black mark' for wearing old-fashioned clothing more suited to Clark Gable.[33]

When *Jailhouse Rock* was reformatted for VHS in the 1980s it was awarded a U certificate – and this was not disputed by the board. In fact, the censors wondered why the theatrical release had required the restrictive A classification. 'I can only think it was because of the notoriety that Elvis's hips had gained for him in the eyes of the older generation', reasoned one examiner.[34] Contrary to this assertion, a survey of contemporary press reviews reveals that Presley's musical sequences and the scene in which he is stripped to the waist and flogged were not excised. These were all potentially erotically charged scenes featuring Presley, yet remained intact.

In 1986, *King Creole* was classified PG and, fortunately, the report generated for this VHS re-release documents that two minutes of celluloid was cut from the original film in 1958. Again, the recent censor assumed that the sexual magnitude of 'Elvis the Pelvis' had 'constituted an automatic threat to the civilised world'.[35] However, contemporaneous film reviews of *King Creole* confirm that all of Presley's dance sequences remained intact. Furthermore, this is another story of a teenager's regeneration. As recalled, Danny (Presley) breaks ties with Shark's gang, and disentangles himself from the 'bad girl' Ronnie, who is accidentally shot and killed. In this, Ronnie conforms to the classic narrative of self-destruction and death that negotiates the troubling issue of cinema's promiscuous women.[36] The ingénue Nellie helps to restore Danny's moral compass and by frustrating his attempts at seduction, sabotages the 'morbid fascination' the teenage girl has for the glamorised delinquent. Hollywood film-makers had learned to use a system of dual address to disguise potentially contentious themes liable to be censored by the PCA.[37] Sophisticated audiences might have recognised the real nature of the revue bar where Danny works – a burlesque club – whereas the more 'innocent' would not.

The likeliest censorship problems with the *King Creole* production would have concerned violence and use of weapons. For example, Maxie's gang uses a cosh to render Danny's father unconscious and there is a prolonged fight between Danny and Shark involving a flick knife. Interestingly, in the 1980s, the examiner describes the *mise en scène* that mitigated the violence for a young audience and warranted a PG classification. The climactic confrontation between Danny and Shark was conveyed in medium long shots, a relatively dark atmosphere, and Danny's expedient – rather than mindless – violence, in which the hero overcomes the 'baddie' in a 'desperate situation'.[38] The same filmic elements that satisfied the recent censor would have demanded stringent measures in the 1950s because of the urgency of juvenile delinquency.

'Those crazy pelvic manoeuvres': Presley and the British critics

Press reviews and commentaries on *Jailhouse Rock* and *King Creole* demonstrate the vicissitude of journalistic reaction to Presley as a singer-turned-actor. Presley was an untrained actor during an epoch of intense interest in, and veneration of, method acting. Biography supplied by the studio pressbooks that furnished early press releases compensated for this lack of training by emphasising Presley's passion for filmgoing, and argued that he had learned his acting techniques from watching his screen idols: Marlon Brando, Tony Curtis and James Dean.[39]

In the cineaste journals *Sight and Sound*, *Monthly Film Bulletin* and *Films in Review*, Presley's acting was never seriously evaluated. However, journalists in the popular dailies and fan magazines were divided on his abilities and wondered whether he had the potential to be the 'next Jimmy Dean' or 'the singing Marlon Brando'.[40] John Balfour in the *Daily Sketch* stated his preference for Presley's 'natural' acting style unhampered by the 'stuttering hesitations or embarrassing mannerisms' that had become characteristic of Brando's method acting.[41] Nonetheless, this positive assessment was rare. More typical was Margaret Hinxman's view that putting Presley on the big screen cruelly magnified his patent lack of acting experience.[42]

Chapter 4 has shown that cineaste film critics and filmmakers such as Tony Richardson, Lindsay Anderson and Walter Lassally disregarded *Rock Around the Clock* as a fad film. Exercising their taste-making function, this elitist group championed Hollywood's social realism as the most effective and imaginative means for film to be as influential and valuable as theatre and literature. Penelope Houston, the editor of *Sight and Sound* since the mid-1950s, denigrated the gimmickry of rock 'n' roll films because they were tailored to display a performer's skill set and had little cinematic value.[43] In a similar missive, Virginia Lewis petitioned Hollywood for more authentic commentary on juvenile themes: 'I want art. I want to see the sordidness and misery transcended by the human spirit', she told the readers of *Film Review*.[44]

Given the popularity and conspicuousness of pop stars on screen, the majority of British teenagers wanted other pleasures from cinema: they embraced the excitement of live musical performance and storylines pertinent to their life experiences. Bourdieu's analysis of taste argues that elitist groups maintain their cultural capital by differentiating between high and low art forms.[45] On this basis, Andrew Caine asserts that *Monthly Film Bulletin* represented the cultural elite and, in affiliation with the BFI, aimed to encourage a wider appreciation for film culture as cinematic art.[46] The negative attitudes to 1950s rock 'n' roll cinema also reflect the generational gap between these film critics and younger filmgoers. To exemplify this, the persistence of Presley's image in prison uniform, one that is still in circulation today, is a valuable point for discussion. The enduring iconography of *Jailhouse Rock*, which framed the young Presley as a rebel and conferred a classic status on the film, owes much to an impressive musical sequence. The memorable scene shows him dancing alongside fourteen cellmates and a truncheon-swinging warden. Despite sharing the high production values of earlier Hollywood musicals, both for its galvanising choreography and elaborate stage set, reviewers in *Sight and Sound and Monthly Film Bulletin* make no mention of the scene. *Jailhouse Rock* was almost entirely disregarded as a clichéd 'formula' of the 'surly unknown' who makes good.[47]

Throughout the book I have referred to the commercial constraints of the industry that inhibited Hollywood's artistic freedoms. To this end, Hollywood producers had restricted the singer's exuberant (and over-sexualised) live stage performances to avoid offending mainstream audiences.[48] In spite of these changes, the consensus of British critics in the popular press was that *Jailhouse Rock* was a confounding pastiche of other Hollywood films. In the *Sunday Times*, Dilys Powell, who admired Presley's singing abilities, considered the plotline implausible.[49] In the *Daily Mirror*, Donald Zec, who described himself as a fan of Bill Haley's style of rock 'n' roll, surmised that *Jailhouse Rock* was no more than 'a crude, ugly musical' because it was 'a muddy brew of delinquency, cheap sentiment, bad taste and violence'.[50]

Jailhouse Rock did not conform to the backstage scenarios explored in *Rock Around the Clock* and *Don't Knock the Rock*. It offered audiences a hybrid of genres that produced a rock 'n' roll musical around juvenile delinquency themes. In marked contrast to Bill Haley, who developed his screen persona around performing songs in an affable style, Presley was enlisted with the unenviable task of proving his merit as a method-type actor as well as delivering his rock 'n' roll stage act. Many British critics had built their reputations on evaluating the craft of acting and were perplexed by these new trends in cinema. As a result, Presley's acting was 'invalidated' by his undulating rock 'n' roll performances.

Following the release of *Jailhouse Rock*, *King Creole* was promoted to British audiences as the singer's 'prestige picture' featuring the 'new Presley'. Yet it was ill received by the *Monthly Film Bulletin*, whose reviewer described it as a disagreeable 'entangled series of clichés' of 'calculated violence and viciousness'.[51] Derek Prouse, a regular contributor to the cineaste journals, believed that Presley's film career was the latest example of the Hollywood star vehicle. According to Prouse, *King Creole* was nothing more than a pretext for Presley to demonstrate his 'gilt-edged securities' (his romantic connotations and his vocal range) that were cleverly 'streamlined' into a coherent story by the adeptness of a seasoned director, Michael Curtiz.[52] Veteran reviewers across the media echoed many of these negative sentiments. In effect, they disliked *King Creole* because the musical numbers failed to counterbalance the darker themes of gangs and hoodlums. Aside from some recognition of Presley's inchoate acting ability, the 'new' Presley appeared much like the 'old'. In the *Daily Telegraph*, Eric Gillet called Presley 'a symptom and a symbol of post-war adolescence' and consigned him to inevitable obscurity as soon as teenagers lost their taste for his music.[53]

As demonstrated, Hal Wallis's decision to align Presley with well-known method actors was counterproductive and disaffected large sectors of the British press. It also proved tedious to one filmgoer from Buckinghamshire, who described the 'miserable failure' of Presley's imitation of method acting and regarded his 'blinking and stuttering' as entirely 'unsuited' to him.[54] For others, Presley's screen personality had 'clicked' with cinema audiences. Thus, one approving fan suggested that he could dispense with singing altogether and concentrate on dramatic roles.[55]

Film critics in the popular daily papers were no more fans of rock 'n' roll music than any others but they were more inclined to concur with – or at least include – ideas suggested in Paramount's pressbook. Presumably, this attitude fulfilled their function in promoting films, and accommodated the interests of their younger readers who were also frequent cinemagoers. Dick Richards' review in the *Daily Mirror* was noticeable for the grudging praise he offered Presley. In a half-humorous apology, Richards wrote, 'Sorry chum, I've never taken you very seriously' and furtively suggested that Presley might have a future as an actor.[56] Fred Majdalany in the *Daily Mail* was more generous in his praise and reminded his readers that: 'The hysteria [aroused] in his younger admirers should not blind anyone to the fact that, in his own line, [Presley] is a remarkably gifted performer.'[57]

In addition to providing varied responses to Presley's acting, media commentary also reconstructs the image of masculinity that Presley offered his British fans. This remains a largely unexplored facet of Presley's stardom: how he invited the cinematic gaze. My survey reveals that British journalists had an intense fascination with the singer's physical attributes from the minutiae of his 'baby lips' or 'pouting' mouth, his 'baleful' or 'insolent' eyes as well as the inevitable fixation on his hips and dancing. What becomes apparent is that pejorative and personal attacks were aimed at Presley for, literally, 'making a spectacle' of himself.

In Chapter 1, I argued that Marlon Brando's proletarian heroes invited the gaze by wearing undergarments that revealed his muscularity or through the ultra-fashion of biker's paraphernalia. Chapter 3 argued that James Dean's boyish blondness invited the gaze through his 'feminised' and childlike displays of emotional intensity. Certainly, Brando and Dean brought an unfamiliar physicality and eroticism to the screen but they were also highly regarded method actors. In contrast, the young and handsome Presley invited the gaze purely for the pleasure of being 'looked-at'; his titillating gyrations were considered emasculating because they appealed to the baser desires of his (female) audiences. Indeed, British critics were unversed in assessing this self-conscious display of male sensuality. Inevitably, with no other points of reference, allusions to cinema's popular 'blonde bombshells' and other oversexualised female tropes persisted in Presley's film reviews. In his film debut, *Love Me Tender*, Presley was described as '[t]he male Jayne Mansfield or Marilyn Monroe'.[58] Further, the epithet of 'Elvis the pelvis', familiar to audiences (then as now), was liberally used by tabloid journalists. Certainly, the moniker achieved comic effect but it also conveyed Presley's inherent immorality and, tacitly, endorsed discussion of the entertainer in reductive terms. John Balfour's assessment in the *Daily Sketch* typifies these contradictions and disregards Presley's acting credentials altogether: '[F]or the first time I understood completely why Presley drives those teenage gals crazy. No gramophone record can catch the physical impact of Elvis The [*sic*] Pelvis. He is the hopped-up male version of the hula-hula performer, the hip-swinging harem dancer, the Arab belly dancer.'[59] Neither was such physical scrutiny or ridicule reserved for the tabloids. In the *Sunday Times*, Dilys Powell described him as having 'the rhythmic style of a galvanised belly-dancer [like] Fatima the Fatal'.[60]

To extend these notions, Steve Neale's work on 'masculinity as spectacle' is instructive. Neale's assertions that cinematic men are 'feminised' when they invite the gaze may be applied to Presley's stardom. For example, when paired with a female co-star, Presley is often positioned as the object, rather than the bearer, of the gaze and assumes the blocking normally reserved for the actress. Furthermore, Presley's appearance in musicals reinforces his 'feminisation'. As Neale argues, this is 'the only genre in which the male body has been unashamedly put on display'.[61]

In his early career, Presley was frequently compared with Rudolph Valentino, who held intense erotic fascination for female audiences in the 1920s. Valentino was an Italian émigré who became an enormously popular matinee idol of the silent screen for his darkly good looks, his athleticism and his dexterous dancing. In particular, Valentino's eroticisation was his association with tango at a time when the dance symbolised a newly transgressive expression of feminine freedom.[62] According to Miriam Hansen, Valentino's fascination for female spectators became a source of social anxiety and, because his exotic looks, sartorial flamboyance and dancing invited the gaze, he was subjected to scrutiny and ridicule in the national press and given the unflattering sobriquet of 'the Powder Puff'.[63] Mark Glancy has argued that Valentino was warmly received by the British press, as a European who expressed a strong anti-Hollywood rhetoric, until an unexpected visit to London elicited the hysterical behaviour of his *British* female fans.[64] Invoking the established prejudices against women spectators – for their impressionability and susceptibility to the star system – Valentino was 'punished' for his part in fascinating them, as was Presley several decades later.

In the 1950s, explicit comparisons between Presley and Valentino recur in the British media. For instance, responding to his Latin looks and brazen choreography in *Loving You*, Margaret Hinxman observed that Presley '[was] the sexiest screen sinner since Valentino'.[65] In his essay on pop culture, Colin MacInnes remarked that Presley's sexual charisma was 'a reversion to the Valentino era with his sleeked, slick locks and sideburns, and his baleful, full-lipped Neronic glare'.[66] Even Presley's British fans recognised their affinity with Valentino's admirers. One young woman from Birmingham called Presley 'the 1957 Rudolph Valentino or John Gilbert' and claimed that 'the Valentino worshippers [could not have] adored Rudolph any more than we Presley fans love Elvis'.[67]

In recognising these similarities, we should also note important differences. First, Valentino showcased the tango – a highly technical dance that required a female partner. In his musical sequences, Presley danced alone, generally at the microphone or swinging a guitar, directly facing his audience as though on stage. The distinctive dance steps so revered by fans were his own invention but were imitable by the untrained, non-professional. Second, as a solo dancer,

Figure 5.2 *King Creole* was adapted from a bestseller as an Elvis Presley vehicle. The film combined the topical themes of juvenile delinquency and the prerequisite dance sequences fans had come to expect. One British fan asked Hollywood not to 'tame' Presley.

Presley was the exclusive site of audience pleasure and provided an unfettered model of imitation for anyone wanting to copy their idol. Third, since dance scenes rarely motivated the action, they also offered audiences a glimpse of a 'live' Presley concert performance. Lastly, the issue of ethnicity is another point of contrast between the two stars. Valentino's stardom was inextricably linked with, and negotiated by, his ethnic 'otherness'. This was not the case with Presley, whose 'Latin looks' were largely manufactured, contrived from black hair dye and heavy eye makeup. He was irrefutably an American.

By the mid-1950s, jazz was an established form of musical expression. Its organic development from older forms of African American music recommended it to British intellectuals, who preferred it to the heady commercialism of rock 'n' roll. Presley's background in this inferior and tribal style of music – as was the learned consensus – galvanised some of the debates around Americanisation. Anti-Americanism motivated the vituperative comments directed at Presley for his musical heritage and for his compliance with the unprecedented commercialisation of his stardom. Profiting from a high percentage of his record sales, Hollywood films and global merchandise and memorabilia brought Presley an unparalleled level of wealth and fame at a very young age. Moreover, although American singers such as Frank Sinatra and Johnnie Ray had enjoyed their fair share of 'bobby-soxer' adulation at the height of their success, their extreme fan hysteria was short-lived. In contrast, the extraordinary behaviour of American youngsters at Presley's live concerts shocked the British media, who were concerned that a national tour would provoke similarly hysterical reactions from British teenagers. Journalists reported the undesirable reverberations of Presley's sexualised stage act among American teenagers. Typically:

> [H]e reduces [them] to shrieks and outbursts of weeping by his moaning and sinuous swayings. … [H]is audience is stimulated to such rhythmical movements as clapping in unison and jumping and dancing in the aisles; often those in the front rows will surge to the platform and grab at Mr. Presley's clothes.[68]

The assiduous effect of such alarmist accounts generated an image of Presley as immoral and lascivious, and British journalists wanted to anticipate and avert this 'audience-fever' at home. Jack Payne, a veteran bandleader, disdained tailoring popular music to uninformed teenage tastes. In the *Daily Mail*, Payne censured the 'obnoxious' Presley for the horrible effect he was having on (immature) American girls and warned him that British parents would 'chase him right back across the Atlantic' if he toured Britain with the same stage show.[69] In *Picturegoer*, Tom Hutchinson, who had ridiculed Bill Haley's ineffectual film appearances, expressed his 'intense dislike' of

Presley's 'crazy cult' and hoped that it would 'not reach England'.[70] Charles Swann similarly described Presley's stage antics as 'indecent' and 'unnecessary' and demanded that the singer 'clean up or shut up'.[71]

'He's got that X-tra something': Presley and his British fans

In the short period between the exuberant riots around Bill Haley's film appearance in *Rock Around the Clock* and Presley's screen debut, one teenager from Middlesex had decided: 'Presley definitely knocks Bill Haley off his throne as king of rock 'n roll.'[72] Presley's rising star and his desirability to (young) women placed him at the centre of cultural discourses that attempted to negotiate his sexualised masculinity. Consigned to the narrow meanings conferred by the epithet of 'The Pelvis' the majority of British critics disregarded his vocal range and his eclectic style of rock and (hillbilly) folk music, and interpreted his fame as vulgar American commercialism.

Whatever reservations the media might have had about him, success in two significant areas of popular culture – music and cinema – meant that Presley was a globally recognised figure who ranked high in young people's hero-worship. When a national poll of four hundred British schoolboys listed 1957's most admired people Presley came fourth among the following: Group Captain Douglas Bader (1st), Winston Churchill (2nd), Lord Nelson and Stanley Matthews (tied 3rd) and the British rock 'n' roller Tommy Steele (5th). Similarly, in a 1958 poll of five hundred Scottish 14-year-olds, Presley was ranked third after Winston Churchill (1st), 'Mother' (2nd) and ahead of the Pope (4th).[73]

In unpicking Presley's iconic status, his Hollywood construction as a charismatic screen rebel is central. Presley's youngest British fans were intrigued by his enigma and the supposed glamour of his unfamiliar origins. 'I remember seeing a photograph with his slick of hair and just falling in love', recalled the British actress and broadcaster, Joanna Lumley, who first glimpsed Presley on an album cover. Growing up in a comfortable middle-class home in Kent, Lumley habitually played Elvis records on her auntie's gramophone, and responded to the singer's exoticism. 'I never thought about where he came from but it was probably somewhere exciting: bright lights, big city', Lumley reminisced. 'I'd never heard of Tupelo and Mississippi was just a spelling test.'[74]

In the same way, children and teenagers responded to the repetitive lyrics and memorable melodies of Presley's style of rock 'n' roll. In parts of the Midlands, lunchtime rock 'n' roll sessions in town centre dance halls attracted groups of local children, who danced alongside older Teddy boys and girls. These midday sessions proved so popular that children were 'skipping lunch' and returning late to resume their lessons. In response, W. G. Jackson, the regional Director of Education, formalised the complaints of Nottingham and Wolverhampton head teachers and enforced a ban on children attending. The local press reported on groups of barred children staging their own forms of rebellion. Children sang Presley's hit song, *Don't Be Cruel* outside dance halls and mature-looking schoolgirls 'dodged the ban' by changing out of their school uniforms. Other groups like 'The Unsatiated Wilfrunians' formalised their disapproval and devised their own charter of demands. As a result, school principals in Rochdale, Nottingham and Wolverhampton resolved the issue of these disruptive lunchtime dance sessions by permitting entry only to children accompanied by an adult or able to produce a permission slip showing parental consent.[75]

In the British fan press, readers were offered the customary pin-ups, personal interviews and biographies to sustain Presley's public persona as a working-class rebel. Typical of Hollywood's machinations to harness a wide fan base, Presley was juxtaposed as the 'bad boy' to the wholesome and popular American singer and actor, Pat Boone.[76] Boone was the perfect foil to Presley: he was married with children, had gained a university degree and openly discussed his strong religious convictions. In personifying a conservative and stalwart masculinity, Boone appealed to older British critics for continuing Bing Crosby's venerated style of crooning. In *Picturegoer*, Derek Walker spurned the contemporary music scene as 'a pop world of Elvis Presleys, pink Cadillacs and scarlet living' and praised Boone 'as a young man whom we can all admire'.[77] Similarly, Mark Carlyle preferred the 'healthy' and 'nice' Boone and chastised Presley as one of the 'gimmick boys' who 'peddle sex under the slim guise of music'.[78] If Boone's clean-cut persona was the obvious choice for parental authority, then Presley's rebellious iconography endeared him to those teenagers who wanted to emphasise their generational differences.

The British media was equally absorbed in divulging details of Presley's accumulating personal fortune and lavish spending. In the fan magazines, this intense scrutiny was partly motivated by the vicarious interest of readers, intrigued by the glamorous lifestyle enjoyed by their idol, and may have resonated with the new affluence of teenage consumers. On closer examination, however, the heavily loaded rhetoric against Presley's success was motivated by wider concerns and should be attributed to Hollywood's dominant position in the Americanisation discourses. Just as Marlon Brando's rising salary was a recurring topic in the British press, Presley's wealth was presumed to be ill-deserved and became a topic for media discussion. In *Photoplay*, Ian Hart used his media platform to discredit Presley as 'a droopy-eyed, swivel-hipped hill-billy' and 'the hound dawg' who had 'made a million'.[79] Hart remonstrated against the expense of joining the singer's official fan club, the cost of branded memorabilia and the proliferation of merchandise that included clothing, trinkets, charms, *Love* perfume and an (ill-advised) glow-in-the-dark Elvis portrait for the bedroom. *The Times* and *Picture Post* similarly interrogated the rock 'n' roll fan phenomenon sending its reporters to factories in the Midlands. Journalists learned that teenage factory girls – often travelling forty miles each morning – brought in their own records to play and pinned up coloured cut-out pictures of their favourite singers to diversify the factory rooms. The majority also wore a 'symbol of devotion' every day ranging from a Bill Haley brooch, an Elvis Presley trinket or a Tommy Steele charm bracelet.[80] Given that fan merchandise was largely aimed at girls, it would appear that media rhetoric was attacking, however obliquely, the machinations of the Hollywood star system, which duped its most gullible female fans.

To traditionalists, or mature audiences, the material wealth of Presley – a young, working-class singer with no discernible talent – was highly objectionable. The growing demand for his fan clubs, increasing sales of merchandise, numerous hit records and Hollywood's development of the Presley vehicle testify to his popularity with young fans. Presley's phenomenal stardom appeared symptomatic of wider concerns about working-class teenagers and their enormous spending potential. According to a study by the economist Mark Abrams, cinemagoing, magazines, records and other leisure products characterised the burgeoning teenage consumer market.[81] In his social history of the period, Harry Hopkins observed that semi-skilled working-class teenagers were endowed with the highest wages and lowest outgoings, producing 'the most spectacular margin for free spending'.[82]

Prevailing attitudes across the media epitomised teenage consumerism as incautious and uninformed and warned of its undesirable consequences. Official consensus denigrated the younger generation's predilection for *carpe diem* and 'living only for leisure' to relieve the monotony of dull jobs, rather than forging a career and saving for the future. Reproving media commentary was sustained by sociological research, academic literature and governmental reports. Arthur Bryant, a well-known historian and biographer, spoke for a learned consensus when he described the rising generation as 'the drifting youth of the Welfare State'. Bryant warned that without an expanded youth service – to provide varied diversion – young people would likely become juvenile delinquents or lead materialistic, purposeless and stunted lives.[83]

Presley's prominence in music and film sustained his stardom. His fans could congregate in their favourite coffee bars to dance to his records, play his music at home or watch his latest feature at the cinema. Dominic Sandbrook argues that Presley and Haley were direct beneficiaries of the new affluence of British teenagers because they were more passionate about music than their elders and could afford to buy records.[84] Similarly, Bill Osgerby, in his study of post-war teenagers, concurs that the expansion of the youth market had its greatest impact on popular music.[85]

Members of the clergy, school committee groups, education boards, religious lobbyists, as well as established stars such as Frank Sinatra, could be counted among the dissenting voices against Presley and rock 'n' roll. The music historian Nik Cohn argues that it was the widespread parental backlash that transfigured Presley as 'very young, private, unshareable, exclusive teenage property' and sustained rather than dismantled his stardom.[86] Joining fan clubs and buying branded memorabilia and records provided fans with opportunities to identify with their idol and conspicuously participate in his stardom. Cliff Richard, for example, recalled that he would immediately tear off the brown paper wrapping from his record purchases, explaining:

'I wanted everyone to say, "Oh look, he's got Elvis's latest album." I wanted to be recognised as being an Elvis fan.'[87]

British critics pilloried Presley for his crossover fame but his fans believed that good film roles would develop his performances and many found the comparison with Brando and Dean plausible. While the British media disregarded Presley's screen persona as contrived and superficial, fans interpreted his controversial image as authentic and well earned. Just as James Dean's fan mail continued to eulogise the late actor's charisma and emotional range, Presley's admirers found resonance with the performer's transgressive qualities and revered him as a 'screen rebel'. 'Elvis represents everything that's uninhibited and unconventional', explained one fan. 'He's an outlet – an escape for our feelings. He demonstrates a wild free emotion that we teenagers would like to express but can't.'[88]

Picturegoer fan magazine continued to have a large and sustained readership throughout the 1950s and, commensurate with the influence of teenage consumerism, was adapted to suit younger readers. To accommodate the popularity of the pop musical, a 'Top Singer' category replaced 'Best Newcomer' in their annual awards. In 1957, Presley came third in this new category for his performance in *Jailhouse Rock*, with Frankie Vaughan ranked first place and Pat Boone the runner-up.[89] As an indicator of teenage support, Presley's performance in *King Creole* was ranked ninth in the 'Top Ten Actor' category, in a list that included the perennially popular Dirk Bogarde, Marlon Brando and Sidney Poitier.[90]

When the film critic Donald Zec used his *Daily Mail* column to attack Presley, hundreds of youngsters sprang to the singer's defence. In contrast to the platonic devotion expressed by boys and girls for James Dean, Presley's 'defenders' were almost exclusively girls and were (unjustly) represented as immature, volatile and overly emotional. In summary, Zec described how 'hopping mad' fans had ridiculed him and accused him of being jealous of their idol. The fans advised Zec to: 'Take poison, get hung, take a long walk off a short pier, drop dead (seventeen suggested this), get lost, gas yourself, shoot yourself, cut your throat, disappear.'[91]

Presley's predominantly female fan base motivated gentle mockery from other journalists. At a preview screening of *Love Me Tender*, Margaret Hinxman reported the screams, gasps, applause and 'Elvis' chanting that enveloped all the teenage girls.[92] Inevitably, the boys at the same screening were demonstrably less enthusiastic and were as likely to ridicule Presley's scenes. When Cliff Richard and his older sister, Donna, saw the film at the Odeon Edmonton, he recalled that she had stifled her moans and screams with a handkerchief, perhaps to maintain the required level of decorum in front of her younger brother.[93]

Young women and teenage girls were paramount in the media's discussion of Presley's fame. Inevitably, the construct of the star system encouraged female audiences to more readily express their devotion or infatuation with a film star, and scholars have tended to shift their focus here.[94] Given his brooding good looks and his trademark hip gyrations, it was unsurprising that female fans should openly discuss Presley as a sex symbol. Pauline Barnard from Cornwall candidly implored Hollywood not to 'tame' Presley but to allow his film career to foster his sexual magnetism.[95]

Regardless of the media's pessimism, Presley's crossover fame encouraged a wider fan base than that of Marlon Brando and even James Dean. For many teenage boys, Presley represented someone to emulate and imitate. Ray Gosling, whose rigorous grammar school education was alleviated by his frequent visits to the cinema, recalled the many reasons underlying his adulation. 'Elvis was terrific', Gosling recalled. 'He spat his songs and shook and murmured with the bottled-up emotion we felt. When he twitched his leg and tossed his lanks we knew it was sex.' In contrast, for Gosling and his teenage friends, Bill Haley only remained popular with 'silly girls' and, once overshadowed by Presley, took on the appearance of 'an imposter'.[96] Furthermore, Gillian Mitchell's academic reappraisal of Haley and the Comets British tour of 1957 argues for the group's rehabilitation of rock 'n' roll, which made him popular with parents as well as youngsters.[97] George Melly, a musician in the 1950s, similarly argues that it was this tour that changed fan perceptions of Haley and, therefore, disrupted his career. As Melly argues, Haley disappointed ardent rock 'n' roll fans because in real life he was 'plump' and looked 'old' whereas Presley remained an enigmatic idol of the screen.[98] These observations on how enigma sustains star mythology are important. Presley's brief stopover at Prestwick only enhanced his mystique.

While male fandom has inevitably been less demonstrative, teenage boys were as feverishly excited by Presley's stardom as were his female fans. Male fans tended to identify first with Presley's music and express their interest by forming fan clubs. For example, Terry Roberts and his friends in Canterbury, began sharing Presley's records before they decided to start the 'first' official Elvis Presley Fan Club in Britain.[99] The combination of Presley's matinee idol looks, his sexual confidence in dance routines and his melodious delivery of songs embodied an idealised masculinity for young men to emulate. Paul McCartney described how Presley had resonated with him: 'I first saw [Elvis's] picture in a magazine … and I thought, "Wow! He's so good looking … he's perfect. The Messiah has arrived.'[100]

In recent years, well-known British performers have shared their memories of Presley and described his influence on their careers. Tommy Steele, presented as the 'British Presley' in the 1950s, was unusual in expressing a 'hatred' for his American contemporary.[101] For others, Presley's rag-to-riches biography was both inspirational and aspirational. Robert Plant, the lead singer of Led Zeppelin, responded to the 'wild howl' and 'searing' intensity of Presley's eclectic music. Using a hairbrush as a microphone, Plant would imitate Presley behind the sofa in the terraced house where he grew up, in West Bromwich.[102] Similarly, years before he formed the Rolling Stones, Keith Richards would spend hours strumming his guitar to Presley's records in his childhood home.[103]

Like Brando and Dean, Presley inspired Teddy boys to adopt his favourite fashions and his distinctive hairstyle. During his teenage years, Cliff Richard and his best friend copied Presley's greasy ducktail (or pompadour) because they found that it 'impressed the girls'.[104] When Richard was heralded as a 'British Elvis', he was quizzed about whether he wanted a similar career: 'Yes, I want to be like Elvis. He's been my idol. He's got to the top as an outstanding film personality. And that's the kind of star I want to be.'[105]

Other famous British fans provide impressionistic accounts of Presley's stardom. Though less known now, the singer Terry Dene was a popular rock 'n' roll entertainer, who began his career by impersonating Presley in London nightclubs. Dene, who grew up in the Elephant and Castle area, provides an alternative perspective on the aspirational Presley model of fame. Expressing his opinions on why Presley inspired him, Dene's colloquialisms are also indicative of his working-class origins: 'Rock 'n' Roll [*sic*] was given to me by Presley, know what I mean.' Comparing himself to 'merry' Tommy

Steele, Dene explained that, like Presley, he preferred to dance with 'more of a jerk' and have 'a mostly serious face'.[106]

That the young John Lennon admired and emulated Presley is a staple of any biography on the musician.[107] As a teenager, Lennon dressed like Presley, talked incessantly about him to his Aunt Mimi, and emulated his dancing in front of a mirror. Lennon, who liked to frequent the cinema, recalled waiting in line for the latest Presley film with 'screaming' teenage girls, when he was struck by a bright idea for his future: 'I thought, now that's a good job.'[108] In one of his last televised interviews, Lennon, in retrospective mood, explained the deeper impact of Presley on his own life: 'If I could pin it on anyone ... It was Elvis who got me out of Liverpool.'[109]

Notwithstanding the proverbial raucous misbehaviours of teenage boys in audiences, it was children and young women who responded with immediacy and urgency to Presley's screen appearances. Thus, children's cinema club sessions were enlivened by the shouting of Presley's name, collective singing and dancing around cinemas without adult interference or censure.[110] Similarly, 'screaming' was a familiar and collective pleasure for groups of exuberant teenage girls in their interactions with Presley's films. When asked to leave a London cinema for causing a disturbance, Veronica Tomkins complained: 'But what does [the manager] expect when fans go to see their singing idol?'[111] During a midnight screening of *King Creole*, the excessive stamping of exhilarated teenage girls had caused the collapse of a balcony in a West End cinema.[112]

These incidents of disrupted cinema programmes were few and far between and suggest that Presley's films did not encourage the extreme responses (or delinquency) which had characterised early screenings of *Rock Around the Clock*. Perhaps cinema managers had by now learned how to anticipate and avert the worst behaviours from young audiences. They may well have utilised the tried and tested precautions that had proved successful during the riots around the *Rock* films. It is also worth considering that Presley's films were musicals of the type that inevitably attracted younger cinemagoers, who were collectively involved in boisterous interactions with the medium. Greater participation was expected and tolerated at these times. Furthermore, older filmgoers had also learned from previous experiences and taken appropriate action so that they could enjoy films in a more conducive atmosphere. John McGowan, a family man from the West Midlands, blamed rowdy and ill-mannered Teddy boys as 'the single greatest factor' in declining audiences, and avoided teenagers altogether by going to quieter screenings.[113]

Conclusion

By the end of the 1950s, Presley's film appearances had forged a popular screen persona as a charismatic rebel. In addition to the pertinent storylines, fans were rewarded with glimpses of 'live' concert performances when Presley delivered his songs in exuberant rock 'n' roll dance sequences. With the advent of MTV in 1981, the music video proliferated but *Rolling Stone* magazine singled out *Jailhouse Rock* as 'the first rock movie to have any aesthetic influence on the rock videos we see today'.[114]As shown, earlier British critics disregarded Presley and his films as a low and transitional form of popular entertainment. Presley was the first crossover artist to establish an enduring Hollywood career and others like Pat Boone, Tommy Steele and Cliff Richard took film in a new direction that catered to teenage tastes. In *The Times* one critic judged these semi-biographical vehicles to be 'bad films' that evoked the hackneyed 'music hall turn' and did not conform to any respected film genre.[115]

Few twentieth-century narratives fulfil the American Dream as satisfyingly as Presley's rags-to-riches mythology. Presley's famed entourage of family and friends, his collection of cars, toys and gadgets, his pursuit of leisure and an idiosyncratic diet, enveloped the performer in an enduring adolescence. One American music journalist considered this lifestyle to be Presley's true 'genius' because he negotiated 'the Jimmy Dean syndrome' and also bought himself 'freedom' from adult supervision.[116] These aspects of his fame were greatly appealing to British teenagers, who continued to identify with him long after his initial flush of success. In 1967, a National Opinion Poll survey ranked Presley ninth in a Top Ten list of people most admired by British teenagers (in a list that included Queen Elizabeth II, the Prime Minister, and 'Mum' and 'Dad').[117]

The 'having it so good' ethos that propagated public concern about a vapid and directionless younger generation found parallels in Presley's commercial successes and financial excesses. Drawing as much attention as his film appearances, Presley's indiscriminate spending on Cadillacs and motorbikes, living in his mansion (Graceland), sporting gaudy Teddy boy fashion and buying lavish gifts for a series of girlfriends proved morbidly fascinating to the British media. To the establishment, this garish and frivolous lifestyle may have typified the worst example of working-class lad 'made good'. Admittedly, these oppositional attitudes were fuelled by Presley being an American: when young Tommy Steele earned a fortune in his crossover career he never received this harsh criticism.[118]

To the older generation, Presley's career appeared to be a specious stardom based on his sex appeal to young women rather than his vocal talents. The Svengali-like Tom Parker, a former circus promoter, who controlled the intricacies of his client's career, also diminished the entertainer's credibility. The book has now shown that Marlon Brando sustained an anti-Hollywood rhetoric; and sudden death had 'authenticated' James Dean's screen rebellion. In contrast, Presley's ostentation exposed the machinations – and reaffirmed the hegemony – of the Hollywood film industry.

Unlike Bill Haley and Pat Boone, Presley never performed in Britain although press releases about an imminent tour periodically appeared in the media throughout his career. This meant that the fans who met Presley in person after his army service at Prestwick airport were the only ones to do so on British soil. After a two-year hiatus, Presley was apprehensive about resuming his movie career. When a Scottish reporter probed him on his future in films, Presley commented: 'Ah [*sic*] would like to branch out and do something more serious. But nothing like Shakespeare. Ah know my limitations.'[119] What are we to assume from this statement? That he wanted to develop his acting craft as Brando and Dean had? That he wanted to resume the high quality work reminiscent of *King Creole*'s pithy narrative? An overview of Presley's later films demonstrates the schism between the types of film work offered him before and after his army service. Paul McCartney was disappointed at the change and has described Presley's earliest star persona – the transgressive anti-hero – as the most compelling for him and his fellow Beatles. 'I think all of us went off Elvis after he went in the army', McCartney commented. 'He was so magical before the army … When he went in the army, it all got "Sir, Sir, yes Sir".'[120]

Whatever acting ambitions Presley harboured, the first film he completed after army service was *GI Blues* (Norman Taurog, 1960).

Exploiting his recent military experiences, Presley plays Tulsa McLean, a tank crewman based in West Germany, who aspires to a singing career and owning a nightclub. This film ruptures the charismatic screen rebel persona developed in early film roles and foregrounds the family-oriented, mainstream Presley. The memorable scene that has Presley singing *Wooden Heart* inside a puppet booth to a crowd of adoring children epitomises the 'new' Presley. Future films repeated the erstwhile 'all-singing, all-fighting man' formula and provided Presley with love triangles, opportunities to introduce new songs and dance on stage – if less sinuously – and beat up opponents in carefully choreographed fights. However, Presley reprised his juvenile delinquent role just once. In *Wild in the Country* (Philip Dunne, 1961), Presley played a troubled young Southerner on probation assigned to a counsellor (Hope Lange), who encourages him to nurture his talent for writing.

By 1958, Hollywood had reformulated a hillbilly singer as a global superstar and, in so doing, prototyped an imitable 'fame formula'. British impresarios, shrewd enough to capitalise on the power of teenage consumers, realised the lucrative possibilities of nurturing a stable of home-grown stars in Presley's mould. Finally, British teenagers would have their own Marlon Brandos, James Deans and Elvis Presleys, who negotiated Hollywood-style glamour and the ordinariness of the boy-next-door.

Notes

1 'Elvis Presley exclusive: "Why do they criticise me?"', *Photoplay* [GB], 8:12 (December 1957), p. 26.

2 Cecil Wilson, '*Jailhouse Rock*', *Daily Mail*, 17 January 1958, p. 4.

3 Ann Murphy quoted in Emma O'Neill, 'In pictures: when Elvis landed at Prestwick Airport', *The Scotsman*, 3 March 2016. Available at: www.scotsman.com/lifestyle/in-pictures-when-elvis-presley-landed-at-prestwick-airport-1–4042750 (last accessed 19 February 2018).

4 Brian Beacom, 'Why Elvis still lives on in Prestwick', *The Herald*, 7 January 2016. Available at: www.heraldscotland.com/news/14187979.Why_Elvis_still_lives_on_in_Prestwick/ (last accessed 19 February 2018).

5 Gregory L. Reece, *Elvis Religion: Exploring the Cult of the King* (London: I. B. Tauris, 2006).

6 David Frost wrote and presented *Elvis: He Touched Their Lives* (David Green, Yorkshire Television, 1980).

7 Andrew Caine, *Interpreting Rock Films: Pop Films and its Critics in Britain* (Manchester: Manchester University Press, 2004).

8 David E. James, *Rock 'n' Film: Cinema's Dance with Popular Music* (Oxford: Oxford University, 2016), p. 16.

9 Sue Harper and Vincent Porter, 'Cinema audience tastes in 1950s Britain', in *Journal of Popular Cinema* (No. 2, 1999), p. 67; Ross McKibbin, *Classes and Cultures: England 1918–1951* (Oxford: Oxford University Press: 2000), pp. 419–21.

10 Bill Osgerby, *Youth in Britain Since 1945* (Oxford: Blackwell 1998), pp. 35–41; Dominic Sandbrook, *Never Had it so Good: A History of Britain from Suez to the Beatles* (London: Abacus, 2006), pp. 435–41.

11 Eric Hopkins provides an authoritative overview in *The Rise and Decline of the English Working Classes 1918–1990: A Social History* (London: Weidenfeld & Nicolson, 1991).

12 Teenager David Lowe was 'The Presley fan', *Daily Mail*, 5 March 1957, p. 3.

13 *Kinematograph Weekly*, No. 2630, 9 January 1958, front cover and '*Jailhouse Rock*', p. 29.

14 Douglas Brode, *Elvis and Popular Culture* (Jefferson, NC: McFarland, 2006), p. 45.

15 Taglines and references to promotional lobby cards and copy are taken from the *Jailhouse Rock* pressbook (MGM, 1957, BFI microfiche).

16 *Ibid.*

17 Thomas Doherty considers the Shark/Artie West roles representative of the psychotic juvenile delinquent who functions as a foil to the more human young hero. See *Teenagers and Teenpics: The Juvenilization of American Movies in the 1950s* (Philadelphia: Temple University Press, 2002), p. 108.

18 Taglines and copy are sourced from the *King Creole* pressbook (Columbia, 1958, BFI microfiche).

19 '*Jailhouse Rock*', *Kinematograph Weekly*, 9 January 1958, p. 29.

20 '*King Creole*', *Kinematograph Weekly*, No. 2659, 31 July 1958, p. 16.

21 Don Iddon, a British news correspondent in New York, reported that juvenile gang members copied Presley's style. See 'Beat the terror gangs or get out!' *Daily Mail*, 4 September 1957, p. 6. Linda Martin and Kerry Segrave examine widespread opposition to Presley and rock 'n' roll in *Anti-Rock: The Opposition to Rock 'n' Roll* (Hamden, CT: Archon, 1988).

22 'Elvis Presley exclusive: 'Why do they criticise me?', p. 26.

23 'Love me tender', *Monthly Film Bulletin*, 24:276, 1 January 1957, pp. 7–8.
24 A. T. L. Watkins, 'Censorship in Britain', *Films in Review*, 2:3, 2 March 1951, p. 17. See also, John Trevelyan, 'Censored! How and why we do it', *Films and Filming*, 4:10, July 1958, pp. 8 and 33.
25 Martin E. Pryke, Guildford, Surrey, 'Those terrible "A"s', *Films and Filming*, 4:5 (February 1958), p. 3.
26 Margaret O'Brien and Allen Eyles (eds), *Enter the Dream-House: Memories of Cinemas in South London from the Twenties to the Sixties* (London: Museum of the Moving Image, 1993), pp. 171–2.
27 Arthur Watkins explained that cuts could shift 'borderline' films to less restrictive categories in Leonard Wallace, 'The censor talks about his X', *Picturegoer*, 23:879, 8 March 1952, pp. 8–9; A. T. L. Watkins, 'We don't like to cut it', *Today's Cinema*, 84:7176, 5 January 1955, p. 107.
28 Arthur Watkins, 'Notes on the play: Serious Charge', 5 March 1955 (*Serious Charge*, BBFC Files).
29 *Victim* (Basil Dearden, 1961) deals with a blackmail plot of several gay men including a married barrister (Dirk Bogarde).
30 Bill Evans, 'Cliff Calls Off his Germany Date with Presley: "Blame the US army not me" says Britain's teenage rock star', *Disc*, 66, 9 May 1959, pp. 8–9.
31 Reader's Report (unnamed), 8 September 1958 (*Serious Charge*, BBFC Files).
32 Examiner's report 'VHS classification', 'Second VHS report in favour of PG', 24 April 1986 and 'Disagreement preference for 15', 7 May 1986 (*Serious Charge*, BBFC Files).
33 Miss J. Brown, Liskeard, Cornwall, 'Clothes line', *Picturegoer*, 35:1203, 24 May 1958, p. 3.
34 These comments are taken from GL/WGT Video Classification report, 11 July 1986. On 18 June 1992, in a subsequent report assessing the impact of the film for a colourised version, the examiner described it as 'an ancient Presley vehicle' (*Jailhouse Rock*, BBFC Files).
35 JW/Tandy, 'Video Classification Report', 25 November 1985 (*King Creole*, BBFC Microfiche).
36 Miriam Hansen, *Babel and Babylon: Spectatorship in American Silent Film* (Cambridge, MA: Harvard University Press, 1991), p. 269.
37 Richard Maltby, *Hollywood Cinema* (Oxford: Blackwell, 1995), pp. 340–1.
38 JW/Tandy, 25 November 1985 (BBFC Microfiche).
39 All of Presley's early biography mentions his passion for cinemagoing. See for example, Charles Kirschner, 'Meet the incredible Elvis Presley', *Picturegoer*, 32:1121, 27 October 1956 and *Picturegoer*, 32:1124, 17

November 1956; Paul Simpson, *Elvis Films FAQ: All That's Left to Know About the King of Rock 'n' Roll in Hollywood* (Kenner, LA: Applause Books, 2013), xix; David Bret, *Elvis: The Hollywood Years* (London: Robson Books, 2001).

40 'Elvis Presley', *Daily Express*, 26 February 1957 (*Elvis Presley*, BFI microfiche).

41 John Balfour, 'Film star Presley sends them too', *Daily Sketch*, 23 November 1956 (*Elvis Presley*, BFI microfiche).

42 Margaret Hinxman, 'Can Presley survive this film?', *Picturegoer*, 32:1129, 22 December 1956, p. 5.

43 Penelope Houston, *The Contemporary Cinema* (Harmondsworth: Penguin, 1966), pp. 175–6.

44 Virginia Lewis, 'A plea for integrity in pictures', *Film Review*, 8:2 (February 1958), pp. 22–3. Lewis had high praise for *On the Waterfront*, *Blackboard Jungle* and *Rebel Without a Cause*.

45 Pierre Bourdieu, *Distinction: A Social Critique of the Judgement of Taste*, trans. Richard Nice (London: Routledge, 1984), pp. 6–7.

46 Andrew James Caine, '"Calculated violence and viciousness": the British critical reaction to Elvis Presley's *King Creole*', *Velvet Light Trap*, 48 (2001), pp. 34–48.

47 '*Jailhouse Rock*', *Monthly Film Bulletin*, 25:288, 1 January 1958, p. 22. Presley reputedly contributed original material to Alex Romero's choreography. See Patrick Humphries, *Elvis: The #1 Hits* (Kansas City: Andrew McMeel Publishing, 2002), p. 52.

48 As observed by James Powers, '*Jailhouse Rock*: good Berman-Thorpe bright attraction', *The Hollywood Reporter*, 16 October 1957, p. 3.

49 Dilys Powell, '*Jailhouse Rock*', *Sunday Times*, 19 January 1958, p. 21.

50 Donald Zec, 'Elvis, you're a bore', *Daily Mirror*, 16 January 1958, p. 11.

51 '*King Creole*', *Monthly Film Bulletin*, 1 January 1958, p. 115.

52 Derek Prouse, 'The gilt-edge', *Sunday Times*, 31 August 1958, p. 8.

53 Eric Gillet, 'Feud in the South', *Daily Telegraph*, 30 August 1958, p. 9. 'King Creole', *Manchester Guardian*, 30 August 1958, p. 3.

54 Philip Sleigh, High Wycombe, Bucks, *Picturegoer*, 35:1224, 10 May 1958, p. 4.

55 M. Gibson, 'Should Presley stop singing?', *Picturegoer*, 36:1224, 18 October 1958, p. 4.

56 Dick Richards, 'Tough guys', *Daily Mirror*, 29 August 1958, p. 12.

57 Fred Majdalany, 'Precision', *Daily Mail*, 29 August 1958, p. 6.

58 Ker Robertson, 'Elvis Presley', 15 October 1956, *Daily Sketch*, p. 8.

59 Balfour, 'Film star Presley sends them too'.

60 Powell, '*Jailhouse Rock*', p. 21.
61 Steve Neale, 'Masculinity as spectacle: reflections on men and mainstream cinema', in Steven Cohan and Ina Race Hark (eds), *Screening the Male: Exploring the Male in Hollywood Cinema* (London and New York: Routledge, 1993), pp. 9–20 (p. 18).
62 Gaylun Studlar, 'Valentino: "optic intoxication" and dance madness', in Cohan and Race Hark (eds), *Screening the Male* (1993), pp. 23–45 (p. 35).
63 Hansen, *Babel and Babylon: Spectatorship in American Silent Film*, p. 272.
64 Mark Glancy, *Hollywood and the Americanization of Britain: From the 1920s to the Present* (London: I. B. Tauris, 2016), pp. 42–77.
65 Margaret Hinxman, 'Elvis Presley – gets his break at last', *Picturegoer*, 34:1165, 31 August 1957, p. 17.
66 Colin MacInnes, *England, Half English* (London: MacGibbon & Kee, 1961), p. 49.
67 Pam Hughes, Birmingham, *Photoplay* [GB], 8:3 (March 1957), p. 4.
68 'US scenes recall "Jungle bird house at the zoo"', *The Times*, 15 September 1956, p. 4.
69 Jack Payne, 'BBC speaks out on those phoney requests', *Daily Mail*, 13 June 1956, p. 4. Payne relayed his strong opposition to styling music to suit young consumers in 'Should we surrender to the teenagers?' *Melody Maker*, 23 June 1956, p. 5.
70 Tom Hutchinson, 'This man is dangerous', *Picturegoer*, 32:1107, 21 July 1956, p. 10.
71 Charles Swann, 'Clean it up Presley', *Picturegoer*, 34:1182, 28 December 1957, p. 18.
72 Anita D. Milson, Hatch End, Middlesex, *Picturegoer*, 33:1136, 9 February 1957, p. 3.
73 The national poll results were reprinted in the *Daily Mail*, 24 September 1957, p. 7; Scottish poll results were reprinted in 'Hero Worship in Schools, Pupils Select Sir W. Churchill', *The Times*, 30 December 1958, p. 3.
74 Quoted in Claire Webb, 'Joanna Lumley: Elvis and me', *Radio Times*, 12 May 2017 Available at: www.radiotimes.com/news/2017–08–12/joanna-lumley-on-finding-elvis-in-memphis-and-meeting-priscilla-presley/ (last accessed 20 October 2017). Additional comments are taken from the TV broadcast *Joanna Lumley: Elvis and Me* (Ian Denyer, Sony Music, 2015).
75 See for example, 'No rock round the mid-day clock', *Daily Mail*, 26 January 1957, p. 3; 'Children at 3d. rock 'n' roll', *Birmingham Daily Post*, 19 January 1957, p. 1; 'Ban on rock so they loiter in the quad',

Birmingham Daily Post, 8 February 1957, p. 27; 'Rock sessions: JPs ban children', *Birmingham Daily Post*, 13 March 1957, p. 36.

76 Pat Boone's persona was developed in stories such as Gordon Campbell, 'He's the odd man out', *Picturegoer*, 32:1111, 18 August 1956, p. 20; Sarah Stoddart, 'Now it's Boone versus Presley', *Picturegoer*, 32:1130, 16 August 1958, p. 5. Donovan Pedelty, 'Pat Boone breaks that kiss ban', *Picturegoer*, 38:1266, 26 September 1959, p. 7.

77 Derek Walker, 'Is Pat Boone too good to be true?', *Picturegoer*, 33:1144, 6 April 1957, p. 7.

78 Mark Carlyle, 'The gimmick boys take a beating', *Picturegoer*, 32:1130, 29 December 1956, p. 20.

79 Ian Hart, 'How Elvis made a million', *Photoplay* [GB], 8:7 (July 1957), pp. 10–11. See also 'Elvis in the money', *Daily Mail*, 31 May 1957, p. 4; Donald Zec, 'Elvis you're a bore', *Daily Mirror*, 16 January 1958, p. 11; 'Singer's father retires at age of 39', *The Times*, 20 September 1956, p. 5.

80 Alison Settle, 'Viewpoint', *The Times*, 23 September 1956, p. 3; 'Those wild, wild girls', *Picture Post*, Issue 13, 1 April 1957, pp. 14–15.

81 Mark Abrams, *Teenage Consumer Spending in 1959* (London: London Press Exchange, 1961).

82 Harry Hopkins, *The New Look: A Social History of the Forties and Fifties in Britain* (London: Secker & Warburg, 1963), p. 427.

83 See for example, Hilde Marchant, 'The truth about Teddy boys and girls', *Picture Post*, 29 May 1954, pp. 25–7; and Trevor Philpott, 'The truth about teenagers: the world at their feet', *Picture Post*, 8 April 1957, pp. 25–6 and 29. Arthur Bryant's foreword in Pearl Jephcott, *Some Young People* (London: Allen & Unwin, 1954), pp. 6–7.

84 Sandbrook, *Never Had it so Good*, p. 461.

85 Osgerby, *Youth in Britain*, p. 38.

86 Nik Cohn, *Awopbopaloobop Alopbamboom: Pop from the Beginning* (London: Macmillan, 1970), p. 16.

87 Cliff Richard broadcast interview, *Kings of Rock 'n' Roll* (Fay Gibson, BBC, 2008).

88 Pip Evans, 'The rebels', *Photoplay* [GB], 8:1 (January 1957), pp. 8–9.

89 'Britain sweeps the board in our annual awards', *Picturegoer*, 35:1204, 31 May 1958, p. 5.

90 'Bogarde triumphs again', *Picturegoer*, 37:1255, 23 May 1959, p. 5. Presley ranked third in the Top Singer category (Boone was first).

91 Donald Zec, 'Angry young letter', *Daily Mirror*, 23 January 1958, p. 6.

92 Margaret Hinxman, 'You go for Presley', *Picturegoer*, 33:1133, 19 January 1957, pp. 12–14.

93 Cliff Richard was interviewed in a TV broadcast. *The Nation's Number One Elvis Song* (Shiver Productions, ITV, 2013).
94 Two influential studies are Helen Taylor, *Scarlett's Women: Gone With the Wind and its Female Fans* (London: Virago, 1989); and Jackie Stacey, *Star Gazing: Hollywood Female Spectatorship* (London: Routledge, 1994).
95 Pauline Barnard, Cornwall, '*The Wild One*', *Picturegoer*, 33:1136, 9 February 1957, p. 3.
96 Ray Gosling, *Personal Copy* (London: Faber & Faber, 1980), pp. 39–40.
97 Gillian A. M. Mitchell, 'Reassessing "the Generation Gap": Bill Haley's 1957 tour of Britain, inter-generational relations and attitudes to rock 'n' roll in the late 1950s', *Twentieth Century British History*, 24:4 (2013), pp. 573–605 (p. 576).
98 George Melly, *Revolt into Style: The Pop Arts in the 50s and 60s* (Oxford: Oxford University Press, 1989 [1970]), p. 45.
99 'Eye on Presley 2', *Photoplay*, January 1957, p. 5; Raymond Hyams (ed.), 'Fanfare', *Photoplay*, July 1957, p. 54.
100 Paul McCartney quoted in Philip Norman, *Paul McCartney: The Biography* (London: Weidenfeld & Nicolson), pp. 53–4.
101 Patrick Doncaster, 'Now Britain gets a Presley! But rock 'n' roll Tommy says "I hate him"', *Daily Mirror*, 27 September 1956, p. 19.
102 Robert Plant broadcast interview. Available at: www.youtube.com/watch?v=gP-zcXtiXhA (last accessed 14 October 2017) and Paul Rees, *Robert Plant: A Life* (London: HarperCollins, 2013), pp. 17–19.
103 Victor Bockris, *Keith Richards: The Biography* (London: Da Capo Press, 2003), pp. 27 and 33.
104 Cliff Richard interview. *The Nation's Favourite Elvis Songs*.
105 Quoted in Ronald Morris, 'Eager Richard', *Picturegoer*, 39:1280, 2 January 1960, p. 4. Cliff Richard achieved a lifelong goal of making a [digitally achieved] duet of *Blue Suede Shoes* with Presley for the album, *Just … Fabulous Rock 'n' Roll* (Sony, 2016).
106 Robert Muller, 'A talk with Terry Dene, *Daily Mail*, 12 February 1958, p. 6. Dene is included in David E. James's chapter, 'Back in the UK: the English Elvises', in his book *Rock 'n' Film: Cinema's Dance with Popular Music*, pp. 123–37.
107 The best anecdotal examples (subsequently recycled by recent biographers) are taken from Albert Goldman, *The Lives of John Lennon* (New York: Bantam Books, 1989), pp. 62–3.
108 John Lennon interview with Tom Snyder, *The Tomorrow Show* (NBC, 1975) Available at: www.youtube.com/watch?v=lAOkNc-7pVU (last accessed 10 October 2017).

109 John Lennon interview. Available at: www.youtube.com/watch?v=BegLdgqf-_s (last accessed 13 October 2017).
110 Unnamed sources, Allison Pressley, *The 50s and 60s, The Best of Times: Growing up and Being Young in Britain* (London: Michael O'Mara Books, 2003), pp. 114–15.
111 Veronica Tomkins (Hanwell, London), 'Let us scream', *Picturegoer*, 35:1201, 10 May 1958, p. 4.
112 '10 injured as cinema ceiling collapses, Marble Arch Odeon audience calm', *The Times*, 19 September 1958, p. 1; and 'Elvis did not bring the house down, expert's assurance on effect of sound', *The Times*, 20 September 1958.
113 John S. McGowan, Stourbridge, 'Teddy ordeal', *Films and Filming*, 4:7 (April 1958), p. 3.
114 Michael Shore, *The Rolling Stone Book of Rock Videos* (New York: Quill, 1984), p. 43.
115 'Films of to-morrow and their public', *The Times*, 6 November 1957, p. 3.
116 Vernon Scott, 'Elvis – ten million dollars later', in Ira Peck (ed), *The New Sound, Yes* (New York: The Four Winds Press, 1965), pp. 62–75. Jonathan Gould also argues the juvenility of rock 'n' roll as a musical form. See, *Can't Buy Me Love: The Beatles and America* (New York: Three Rivers Press, 2008), p. 103.
117 Julian Holland, 'Who'd have expected this teenage top ten?', *Daily Mail*, 29 November 1967, p. 6. The Beatles received less than twenty votes between them.
118 Rivalry between Tommy Steele and Elvis Presley played out in fan magazines. See Caine, *Interpreting Rock Films*, pp. 121–6. Colin MacInnes suggests that Tommy Steele was 'nicer' and a 'more ordinary' option for British teenagers in 'Pop stars and teenagers' (February 1958), reprinted in H. Kureishi and J. Savage (eds), *The Faber Book of Pop* (London: Faber & Faber, 1995), p. 89.
119 'Elvis rocks Scot fans for an hour', *Daily Record*, 2 March 1960.
120 Paul McCartney, broadcast interview with Charlie Rose (PBS, 1992). Available at: https://charlierose.com/guests/1855 (last accessed 14 May 2018).

Conclusion
The rise of the Angry Young Men

> It was pre-sixties. People were looking for rebellion. I happened to be in the right place at the right time with the right state of mind. In a sense, [*The Wild One*] was my own story, rebelling for the sake of rebelling.
>
> Marlon Brando, *Listen to Me Marlon* (2015)[1]

Entitling the book *Screening the Hollywood rebels* serves its main objectives: namely, to re-evaluate how the British censors screened these cinematic images of masculine rebellion before home audiences saw them; and to explore how British critics and audiences interacted with these screen images. With the exception of *Rock Around the Clock*, the wrangles for creative control between the British censors and the Hollywood studios reconfigured all the case study films. The censors modified these classic American films and restricted exhibition to adults aged 16 or above. As discussed, they banned *The Wild One* in 1953 and did not grant it a certificate of general exhibition until 1968. These extreme actions were a response to the widespread public concern about the 'Teddy boy problem' and attest to the BBFC's similarly negative attitudes to young people. The film examiners held to the 'hypodermic needle effect' of glamorised screen rebellion and used the protection of the X certificate to wield control over viewing pleasures. No other country banned *The Wild One*, consequently the film's British history is particularly significant.

While James Dean is central to American cultural memory of 1950s rebellion, Marlon Brando's anti-hero status persisted in Britain. When Brando died in 2004, two images proliferated in the British press to emblematise the actor's successes and his own turbulent life: young Brando as the freewheeling motorcyclist Johnny Strabler and mature Brando as the Italian mobster, Vito Corleone in *The Godfather* (Francis Ford Coppola, 1972).

Hollywood's films about juvenile delinquents predated and arguably influenced the Angry Young Men of the British New Wave. When John Osborne's play *Look Back in Anger* was adapted for the screen, and directed by Tony Richardson in 1959, the attractive stage-trained Richard Burton, himself a poor Welsh coalminer's son, imbued the role of Jimmy Porter with an exciting, rough-edged authenticity. However, the film, which retained Osborne's discursive dialogue, proved unpopular with cinema audiences. Conversely, the enormously successful films, *Room at the Top* (Jack Clayton, 1959) and *Saturday Night and Sunday Morning* (Karel Reisz, 1960) disrupted British cinema and reoriented screen masculinities. In *Room at the Top*, Joe Lampton (Laurence Harvey), a lowly town clerk, seizes the opportunity to seduce the local industrial magnate's daughter for social gain. 'Things have changed since the war,' Lampton declares. 'If I want her, I'll have her.' In *Saturday Night*, Arthur Seaton (Albert Finney), a Nottingham factory worker, sets the tone for his high-spirited social rebellion in the film's opening scene with the statement: 'What I'm out for is a good time – all the rest is propaganda.' Evocative of Johnny Strabler's combative declarations, Arthur asserts his fierce independence with comments such as, 'I'm me and nobody else and whatever people think I am or say I am, that's what I'm not, because they don't know a bloody thing about me.'

Earlier British films about rebel men referenced an archetype familiar to post-war audiences. This type was physically attractive and desirable but ultimately doomed; narrative devices stripped him of kudos and revealed underlying psychosexual disorders. Unlike this trope, Arthur Seaton and Joe Lampton are not punished for freely pursuing their desires or indulging in sexual experimentation. The textual analyses undertaken in this research argue that the change in Hollywood masculinities was largely the result of inviting the cinematic gaze to the male. Screen rebels became the 'spectacle' through an industrialised production of charisma that foregrounded newly sexy-vulnerable masculinities. Brando and Dean were method actors, whose physically and emotionally unrestrained performances explored the range of human experience. In his juvenile delinquent roles, Elvis Presley projected his exoticism and earthiness in erotic dancing and unique delivery of songs. Significantly, Arthur Seaton and Joe Lampton transgress from earlier British tropes and display the tender-tough duality of the Hollywood rebels. Correspondingly, they are framed as the object of the cinematic gaze in the experimental narratives and formal techniques of British New Wave cinema. For example, Arthur's rambunctious nature is demonstrated in fight scenes and his youthful good looks and immaculate costuming are juxtaposed with the dowdy appearance of his older married lover (Rachel Roberts). Similarly, Joe's classically handsome features are privileged in scenes with his homely wife Susan (Heather Sears) and his middle-aged mistress, Alice (Simone Signoret).

This study has appraised how Brando's magnetic performances and Dean's posthumous stardom popularised method acting. The film reviewers of specialist cinema journals, who championed this experimental American acting, were dubious about the proliferation of the Young Rebel trope in European cinema.[2] *Violent Playground* (Basil Dearden, 1958) was the first of many British films that exploited their leading man's resemblance to James Dean and drew inspiration from the familiar Hollywood motifs of juvenile delinquency and rock 'n' roll. In the film, David McCallum – who had been promoted as 'the British James Dean' – plays Johnny, a maladjusted teenager whose troublesome behaviour is being monitored by a police sergeant (Stanley Baker). A particularly striking scene shows Johnny's teenage friends become entranced by the hypnotic power of American-style rock 'n' roll. In this scene, Johnny steps away from the police sergeant, unable to resist the frenzied rhythm and aggressive lyrics of the song. As Johnny begins to mirror the menacing dance moves of the other teenagers, the police sergeant comes to realise that Johnny is beyond rehabilitation.

The book has illustrated how the power of teenage consumerism sustained the stardom of the rebel males in Hollywood films. British working-class teenagers were the benefactors of the welfare state's expanded provision for longer state education, comprehensive healthcare and improvements to social housing. Fuller employment resulted in teenagers having the lowest outgoings and the largest margin for free spending. Colin MacInnes's pertinent contemporary essay recognised that a 'kitty' of teenage spending (in excess of £300,000,000) had the power to influence the British economy and change social patterns.[3] Various chapters have now outlined the trends of teenage spending and shown how British youngsters developed and sustained the stardom of Hollywood stars, often in contradiction to hostile media commentary. Kenneth Allsop, whose elitist views on literature and film have been mentioned, rebuked teenage consumerism for redefining the 1950s as 'a sick and meretricious society, with instability endemic and the values of a corrupt bobby-soxer'.[4]

Commentaries such as these disregard the agency of British teenagers and depict them as the unwitting victims of Americanisation. Just because British youngsters openly embraced aspects of American popular culture did not mean that they had been 'duped' by Hollywood. As the book shows, British teenagers of the 1950s used the platform offered to them by the Hollywood rebel film stars to create their own distinctive youth culture and eventually their own film stars. This agency is aptly demonstrated in the career trajectory of Adam Faith, who modelled himself on James Dean's characterisation of Jim Stark. '[Dean] was the model I'd been searching for. My hero did what he liked,' recounted Faith. 'He was the first teenager to say, "Sod what's gone. This is how it's going to be, from now on." … He was a REBEL. And that's what I wanted to be.'[5] Interpreting Dean's characterisation as open defiance of adult authority and hypocrisy, Faith transcended his class limitations to become a star of his own making. By similar means, Joe Brown, an actor-singer and a musician, referenced American popular culture to begin his career. Brown, who formed a skiffle band after seeing *Rock Around the Clock* in 1956, recalled: 'Kids in England, had nothing really. No fashion, there was no music. It was all blokes in white suits singing through a megaphone and that sort of thing.'[6] The chapter on Elvis Presley's early career demonstrates how the rebel trope transitioned and incorporated the iconography of rock 'n' roll. Teenage consumerism similarly created a niche for home-grown pop stars, which in turn reoriented British cinema.

Larry Parnes, an astute English impresario, was one of the first to exploit these cultural trends and groomed a group of British actor-singers in the Hollywood mould. One of the most successful was Billy Fury, who secured the lead role in a derivative film, *Play It Cool* (Michael Winner, 1962), about an immoral nightclub singer.[7] Early publicity capitalised on Fury's resemblance to Dean and drew further parallels by describing him as an emotional teenager looking to fall in love.[8] In fan materials, Fury became popular enough to articulate the generational gap that privileged newcomers and replaced seasoned entertainers: 'It all boils down to the fact that the teenagers want entertainers of their own age. It's just a change in taste.'[9]

This project has shown that the meanings and pleasures of Presley's stardom were connotative of his exoticism, transgressive rock 'n' roll meanings, and in his idealisation of the rags-to-riches mythology. Ordinary working-class fans participated in his stardom while others aspired to a similar career in film and music. Chapter 5 examined *Serious Charge*, the British film that introduced cinema audiences to Cliff Richard. The teenaged Richard worked in a factory in Cheshunt and used his adulation of Presley to propel his own career trajectory. 'My music changed my life – it stopped [my family] being poor,' Richard reminisced. 'But I didn't do it to stop being poor – I did it because I wanted to look and sound and sing like Elvis. Pure and simple.'[10]

Research in the book has shown that Presley's phenomenal fame was criticised for its ostentation and the singer's purported duplicity in exploiting British youngsters. Nik Cohn argues that parental authority was affronted because Presley 'brought it home just how economically powerful teenagers really could be', and further asserts that what began as a nebulous rebellion 'spawned its own style on clothes and language and sex, a total independence in almost everything'.[11] Indeed, Presley's iconography and motifs – scorned by an older generation – became the benchmark of success for imitative British pop stars. Billy Fury, for example, copied Presley's gold lamé suit and proudly wore it on stage; and he began to amass a collection of sports cars.[12] John Kennedy, who managed Tommy Steele – Presley's nominal arch-rival – similarly adopted aspects of Colonel Tom Parker's commodification of Presley's persona in producing branded merchandise for the express pleasure of Steele's teenage fans.[13]

The American press characteristically negotiated Presley's celebrity by reminding their readers of his family's extreme poverty and that before stardom he had driven a truck. In Britain, Presley's rags-to-riches biography spawned a new type of British pop star. For many young men, music and film careers had seemed inconceivable but now their working-class origins became essential motifs of authenticity and contemporaneity. Hence, Tommy Steele and his younger brother, Colin Hicks, Terry Dene, Marty Wilde and Joe Brown, among others, from London's most deprived neighbourhoods were

Figure 6.1 Billy Fury became very successful as a 'James Dean type'. As Fury gained popularity, he wore a gold lamé suit like Elvis Presley's on stage and began a sports car collection.

not impeded by their backgrounds or distinctive Cockney diction. In fact, their popularity was sustained by their identification with working-class (but affluent) teenage fans. 'The current trend is for Cockney voices', explained Paul Lincoln, the owner of the Two I's, a Soho cafe where emerging British pop stars were showcased. Lincoln concluded that times had changed and commented, 'Good diction's a handicap.'[14]

This book has demonstrated that Hollywood's rebel stars satisfied specific social and cultural functions for British audiences in the post-war period. In their interactions with Hollywood films, British teenagers generated their own meanings from star images and, because of their purchasing power, participated in and characterised a transcultural dialogue between the USA and Britain. By the mid-1960s, the so-called 'British invasion' – spearheaded by Beatlemania – marked a period of enormous influence of British popular culture in the USA. A new generation of young Americans celebrated British pop stars and film stars, writers and satirists, artists and photographers,

Figure 6.2 Evoking Elvis Presley's 'rebel of song' persona, Cliff Richard debuted in *Serious Charge* (1959) as a juvenile delinquent who sang and danced to rock 'n' roll.

hair stylists and fashion designers. Eventually, this transcultural exchange would inform and influence the counterculture that came to define the 1960s for subsequent generations. The American sociologist, Herbert Gans, was one of the first academics to theorise on Beatlemania in the USA and argued for the significance of cross-cultural exchange: 'Nations develop the images they hold of other nations in order to satisfy social and emotional needs that cannot be met at home.'[15]

This analysis of classic Hollywood films and iconic American stars marks a key intervention in the burgeoning field of transnational film reception studies. In so doing, it reiterates the power of the teenage consumer and argues for the enduring legacies of Hollywood's rebel trope in British popular culture of the 1960s. In its wider application, it is hoped that the book has enriched our knowledge and understanding of transcultural exchange during a fascinating era of societal transition.

An epilogue: Beatlemania in the USA

Between the 1950s and early 1960s, British youth culture had absorbed and reconfigured some of the motifs of the Hollywood rebel films in what may be termed a 'cross-cultural' exchange. Perhaps the best example of this assimilation and export of American popular culture back to its natural home was the spectacular success of 'Beatlemania' or 'The Beatles invasion' of the USA. Paul McCartney and John Lennon, as recounted, were fans of Presley's rock 'n' roll and went regularly to the cinema to watch his films. Early publicity photos of the Beatles reveal that before they adopted their recognisable Europeanised suits and distinctive haircuts, they borrowed motifs and iconography from the Hollywood rebel films.

Reminiscent of the British teenagers who had descended en masse to greet Bill Haley at Southampton dockside in 1957, thousands of American teenagers greeted the Beatles when they arrived at JFK Airport in 1964. Commonalities between Elvis Presley and the Beatles were immediately noted by the American media. One American reporter observed: 'Multiply Elvis Presley by four, subtract six years from his age, add British accents and a sharp sense of humor [*sic*]. The answer: It's the Beatles (Yeah, Yeah, Yeah).'[16] To negotiate the Beatles phenomenon, the American media – adopting superior notions of a host culture – projected negative opinions on the lesser talents of these British pop stars compared to their home-grown musicians.[17] However, American teenagers responded to the exoticism of the Beatles in not altogether dissimilar terms that tempered how British teenagers had reacted to Presley, a few years earlier. 'They're just so different,' enthused one American teenage girl, waiting to meet the Beatles at JFK. 'I mean, all that hair. American singers are so clean-cut.'[18]

The British media's discussion of Presley's humble beginnings found parallels in the American press which now emphasised the Beatles' working-class origins. Press conferences were enlivened by the group's ebullience, their candidness and their irreverence to serious issues. These traits characterised the Beatles as authentic and contemporary, iconoclastic and exciting.[19] While Ringo Starr's upbringing was modest, there was little mention that John Lennon, Paul McCartney and George Harrison had attended grammar school and lived fairly comfortably in the suburbs of Liverpool. What was important was to present these four Liverpudlian lads as slightly transgressive and resistant to parental authority and establishment codes. The dynamism and sumptuous material excess of American popular culture of the 1950s had fascinated British teenagers emerging from the gloom of post-war austerity. By the 1960s, the cheerful, optimistic sound of the Beatles ameliorated a pessimistic era of American politics, still recovering from President Kennedy's shocking assassination. The Beatles exported a peculiarly British quirkiness, buoyed by the popularity of the Cambridge satirists such as Jonathan Miller, the emergence of the ultra-British gentleman James Bond, the fashions of Mary Quant, and the tradition and glamour of a young Royal family.

In response to Beatlemania, an older generation of Americans attempted to rationalise the group's appeal and popularity in much the same way that Presley's early stardom had generated reappraisals of popular American culture in the British media.[20] The harsher American critics disparaged the commodification of the group and the enormous revenues accrued through the sale of their branded merchandise. Teenage identification with the Beatles took many forms but none more conspicuous than American boys discarding the GI haircut and wearing Beatles wigs or growing their hair longer.[21] Significantly, when the Beatles appeared on the prestigious *Ed Sullivan Show* – the TV programme that had launched the young Presley – more than 50,000 young fans applied for 1,500 tickets and 'outdrew' Presley's TV appearance.[22]

The Hollywood rebels of the 1950s and the Beatles endure as twentieth-century icons of popular culture. This book is about what happens when commodified star images cross borders. One Hollywood rebel is among the famous faces that feature on the iconic album cover of *Sgt Pepper's Lonely Hearts Club Band*. Behind the wax models of the Beatles is Marlon Brando's image as Johnny Strabler in *The Wild One*.

Notes

1 The quote is taken from *Listen to Me Marlon* (Steven Riley, 2015), a documentary film that sustains its continuous narration through a compilation of Marlon Brando's personal archived recordings.

2 Peter John Dyer, 'The Teenage Rave: youth and cinema: part one', *Sight and Sound*, 29:1 (Winter 1959), pp. 26–30 (p. 26) and 'Candid camera: youth and cinema: part two', *Sight and Sound*, 29:2 (Spring 1960), pp. 61–4 (p. 62).

3 Colin MacInnes, *England, Half English* (London: MacGibbon & Kee, 1961), p. 54.

4 Kenneth Allsop, *The Angry Decade: A Survey of the Cultural Revolt of the Nineteen-fifties* (Wendover: John Goodchild Publishers, 1985 [1958]), p. 32.

5 Adam Faith, *Acts of Faith: The Autobiography of Adam Faith* (London: Bantam Books, 1996 [large print]), p. 25.

6 Joe Brown quoted in *The Kings of Rock and Roll* (Fay Gibson, BBC, 2009).

7 'Billy Fury will do a James Dean in a new film', *Disc*, 2 March 1963, p. 6.

8 Fury was described as an overly emotional and vulnerable figure. See Chris Peters, 'Billy Fury: "I'm Forever Falling in Love"', *Disc*, 107, 9 April 1960, p. 4.

9 Tony Wells, 'And 2 rock men reply', *Picturegoer*, 38:1263, 5 September 1959, p. 8.

10 Cliff Richard, broadcast interview. *The Kings of Rock 'n' Roll* (Fay Gibson, BBC, 2009).

11 Nik Cohn, *Awopbopaloobop Alopbamboom: Pop from the Beginning* (London: Macmillan, 1970), p. 19.

12 Peters, 'Billy Fury: "I'm Forever Falling in Love"', p. 4.

13 Cynthia Figg, 'The coffee-bar sensation', *Picturegoer*, 32:1126, 1 December 1956, p. 18.

14 Tony Brown, 'Our singing kids take over', *Picturegoer*, 34:1171, 12 October 1957, p. 8.

15 Herbert J. Gans, 'Who's o-o-oh in America', *Vogue* [US], 145:6, 15 March 1965, pp. 108, 151.

16 Paul Gardner, '3,000 fans greet British Beatles', 8 February 1964, *New York Times*, pp. 25, 49.
17 Alfred G. Aronowitz, 'Music's gold bugs: The Beatles', in Ira Peck (ed.), *The New Sound/Yes* (New York: The Four Winds Press, 1965); 'The Beatles, four parody singers, now the passion of British young', *Vogue*, 143:1, 1 January 1964, pp. 100–1. Both authors draw parallels between American rock 'n' roll, Presley and The Beatles.
18 Danielle Landau, 15, quoted in Gardner, '3000 fans greet British Beatles', *New York Times*, p. 25.
19 David E. James, *Rock 'n' Film: Cinema's Dance with Popular Music* (Oxford: Oxford University Press, 2016), p. 138; Jonathan Gould, *Can't Buy Me Love: The Beatles and America* (New York: Three Rivers Press, 2008), pp. 177–8.
20 Aronowitz, 'Music's gold bugs: The Beatles', pp. 45–61. See also, Bruce Jay Friedman, 'The new sounds' for an American perspective on the young record-buyer in Peck (1965), pp. 11–20.
21 Paul Gardner, 'The British boys: high-brows and no-brows', 9 February 1964, *New York Times*, p. 19.
22 'At deadline: Beatles outdraw Presley', *New Yorker Times*, 3 February 1964, p. 9.

Filmography

A Streetcar Named Desire (Elia Kazan, 1951, USA)
Blackboard Jungle (Richard Brooks, 1955, USA)
Cosh Boy (Lewis Gilbert, 1953, UK)
Dead End (William Wyler, 1937, USA)
Don't Knock the Rock (Fred F. Sears, 1956, USA)
East of Eden (Elia Kazan, 1955, USA)
Giant (George Stevens, 1955, USA)
GI Blues (Norman Taurog, 1961, USA)
Island of Lost Souls (Erle C. Kenton, 1932, USA)
Jailhouse Rock (Richard Thorpe, 1957, USA)
Julius Caesar (Joseph L. Mankiewicz, 1953, USA)
King Creole (Michael Curtiz, 1958, USA)
Lilies of the Field (Ralph Nelson, 1963, USA)
Listen to Me Marlon (Stephen Riley, 2015, USA)
Look Back in Anger (Tony Richardson, 1956, UK)
Love Me Tender (Robert D.Webb, 1956, USA)
Loving You (Hal Kanter, 1957, USA)
Mad at the World (Robert Essex, 1955, USA)
My Teenage Daughter (Herbert Wilcox, 1956, UK)
One-Eyed Jacks (Marlon Brando, 1961, USA)
On The Waterfront (Elia Kazan, 1954, USA)
Play It Cool (Michael Winner, 1962, UK)
Rebel Without a Cause (Nicholas Ray, 1955, USA)
Rock Around the Clock (Fred F. Sears, 1956, USA)
Rock Pretty Baby (Richard Bartlett, 1956, USA)
Room at The Top (Jack Clayton, 1959, UK)
Running Wild (Abner Biberman, 1955, USA)
Saturday Night and Sunday Morning (Karel Reisz,1960, UK)

Serious Charge (Terence Young, 1959, UK)
Shake, Rattle and Rock (Edward L. Cahn, 1956, USA)
Spare the Rod (Leslie Norman, 1961, UK)
The Blue Lamp (Basil Dearden, 1950, UK)
The Girl Can't Help It (Frank Tashlin, 1956, USA)
The Godfather (Francis Ford Coppola, 1972, USA)
The James Dean Story (Robert Altman and George W. George, 1957, USA)
The Lion Has Wings (Adrian Brunel, Brian Desmond Hurst, Alexander Korda and Michael Powell, 1939, UK)
The Wild One (Laslo Benedek, 1953, USA)
To Sir With Love (James Clavell, 1967, UK)
Violent Playground (Basil Dearden, 1958, UK)
We Are the Lambeth Boys (Karel Reisz, 1958, UK)
Wild in the Country (Philip Dunne, 1961, USA)

Bibliography

Please note that individual articles published between 1942 and 1965 from the following periodicals are cited at the end of each chapter: *Films and Filming*, *Films in Review*, *Film Review*, *Kinematograph Weekly*, *Monthly Film Bulletin*, *Photoplay* [GB], *Picturegoer*, *Picture Post*, *Picture Show*, *Sight and Sound* and *Variety*.

Articles

Aldgate, Tony, '*I Am a Camera*: film and theatre censorship in 1950s Britain', *Contemporary European History*, 8:3 (November 1999), pp. 425–38.

Aronowitz, Alfred G., 'Music's gold bugs: The Beatles', in Ira Peck (ed.), *The New Sound/Yes* (New York: The Four Winds Press, 1965), pp. 45–61.

Baker, David, 'Rock rebels and delinquents: the emergence of the rock rebel in 1950s "Youth Problem" Films', *Continuum*, 19:1 (2005), pp. 39–54.

Barlow, M. L., 'Coming of age 1926–1976', *American Vocational Journal*, 51:5 (May 1976), pp. 63–88.

Bathurst, M. E., 'Juvenile delinquency in Britain during the war', in *Journal of Criminal Law and Criminology*, 34:5 (Article 1, 1944), pp. 291–302.

Bell, Amy Helen, 'Teddy boys and girls as neo-flâneurs in post-war London', *The Literary London Journal*, 11:2 (Autumn 2014), pp. 3–17.

Caine, Andrew James, '"Calculated violence and viciousness": The British critical reaction to Elvis Presley's *King Creole*', *Velvet Light Trap* 48 (2001), pp. 34–48.

Chibnall, Steve, 'Whistle and zoot: the changing meaning of a suit of clothes', *History Workshop Journal*, 20:1 (1 October 1985), pp. 56–81.

Cross, Robert J., 'The Teddy boy as scapegoat', *Doshisha Studies, Language and Culture* 1–2 (1998), pp. 263–91.

Friedman, Bruce Jay, 'The New Sounds', in Ira Peck (ed.), *The New Sound/ Yes* (New York: The Four Winds Press, 1965), pp. 11–20.

Glancy, Mark, '*Picturegoer*: The fan magazine and popular film culture in Britain during the Second World War', *Historical Journal of Film, Radio and Television*, 31:4 (2011), pp. 453–78.

Golub, Adam, 'They turned a school into a jungle!' How *Blackboard Jungle* redefined the education crisis in post-war America', *Film and History*, 39:1 (Spring 2009), pp. 21–30.

Hanich, Julian, 'A weep in the dark: tears and the cinematic experience', in Ralph J. Poole and Ilka Saal, *Passionate Politics: The Cultural Work of the American Melodrama from the Early Republic to the Present* (Cambridge Scholar Publishing, 2008), pp. 27–45.

Helman, Alicija, 'The film viewer: an unknown entity', *Continuum*, 2:2 (1989), pp. 96–115.

King, Rob, 'Introduction: early Hollywood and the archive', *Film History: An International Journal*, 26:2 (2014), pp. vii–xiv.

Kinkade, T. Patrick and Michael Katovich, 'Toward a sociology of cult films: reading "Rocky Horror"', *A Sociological Quarterly*, 33:2 (Summer 1992), pp. 191–209.

Klinger, Barbara, 'Digressions at the cinema: reception and mass culture', *Cinema Journal*, 28:4 (Summer 1989), pp. 3–19.

——, 'Film history terminable and interminable: recovering the past in reception studies', *Screen*, 38:2 (July 1997), pp. 107–29.

MacInnes, Colin, 'The Pied Piper from Bermondsey', in *England, Half English* (London: MacGibbon & Kee, 1961), pp. 11–18.

McLean, Adrienne L., '"New films in story form": movie story magazines and spectatorship', *Cinema Journal*, 42:3 (Spring), pp. 3–26.

Mulvey, Laura, 'Visual and narrative pleasures', *Screen*, 16:3 (Autumn 1975), pp. 6–18.

Orgeron, Marsha, 'Making "It" in Hollywood: Clara Bow, fandom, and consumer culture', *Cinema Journal*, 42:4 (Summer 2003), pp. 76–97.

——, '"You are invited to participate": interactive fandom in the age of the movie magazine', *Journal of Film and Video*, 61:3 (2009), pp. 3–23.

Osgerby, Bill, 'Well, it's Saturday night an' I just got paid': youth, consumerism and hegemony in post-war Britain', *Contemporary Record*, 6:2 (Autumn 1992), pp. 287–305.

Rosenbaum, Jonathan, 'The Rocky Horror picture cult', *Monthly Film Bulletin*, 49:2 (Spring 1980), pp. 78–9.

Simmons Jerold, 'The censoring of *Rebel Without a Cause*', *Journal of Popular Film & Television*, 1 July 1995 (23:2), pp. 57–63.

——, 'A damned nuisance: The Production Code and the Profanity Amendment of 1954', *Journal of Popular Film and Television*, 25:2 (Summer 1997), pp. 76–82.

——, 'Violent youth: the censoring and public reception of *The Wild One* and *The Blackboard Jungle*', *Film History*, 20:3 (2008), pp. 381–91.

Smoodin, Eric, '"Compulsory" viewing for every citizen: *Mr Smith* and the rhetoric for reception', *Cinema Journal*, 35:2 (Winter 1996), pp. 3–23.

Stacey, Jackie, 'Textual obsessions: methodology, history and researching female spectatorship', *Screen*, 34:3 (Autumn 1993), pp. 260–74.

Staiger, Janet, 'The handmaiden of villainy: methods and problems in studying the historical reception of film', *Wide Angle*, 8:1 (1986), pp. 19–27.

——, 'Writing the history of American film reception', in Richard Maltby and Melvyn Stokes (eds), *Hollywood Spectatorship: Changing Perceptions of Cinema Audiences* (London: British Film Institute, 2001), pp. 19–32.

Thomas, Nick, 'Will the real 1950s please stand up?: views of a contradictory decade', *Cultural and Social History*, 5 (2008), pp. 227–36.

Todd, Selina and Hilary Young, 'Baby-boomers to "beanstalkers"': making the modern teenager in post-war Britain', *Cultural and Social History*, 9 (2012), pp. 451–67.

Books

Abrams, Mark Alexander, *The Teenage Consumer* (London: London Press Exchange, 1959).

Abrams, Mark, *Teenage Consumer Spending in 1959* (London: London Press Exchange, 1961).

Ackroyd, Harold, *Picture Palaces of Liverpool* (London: Bluecoat Press, 1998).

Aldgate, Anthony *Censorship and The Permissive Society: British Cinema & Theatre 1955–1965* (Oxford: Clarendon Press, 1995).

Aldgate, Anthony and James Robertson, *Censorship in Theatre and Cinema* (Edinburgh University Press, 2005).

Allsop, Kenneth, *The Angry Decade: A Survey of the Cultural Revolt of the Nineteen-Fifties* (Wendover: John Goodchild Publishers, 1985 [1958]).

Alpert, Hollis, *The Dreams and the Dreamers: Adventures of a Professional Moviegoer* (New York: Macmillan, 1962).

Andrew, Geoff, *The Films of Nicholas Ray: The Poet of Nightfall* (London: British Film Institute, 2008).

Arnold, Rebecca, *Fashion, Desire and Anxiety: Image and Morality in the 20th Century* (New Brunswick, NJ: Rutgers University Press, 2001).

Aquila, Richard, *That Old Time Rock 'n' Roll: A Chronicle of an Era 1954–63* (Urbana and Chicago: University of Illinois Press, 2000).

Austin, Bruce A., *Immediate Seating: A Look at Movie Audiences* (California: Wadsworth Publishing Company, 1989).

Auty, Martyn, *Films of the Fifties* (London: Orbis, 1982).

Bailey, Beth L., *From Front Porch to Back Seat: Courtship in Twentieth-Century America* (Baltimore: Johns Hopkins University Press, 1988).

Balio, Tino (ed.), *The American Film Industry* (Madison, WI: University of Wisconsin Press, 1976).

Banks, Olive, *Parity and Prestige in English Secondary Education: A Study in Educational Sociology* (London: Routledge & Kegan Paul, 1955).

Barbas, Samantha, *Movie Crazy: Fans, Stars and the Cult of Celebrity* (New York: Palgrave, 2001).

Basinger, Jeanine, *The Woman's View: How Hollywood Spoke to Women 1930–1960* (New York: Random House, 1993).
Belton, John, *Widescreen Cinema* (Cambridge, MA: Harvard University Press, 1992).
Bennett, Tony, Susan Bowman-Boyd, Colin Mercer and Janet Woollacott (eds), *Popular Television and Film* (London: BFI, 1985).
Bernstein, George L., *The Myth of Decline: The Rise of Britain Since 1945* (London: Pimlico, 2004).
Bernstein, Matthew, *Pretty in Pink: The Golden Age of Teenage Movies* (New York: St Martin's Griffin, 1997).
Biskind, Peter, *Seeing is Believing: Or how Hollywood Taught us to Stop Worrying and Love the 50s* (London: Bloomsbury, 1983).
Bockris, Victor, *Keith Richards: The Biography* (London: Da Capo Press, 2003).
Boffin, T. and L. Fraser, *Stolen Glances: Lesbians Take Photographs* (London: Pandora, 1991).
Bordowitz, Hank, *Turning Points in Rock 'n' Roll* (New York: Citadel Press, 2004).
Bordwell, David, Janet Staiger, and Kristin Thompson, *The Classical Hollywood Cinema: Film Style & Mode of Production to 1960* (London: Routledge, 1988).
Bourdieu, Pierre, *Distinction: A Social Critique of the Judgement of Taste*, trans. Richard Nice (London: Routledge, 1984).
——, *On Television and Journalism*, trans. Priscilla Parkhurst Ferguson (London: Pluto Press, 1998).
Braine, John, *Room At The Top* (Harmondsworth: Penguin, 1959 [1957]).
Brando, Marlon with Robert Lindsey, *Songs My Mother Taught Me* (London: Century, 1994).
Bret, David, *Elvis: The Hollywood Years* (London: Robson Books, 2001).
Brode, Douglas, *Elvis and Popular Culture* (Jefferson, NC: McFarland, 2006).
Bruzzi, Stella, *Bringing up Daddy: Fatherhood and Masculinity in Post-War Hollywood* (London: BFI, 2006).
Caine, Andrew, *Interpreting Rock Movies: The Pop Film and its Critics in Britain* (Manchester: Manchester University Press, 2004).
Chapman, James, Mark Glancy and Sue Harper (eds), *New Film History: Sources, Methods, Approaches* (London: Palgrave Macmillan, 2007).
Chopra-Gant, Mike, *Hollywood Genres and Post-War America: Masculinity, Family and Nation in Popular Film And Film Noir* (London and New York: I. B. Tauris, 2006).
Christie, Ian (ed.) *Audiences: Defining and Researching Screen Entertainment Reception* (Amsterdam: Amsterdam University Press, 2012).
Church-Gibson, Pamela and John Hill (eds), *American Cinema and Hollywood: Critical Approaches* (Oxford: Oxford University Press, 2000).

Cohan, Steve, *Masked Men: Masculinity and the Movies in the Fifties* (Bloomington, IN: Indiana University Press, 1997).

Cohan, Steve and Ina Race Hark (eds), *Screening the Male: Exploring Masculinity in the Hollywood Cinema* (Oxon: Routledge, 1993).

Cohen, Stanley, *Folk Devils and Moral Panics* (London and New York: Routledge, 1972).

Cohn, Nik, *Awopbopaloobop Alopbamboom: Pop from the Beginning* (London: Macmillan, 1970).

Considine, David, *The Cinema of Adolescence* (Jefferson, NC: McFarland, 1985).

Coontz, Stephanie, *The Way We Never Were: American Families and the Nostalgia Trap* (New York: Basic Books, 1992).

Corner, John (ed.), *Popular Television in Britain: Studies in Cultural History* (London: BFI, 1991).

D'Emilio, John and Estelle Freedman, *Intimate Matters: A History of Sexuality in America* (New York: Harper & Row, 1988).

Dent, H. C., *Changes in English Education: A Historical Survey* (London: University of London Press, 1952).

Dickinson, Margaret and Sarah Street, *Cinema and State* (London: BFI, 1985).

Dixon, Thomas, *Weeping Britannia: Portrait of a Nation in Tears* (Oxford: Oxford University Press, 2015).

Dixon, Wheeler (ed.), *American Cinema of the 1940s: Themes and Variations* (New Brunswick, NJ: Rutgers University Press, 2005).

Doherty, Thomas, *Teenagers and Teenpics: The Juvenilization of American Movies in the 1950s* (Philadelphia: Temple University Press, 2002).

Douglas, Mary, *Purity and Danger: An Analysis of Concepts of Pollution and Taboo* (London: Routledge & Kegan Paul, 1966).

Driscoll, Catherine, *Teen Film. A Critical Introduction* (Oxford and New York: Berg, 2011).

Dyer, Richard, *Stars* (London: BFI, 1979).

——, *Heavenly Bodies: Film Stars and Society* (Basingstoke and London: Macmillan Education Ltd, 1987).

——, *The Culture of Queers* (London: Routledge, 2001).

——, *Only Entertainment* (Oxford: Routledge, 2005).

Ehrenreich, Barbara, *The Hearts of Men: American Dream and the Flight from Commitment* (London: Pluto Press, 1983).

Evans, Caroline, *Fashion at the Edge* (New Haven, CT: Yale University Press, 2007).

Faith, Adam, *Acts of Faith: The Autobiography of Adam Faith* (London: Bantam Books, 1996 [large print]).

Farrand Thorp, Margaret, *America at the Movies* (London: Faber & Faber, 1945).

Feeney, Paul, *A 1960s Childhood: From Thunderbirds to Beatlemania* (Cheltenham: The History Press, 2010).

Fischer, Lucy and Marcia Landy (eds) *Stars: The Film Reader* (New York and London: Routledge, 2004).

Flugel, J. C., *The Psychology of Clothes* (London: Institute of Psycho-Analysis and Hogarth Press, 1930).
Ford, Peter, *Glenn Ford: A Life* (Madison, WI: The University of Wisconsin Press, 2011).
Fowler, David, *The First Teenagers: The Lifestyle of Young Wage-Earners in Interwar Britain* (London: Woburn Press, 1995).
Frascella, Lawrence and Al Weisel, *Live Fast Die Young* (New York and London: Simon & Schuster, 2005).
Fuchs, Otto, *Bill Haley: The Father Of Rock 'n' Roll* (Kornwestheim, Germany: Wagner Verlag, 2011).
Fyvel, T. R., *The Insecure Offenders: Rebellious Youth in the Welfare State* (London: Chatto & Windus, 1961).
Geraghty, Christine, *British Cinema in the Fifties: Gender, Genre and The 'New Look'* (London: Routledge, 2000).
Gerstner, David A. and Janet Staiger *Authorship and Film* (London: Routledge, 2003).
Gibbs, John, *Mise-en-Scene: Film Style and Interpretation* (London: Wallflower Press, 2002).
Gielgud, John, *Gielgud Letters* (London: Weidenfeld & Nicolson, 2004).
Gilbert, James, *A Cycle of Outrage: America's Reaction to the Juvenile Delinquent in the 1950s* (Oxford: Oxford University Press, 1989).
Gillett, Philip, *The British Working Class in Post-War film* (Manchester: Manchester University Press, 2003).
Glancy, Mark, *Hollywood and the Americanization of Britain* (London: I. B. Tauris, 2014).
Gledhill, Christine (ed.), *Stardom: Industry of Desire* (London and New York: Routledge, 1991).
Glynn, Stephen, *The British Pop Music Film: The Beatles and Beyond* (New York: Palgrave Macmillan, 2013).
Goldman, Albert, *The Lives of John Lennon* (New York: Bantam Books, 1989).
Gorer, Geoffrey, *Exploring English Character* (London: Criterion Books, 1955).
Gorst, Anthony, Lewis Johnman and W. Scott Lucas (eds), *Post-War Britain, 1945–64: Themes and Perspectives* (London: Pinter Publishers, 1989).
Gosling, Ray, *Personal Copy: A Memoir of the Sixties* (London and Boston: Faber & Faber, 1980).
Gould, Jonathan, *Can't Buy Me Love: The Beatles and America* (New York: Three Rivers Press, 2008).
Gow, Gordon, *Hollywood in the Fifties* (New York: A. S. Barnes & Co., 1971).
Grant, Barry Keith (ed.), *Schirmer Encyclopedia of Film* (Detroit: Thomson Gale, 2006).
Grant, Neil, *James Dean: In his Own Words* (New York: Crescent Books, 1994).

Griffin, Christine, *Representations of Youth: The Study of Youth and Adolescence in Britain and America* (Cambridge: Polity Press, 1993).

Griswold, Robert, *Fatherhood in America: A history* (New York: Basic Books, 1993).

Grubb, Norton W. and Marvin Lazerson, *Broken Promises: How Americans Fail their Children* (Chicago: University of Chicago Press, 1988).

Hall, Stuart, Dorothy Hobson, Andrew Lowe and Paul Willis (eds), *Culture, Media, Language: Working Papers in Cultural Studies, 1972–79* (London: Routledge, 1980).

Hall, Stuart and Tony Jefferson (eds), *Resistance Through Rituals: Youth Subcultures in Post-War Britain* (London: Hutchinson, 1976).

Hall, Stuart and Paddy Whannel, *The Popular Arts* (London: Hutchinson Educational, 1964).

Halliwell, Leslie, *Seats in all Parts: Half a Lifetime at the Movies* (London: Granada, 1985).

Handel, Leo A., *Hollywood Looks at its Audience* (Urbana, Illinois: University of Illinois Press, 1950).

Hansen, Miriam, *Babel and Babylon: Spectatorship in American Silent Film* (Cambridge, MA: Harvard University Press, 1991).

Hanson, Helen, *Hollywood Soundscapes: Film Sound Style, Craft & Production in the Classical Era* (London: BFI/Palgrave, 2017).

Hanson, Stuart, *From Silent Screen to Multiplex: A History of Cinema Exhibition in Britain since 1896* (Manchester: Manchester University Press, 2010).

Harper, Sue and Vincent Porter, *British Cinema of the 1950s: A Decline in Deference* (Oxford: Oxford University Press, 2003).

Harvey, James, *Movie Love in the Fifties* (Cambridge, MA: Da Capo Press, 2001).

Haskell, Molly, *From Reverence to Rape: The Treatment of Women in the Movies* (Chicago and London: The University of Chicago Press, 1987).

Hebdige, Dick, *Subculture: The Meaning of Style* (London and New York: Routledge, 1979).

——, *Hiding in the Light* (New York and London: Routledge, 1988).

Hennessy, Peter, *Having it so Good: Britain in the Fifties* (London: Penguin, 2007).

Higashi, Sumiko, *Stars, Fans, and Consumption in the 1950s: Reading Photoplay* (New York: Palgrave Macmillan, 2014).

Hill, John, *Sex, Class and Realism: British Cinema 1956–1963* (London: BFI Publishing, 1986).

Hoggart, Richard, *The Uses of Literacy: With a New Introduction by Andrew Goodwin* (New Brunswick and London: Transaction Publishers, 1992 [1958]).

Hollows, Joanne, Peter Hutchings and Mark Jancovich (eds), *The Film Studies Reader* (London: Arnold, 2000).

Hopkins, Eric, *The Rise and Decline of the English Working Classes 1918–1990: A Social History* (London: Weidenfeld & Nicolson, 1991).

Hopkins, Harry, *The New Look: A Social History of the Forties and Fifties in Britain* (London: Secker & Warburg, 1963).

Horn, Adrian, *Juke Box Britain: Americanisation and Youth Culture, 1945–60* (Manchester and New York: Manchester University Press, 2009).

Houston, Penelope, *The Contemporary Cinema* (Harmondsworth: Penguin, 1966).

Humphries, Patrick, *Elvis: The #1 Hits* (Kansas City: Andrew McMeel Publishing, 2002).

Hunter, Evan, *The Blackboard Jungle* (New York: Dell Books, 1966 [1954]).

Izod, John, *Hollywood and the Box Office 1895–1986* (London: Macmillan, 1988).

Jackson, Brian and Dennis Marsden, *Education and the Working Class* (Harmondsworth: Penguin, 1962).

Jackson, Louise, *Policing Youth, Britain 1945–70* (Manchester: Manchester University Press, 2014).

James, David E., *Rock 'n' Film: Cinema's Dance with Popular Music* (Oxford: Oxford University Press, 2017).

Jarvie, Ian, Garth Jowett and Kathryn Fuller, *Children at the Movies: Media Influence and the Payne Fund Controversy* (New York: Cambridge University Press, 2007).

Jeffers McDonald, Tamar, *Doris Day Confidential: Hollywood, Sex and Stardom* (London: I. B. Tauris, 2013).

Jephcott, Pearl, *Some Young People* (London: Allen & Unwin, 1954).

——, *Time of One's Own* (London: Oliver & Boyd, 1967).

Kazan, Elia, *Elia Kazan: A Life* (London: Andre Deutsch, 1988).

Kerr, Paul (ed.), *The Hollywood Film Industry: A Reader* (London: Routledge & Kegan Paul, 1986).

Klein, Amanda Ann, *American Film Cycles: Reframing Genres, Screening Social Problems and Defining Subcultures* (Austin, TX: University of Texas Press, 2011).

Klinger, Barbara, *Melodrama and Meaning: History, Culture and the Films of Douglas Sirk* (Bloomington, IN: Indiana University Press, 1994).

Kolin, Philip C., *Williams: A Streetcar Named Desire* (Cambridge: Cambridge University Press, 2000).

Koppes, Clayton R. and Gregory D. Black, *Hollywood Goes to War: How Politics, and Propaganda Shaped World War II Movies* (London: I. B. Tauris, 1987).

Krauss, Kenneth, *Male Beauty: Post-War Masculinity in Theater, Film, and Physique Magazines* (New York: Suny Press, 2014).

Krutnik, Frank, Steve Neale, Brian Neve and Peter Stanfield (eds), *'Un-American' Hollywood: Politics and Film in the Blacklist Era* (New Brunswick and London: Rutgers University Press, 2007).

Krzywinska, Tanya, *Sex and the Cinema* (London: Wallflower Press, 2006).

Kuhn, Annette, *An Everyday Magic: Cinema and Cultural Memory* (London and New York: I. B. Taurus, 2002).

Kureishi, H. and J. Savage (eds), *The Faber Book of Pop* (London: Faber & Faber, 1995).
Kynaston, David, *Austerity Britain 1945–51* (London: Bloomsbury, 2008).
——, *Family Britain 1951–57* (London: Bloomsbury, 2010).
Landy, Marcia, *British Genres: Cinema and Society, 1930–1960* (Princeton, NJ: Princeton University Press, 1991).
Laurie, Peter, *The Teenage Revolution* (London: Antony Blond, 1965).
Lester Smith, W. O., *The Government of Education* (Harmondsworth: Penguin, 1966).
Lewis, Jon, *The Road to Romance and Ruin: Teen Films and Youth Culture* (New York: Routledge, 1992).
Lewis, Peter, *The Fifties* (London: Book Club Associates, 1978).
Lyons, John F., *America in the British Imagination: 1945 to the Present* (New York: Palgrave Macmillan, 2013).
MacInnes, Colin, *Absolute Beginners* (London: MacGibbon & Kee, 1959).
——, *England, Half English* (London: MacGibbon & Kee, 1961).
Mackillop, Ian and Neil Sinyard (eds), *British Cinema of the 1950s: A Celebration* (Manchester: Manchester University Press, 2003).
Maltby, Richard, *Hollywood Cinema* (Oxford: Blackwell Publishers, 1995).
Martin, Linda and Kerry Segrave, *Anti-Rock: The Opposition to Rock 'n' Roll* (Hamden, CT: Archon, 1988).
Marwick, Arthur, *The Penguin Social History of Britain: British Society Since 1945* (London: Penguin Books, 1982).
——, *Culture in Britain Since 1945* (Oxford: Basil Blackwell, 1991).
Mayer, J. P., *Sociology of Film: Studies and documents* (London: Faber & Faber, 1946).
Mayer, Vicki, Miranda J. Banks and John T. Caldwell (eds), *Production Studies: Cultural Studies of Media Industries* (New York and London: Routledge, 2009).
McDonald, Paul, *The Star System: Hollywood's Production of Popular Identities* (London and New York: Wallflower Press, 2005).
——, *Hollywood Stardom* (Chichester: Wiley-Blackwell, 2013).
McKibbin, Ross, *Classes and Cultures: England 1918–51* (Oxford: Oxford University Press, 1998).
McLean, Adrienne L. and David A. Cook, *Headline Hollywood: A Century of Film Scandal* (New Brunswick, NJ: Rutgers University Press, 2001).
McRobbie, Angela, *Feminism and Youth Culture* (Basingstoke: Macmillan Press, 2000).
Melly, George, *Revolt into Style: The Pop Arts* (Oxford: Oxford University Press, 1989).
Moore, Tony, *Policing Notting Hill: Fifty Years of Turbulence* (Hampshire, UK: Waterside Press, 2013).
Morgan, Ivan W. and Neil A. Wynn, *America's Century: Perspectives on US History Since 1900* (New York: Holmes & Meier, 1996).
Morin, Edgar, *The Stars* (New York: Grove Press, 1960).

Murphy, Robert, *Sixties British Cinema* (Bloomington, IN: Indiana University Press, 1992).

—— (ed.), *The British Cinema Book* (London: BFI, 1997).

Neale, Steve, *Genre and Hollywood* (London: Routledge, 1999).

Niven, Richard, *National Service: Britain in Uniform 1946–1963* (London: Allen Lane, 2014).

Norman, Philip, *John Lennon: The Life* (London: HarperCollins Publishers, 2008).

——, *Paul McCartney: The Biography* (London: Hachette, 2016).

Nowell-Smith, Geoffrey and Steven Ricci (eds), *Hollywood & Europe: Economics, Culture, National Identity* (London: BFI, 1998).

Obelkevich, James and Peter Catterall (eds), *Understanding Post-War British Society* (London: Routledge, 1994).

O'Brien, Margaret and Allen Eyles (eds), *Enter the Dream-House: Memories of Cinemas in South London from the Twenties to the Sixties* (London: Museum of the Moving Image, 1993).

Ohmer, Susan, *George Gallup in Hollywood* (New York: Columbia University Press, 2006).

Oldham, Andrew Loog, *Stoned* (London: Vintage, 2001).

Olivier, Laurence, *Laurence Olivier: Confessions of an Actor* (London: Weidenfeld & Nicolson, 1982).

Osgerby, Bill, *Youth in Britain Since 1945* (Oxford: Blackwell Publishing, 1998).

Pearson, Geoffrey, *Hooligan: A History of Respectable Fears* (London: Macmillan, 1983).

Perkins, V. F., *Film as Film: Understanding and Judging Movies* (London: BFI, 1975).

Philips, Alastair and Ginette Vincendeau (eds), *Journeys of Desire: European Actors in Hollywood* (London: BFI, 2008).

Pilkington, Edward, *Beyond the Mother Country: West Indians and the Notting Hill White Riots* (London: I. B. Tauris, 1988).

Pomerance, Murray (ed.), *American Cinema of the 1950s: Themes and Variations* (New Brunswick, NJ: Rutgers University Press, 2005).

Porter, Vincent, *On Cinema* (London: Pluto Press, 1985).

Pountain, Dick and David Robins, *Cool Rules: Anatomy of an Attitude* (London: Reaktion Books, 2000).

Powdermaker, Hortense, *Hollywood the Dream Factory: An Anthropologist Looks at the Movie-Makers* (London: Secker & Warburg, 1951).

Pressley, Allison, *The 50s and 60s: The Best of Times: Growing Up and Being Young in Britain* (London: Michael O'Mara Books, 2003).

Pye, Douglas and John Gibbs (eds), *Film Style and Meaning: Detailed Studies in the Analysis of Film* (Manchester: Manchester University Press, 2005).

Ray, Robert, *A Certain Tendency of Hollywood Cinema, 1930–1980* (Princeton, NJ: Princeton University Press, 1985).

Reece, Gregory L., *Elvis Religion: Exploring the cult of the King* (London: I. B. Tauris, 2006).

Rees, Paul, *Robert Plant: A Life* (London: HarperCollins, 2013).
Remmers, Henry Hermann and Don H. Radler, *The American Teenager* (New York: Bobbs-Merrill, 1957).
Richards, Jeffrey, *Films and British National Identity: From Dickens to Dad's Army* (Manchester University Press, 1997).
Richards, Jeffrey and Dorothy Sheridan (eds), *Mass-Observation at the Movies* (London and New York: Routledge & Kegan Paul, 1987).
Robbins, Harold, *A Stone for Danny Fisher* (New York: Alfred Knopf, 1952).
Robertson, James, *The British Board of Film Censors: Film Censorship in Britain, 1896–1950* (London: Taylor & Francis, 1985).
——, *The Hidden Cinema: British Film Censorship in Action 1913–1972* (London: Routledge, 2006).
Roffman, Peter and Jim Purdy, *The Hollywood Social Problem Film* (Bloomington, IN: Indiana University Press, 1983).
Rosen, Andrew, *The Transformation of British Life 1950–2000: A Social History* (Manchester: Manchester University Press, 2003).
Rosen, Marjorie, *Popcorn Venus: Women, Movies and the American Dream* (New York: Coward, McCann & Geoghegan, 1973).
Ross, Lillian, *Picture* (New York: Da Capo Press, 1950).
Rosten, Leo Calvin, *Hollywood: The Movie Colony, the Movie Makers* (New York: Harcourt, Brace and Company, 1941).
Rotundo, Anthony E., *American Manhood: Transformations in Masculinity from the Revolution to the Modern Era* (New York: Basic Books, 1993).
Rowbotham, Sheila, *A Century of Women: The History of Women in Britain and the United States* (London: Viking, 1997).
Sandbrook, Dominic, *Never Had it so Good: A History of Britain from Suez to the Beatles* (London: Abacus, 2006).
Scala, Mim, *The Diary of a Teddy Boy: A Memoir of the Long Sixties* (London: The Goblin Press, 2009).
Schaefer, Eric, *'Bold! Daring! Shocking! True!' A History of Exploitation Films, 1919–1959* (Durham and London: Duke University Press, 1999).
Schary, Dore, *Case History of a Movie* (New York: Random House, 1950).
Schatz, Thomas, *Hollywood Genres: Formulas, Film-Making and the Studio System* (New York: McGraw-Hill, 1981).
——, *Genius of the System: Hollywood Filmmaking in the Studio Era* (London: Simon & Schuster, 1989).
Schickel, Richard, *Movies: The History of an Art and an Institution* (London: MacGibbon & Kee, 1965).
Shary, Timothy, *Generation Multiplex: The Image of Youth in Contemporary American Cinema* (Austin, TX: University of Texas Press, 2002).
Shary, Vincent, *Teen Movies: American Youth on Screen* (London: Wallflower Press, 2005).
Sheff, David, *All We Are Saying: The Last Major Interview with John Lennon and Yoko Ono* (New York: St Martin's Griffin, 2000).
Shore, Michael, *The Rolling Stone Book of Rock Videos* (New York: Quill, 1984).

Sillitoe, Alan, *Saturday Night and Sunday Morning* (London: Pan Books Ltd, 1963).

Simpson, Paul, *Elvis Films FAQ: All That's Left to Know about the King of Rock 'n' Roll in Hollywood* (Kenner, LA: Applause Books, 2013).

Sklar, Robert, *Movie-Made America: A Cultural History of American Movies* (New York: Vintage Books, 1994).

Slide, Anthony, *Inside the Hollywood Fan Magazine: A History of Star Makers, Fabricators and Gossip Mongers* (Jackson, MS: University Press of Mississippi, 2010).

Slocum, J. David, *Rebel Without a Cause: Approaches to a Maverick Masterwork* (Albany, New York: State University of New York Press, 2005).

Smith, Sarah J., *Children, Cinema & Censorship: From Dracula to the Dead End Kids* (London: I. B. Tauris, 2005).

Speed, F. Maurice, *Film Review 1951–1952* (London: Macdonald and Co Ltd, 1951).

Spicer, Andrew, *Typical Men: The Representation of Masculinity In Popular British Cinema* (London: I. B. Tauris, 2001).

Spock, Benjamin, *Baby and Child Care* (New York: Pocket Books, 1957).

Springer, Claudia, *James Dean Transfigured: The Many Faces Of Rebel Iconography* (Austin, TX: The University of Texas, 2007).

Stacey, Jackie, *Star Gazing: Hollywood Cinema and Female Spectatorship* (London: Routledge, 1993).

Staiger, Janet, *Interpreting Films: Studies in the Historical Reception of American Cinema* (Princeton, NJ: Princeton University, 1992).

——, *Perverse Spectators: The Practices of Film Reception* (New York: New York University Press, 2000).

Stokes, Melvyn and Richard Maltby (eds), *Identifying Hollywood's Audiences: Cultural Identity and the Movies* (London: BFI Publishing, 1999).

—— (eds), *Hollywood Spectatorship: Changing Perceptions of Cinema Audiences* (London: BFI, 2001).

—— (eds), *Hollywood Abroad: Audiences and Cultural Exchange* (London: BFI, 2007).

Storey, John, *Cultural Theory and Popular Culture: A Reader* (London: Pearson, 2007).

Street, Sarah, *British Cinema in Documents* (London and New York: Routledge, 2000).

——, *British National Cinema* (London: Routledge, 2009).

Taylor, Greg, *Artists in the Audience: Cults, Camp and American Film Criticism* (Princeton: Princeton University Press, 2001).

Taylor, Helen, *Scarlett's Women: Gone with the Wind and its Female Fans* (London: Virago, 1989).

Taylor, John Russell, *Strangers in Paradise: The Hollywood Emigres, 1933–1950* (London: Faber & Faber, 1983).

Thompson, Hunter S., *Hell's Angels* (London: Penguin, 1988).

Thornham, Sue (ed.), *Feminist Film Theory: A Reader* (Edinburgh: Edinburgh University Press, 1999).

Trevelyan, John, *What the Censor Saw* (London: Michael Joseph, 1973).
Trumpbour, John, *US Selling Hollywood to the World: US and European Struggles for Mastery of the Global Film Industry, 1920–1950* (Cambridge and New York: Cambridge University Press, 2002).
Tudor, Andrew, *Images and Influence: Studies in the Sociology of Film* (London: Routledge, 2014).
Tyler May, Elaine, *Homeward Bound: American Families in the Cold War Era* (New York: Basic Books, 1988).
Walker, Alexander, *Stardom: The Hollywood Phenomenon* (London: Michael Joseph, 1970).
Walters, James and Tom Brown (eds), *Film Moments: Criticism, History and Theory* (London: Bloomsbury Academic, 2010).
Wardle, David, *English Popular Education 1870–1975* (Cambridge University Press, 1975).
Wasko, Janet, *Movies and Money* (Norwood, NJ: Ablex Publishing, 1982).
Weeks, Jeffrey, *Sex, Politics and Society: The Regulation of Sexuality Since 1800* (New York: Longman Group Ltd, 1981).
West, Elliott, *Growing up in Twentieth-Century America: A History and Reference Guide* (New York: Greenwood Press, 1996).
Wexman, Virginia, *Creating the Couple: Love, Marriage and Hollywood Performance* (New Jersey: Princeton University Press, 1993).
Willmott, Peter and Michael Young, *Family and Kinship in East London* (Harmondsworth: Penguin, 1969 [1957]).
White, John and Sabine Haenni (eds), *Fifty Key American Films* (London: Routledge, 2009).
Wolfenstein, Martha and Nathan Leites, *Movies: A Psychological Study* (New York: Atheneum, 1950).
Wollen, Peter, *Signs and Meanings in Cinema* (Bloomington, IN: Indiana University Press, 1972).
Wright, Will, *Sixguns and Society: A Structural Study of Westerns* (Berkeley, CA: University of California Press, 1977).
Vasey, Ruth, *The World According to Hollywood, 1939–1989* (Madison, WI: University of Wisconsin Press, 1997).
Veness, Thelma, *School Leavers: Their Aspirations and Expectations* (London: Methuen, 1962).

Unpublished PhD theses

Cohen, Stanley, 'Hooligans, vandals and the community: a study of social reaction to juvenile delinquency', PhD dissertation (The London School of Economics and Political Science, 1969).
Dolinger, Amy D., 'Playboys, single girls, and sexual rebels: sexual politics 1950–1965: a trilogy of significant developments', PhD dissertation (University of East Tennessee State University, 2001).

Jeffers, Tamar Elizabeth Louise, '"Should I surrender?" Performing and interrogating female virginity in Hollywood films, 1957–64', PhD dissertation (University of Warwick, 2005).

Kelly, Gillian Patricia, 'A Taylor made star: male beauty, changes in masculinity and the 'lost' stardom of Robert Taylor, Hollywood 1934–1969', PhD dissertation (University of Glasgow, 2015).

McDonald, Paul, 'Public bodies, private moments: method acting and American cinema in the 1950s', PhD dissertation (University of Warwick, 1997).

Reports and surveys

Kefauver, Senator Estes, The Hearings of the Subcommittee to Investigate Juvenile Delinquency (1954).

King George's Jubilee Trust. Council, *Citizens of Tomorrow: A Study of the Influences Affecting the Upbringing of Young People* (London: Odhams Press Ltd, 1955).

Trevelyan, John, *Censored* (Southampton: The Millbrook Press Ltd, 1962).

Wilcox, H. D., *Report on Juvenile Delinquency* (London: Falcon Press, 1949).

Photo essay

Russell, Ken, *Photo Essay on London Teddy Girls* (*Picture Post*, 4 June 1955).

Index

Abeles, Arthur 120
Abrams, Mark 30, 57, 58, 173, 212
Actors Studio 22, 122, 141
  see also method acting
Adams, Nick 131
Adler, Stella 43
affluence 28, 115, 185, 211–12, 217
Albermarle Report (1960) 28
All About Eve 13
Allen, Corey 112
Allsop, Kenneth 83, 127–8, 230
Americanisation
  American influences on British teenagers 17, 117, 119, 121, 128, 131, 134, 153, 161, 163, 164–5, 202, 212
  cultural protectionism 18, 19, 132, 165
  US monopoly of mass media 18, 163, 208–9, 211
Anderson, Lindsay 127, 202
Angeli, Pier 130, 141
Angry Young Man 17, 129, 228–30
Arnold, Rebecca 57
audiences
  adolescent and teenage 3, 58, 117, 118, 188
  appeal of American stars 6, 69, 128, 140, 235
  change in demographics 3, 69, 121, 161, 166, 173–4, 185, 216–17
  gay and lesbian 13, 15
  historical 5, 6
  TV 28, 67, 102, 155, 227
  viewing practices 165–8, 173–4, 216
Austin, Guy 135

Backus, Jim 112, 118
Bailey, Beth L. 14
Baker, Stanley 229
Balfour, John 201, 205
Banks, Olive 83
Barbas, Samantha 131
Barton, Earl 152, 160, 162
Beat generation (Beatniks) 58, 80
Beatles, the (Beatlemania) 5, 218, 232, 234–5
Beaulieu, Lord Montagu of 197
Benedek, Laszlo 41, 66
Bentley, Derek 26, 50–1, 53, 115
Berman, Pandro S. 195
Biltereyst, Daniel 115
Biskind, Peter 85, 113
Blackboard Jungle 2, 71, 79–105, 111, 118, 121, 138, 151, 175, 190, 192, 195, 199
  BBFC and 81, 84–90
  critics and 91–3, 96
  promotion and publicity 89–91, 93–8

syndrome in schools 83, 99, 102
Venice Film Festival (1955) 81–2, 91
Bloom, Ursula 67
Blue Lamp, The 93, 112, 198–9
Bogarde, Dirk 60–1, 93, 213
Doctor films 61, 63
Bogart, Humphrey 51
Boone, Pat 210–11, 213, 217, 218
Borgnine, Ernest 131
Bourdieu, Pierre
field theory and 1950s films 10, 20, 46, 92
theories of taste and distinction 10, 19, 202
Branch, Newton K. 101, 153
Brando, Marlon 1, 2, 12, 15, 39–72, 91, 94, 96, 103, 112, 113, 124, 126, 128, 174, 184, 185, 187, 192, 193, 198, 201, 205, 211, 213, 214, 228–9, 236
as Mark Antony 46, 62
non-conformity 3, 40, 55–6, 61–3, 71, 95
as Stanley Kowalski 13, 20, 42, 43, 45, 62, 63, 187
Brew, Dr Josephine McAlister 56, 164
British Board of Film Censors (BBFC) 2, 3, 7, 13, 21–3
'43 Rules of the BBFC' 21, 48, 116, 118–19, 161
local watch committees 39, 49, 65–6, 157, 159
Memorandum to Film Producers (1949) 87, 120
British Broadcasting Corporation (BBC) 18, 134
British Film Institute (BFI) 11, 202
British Nationality Act (1948) 69
British New Wave 17, 141, 228–9
Brooks, Richard 83, 88, 96, 101
Brown, Joe 230, 232
Brown, Tom 164–5, 175
Brown, William 67
Bruzzi, Stella 124
Bryant, Arthur 212
Burnup, Peter 129
Burton, Richard 228
Butler, Judith 125
Butler, R. A. 170
Bygraves, Max 88

Caine, Andrew 8, 113, 184, 202
Caine Mutiny, The 172
Calhern, Louis 80, 101
Carlyle, Mark 210
Carter, Marie 125
Carthew, Andrew 150
Catcher in the Rye, The 127
Centre for Contemporary Cultural Studies 24
Chapman, James 5
cinema
chains (British) 22, 48, 155, 156, 157, 158, 167, 168, 169, 173
popularity 48
private clubs and societies 66, 67
professional organisations 50, 157–9
cinema riots 2, 38, 49–54, 104, 150–1, 154–8, 166, 168–9, 171, 209, 216
Clapham Common murder trial (1953) 27, 52–3, 115
Cochrane, Kelso 26, 65
Cohan, Steve 14–15, 64
Cohen, Phil 24
Cohn, Nik 212, 231
Cold War, the 16, 91
Colleano, Bonar 45
Collier, Lionel 46, 66
Columbia (film studio) 47, 52–3, 65, 68, 70, 153, 160–1
Committee on Maladjusted Children (1950) 116

Conway, Harry 140, 161
corporal punishment 88, 99
Cosh Boy 50–3, 93, 112, 198
Craig, Christopher 26–7, 50–1, 53, 115, 158
Crawford, Cheryl 20
Crosby, Bing 210
Curtis, Tony 64, 201
Curtiz, Michael 191, 203

Daily Mirror 28, 164, 171
Damone, Vic 130
Davis, Bette 13
Day, Doris 11
Dead End 51, 123
Dean, James 1, 2, 10, 15, 46, 95, 104, 111–42, 174, 184, 185, 188–9, 193, 198, 201, 205, 213, 214, 217, 227–30
  death cult 10, 111, 130–33, 139, 153
  emotional acting 14, 112, 117–18, 124, 139, 141, 213
  fan clubs 132–3
  fan culture 112, 114, 118, 129
    Deanagers 129–39, 141, 163
  in lesbian academia (gender fluidity) 16, 125
Dene, Terry 215, 232
Dent, Harold 83
Dixon, Thomas 16, 165, 170
Docker, Lady Norah 102
Doherty, Thomas 8, 114
Doncaster, Patrick 137
Don't Knock the Rock 151, 159, 161, 173, 203
Doran, Ann 112, 118
Dyer, Richard 12–13, 16, 62, 64, 93

East of Eden 128, 131, 132
Eckman, Sam 85–6, 88
education
  British 99–100
  Education (Butler) Act (1944) 83–4
  US 81, 83
Elsaesser, Thomas 6

Faith, Adam 130, 134, 230
Family Doctor 56–7
fan culture
  theories on 70, 100–2, 153, 184
fan magazines 11, 12, 97, 164, 211
  see also Photoplay, Picturegoer, Picture Show
Fear Strikes Out 141
Field, Audrey 88–9, 169
film classification
  A certificate 22, 67, 85, 89, 116, 120, 194–5, 197, 200
  H certificate 22
  PG certificate 22, 71, 142, 199, 200
  U certificate 22, 153, 157, 159, 194, 200
  X certificate 22, 47, 48, 49, 53, 71, 83, 85, 89, 101, 102, 116, 120, 194–5, 197, 227
Films and Filming 62
Films in Review 10, 201
Film Review 42, 202
film theory
  films as cultural artefacts 7
  gaze theory 14, 204
    see also Mulvey, Laura
  neo-formalism 6
  realism (social) 1, 20, 45, 55, 67, 83, 92, 102, 103–4, 114, 121, 123, 194, 202
  reception studies 6, 8, 9, 10, 11, 60, 128, 184, 201, 232

historical-materialist approach 13; *see also* Staiger, Janet
queer theory 15–16, 125
Finney, Albert 61, 141, 228–9
Fischer, Lucy 11, 93
see also star text
Ford, Glenn 4, 80, 91, 92–6
Forrest, Elizabeth 61
Francis, Anne 80, 91
Frank, Elizabeth 161
Freddie and the Bellboys 153
Free Cinema 28, 127
Freed, Alan 153
Freudian theory
in films and popular culture 14, 43, 82, 124, 128, 192
Frost, David 184
Fury, Billy 7, 230–2
Fyvel, T. R. 24, 56

Gable, Clark 200
Gallup poll 99
Gans, Herbert 233
Gaye, Lisa 152, 160–1, 162
Giant 114, 131, 137, 139
Gibbs, Patrick 162
GI Blues 218–9
Gielgud, John 46
Gilda 94
Gillet, Eric 204
Girl Can't Help It, The 159
Glancy, Mark 5, 8, 206
Godfather, The 228
Gorer, Geoffrey 17, 28, 100
Gosling, Ray 56, 104, 140, 169, 214
Gray, Donald 67
Grease 8, 174
Griffiths, Sir David E. 49
Gris, Henry 61

Haley, Bill 2, 15, 104, 150–3, 161–4, 165–75, 189, 203, 208, 209, 211, 212, 218, 234
and the Comets 2, 80, 151, 161, 165, 167, 169, 214
Halliwell, Leslie 39–40
Hanich, Julian 166
Hansen, Miriam 206
Hanson, Helen 54
Harman, Jympson 92, 123, 129, 161
Harper's Magazine 41
Harper, Sue 5, 69, 165
Harris, Julie 128
Harris, (Sir) Sidney 21, 47, 51, 53, 68, 69, 71, 118, 157
Harrison, George 235
Hart, Dolores 190
Hart, Ian 211
Harvey, Laurence 228–9
Hastings, Michael 134
Hayes, Margaret 80
Hebdige, Dick 24, 53
Hell's Angels 42, 47, 55
Hicks, Colin 232
Hill, Derek 89, 92, 96
Hinxman, Margaret 71, 102, 141, 202, 206, 213
Hoggart, Richard 19, 24, 83, 128
Holden, Jennifer 188
Hollister (California) 41, 42, 47
Hollywood
anti-hero 2, 112, 125, 172, 186, 218, 227
British attitudes to 40, 43, 122–3, 172, 202, 218, 206, 208, 211, 217
classic period 12
competition from TV 68, 82
promotion and publicity 5, 8, 9, 12, 13, 14, 60, 187
star system 8, 206, 211, 214
star vehicle 60, 85, 184, 186, 203, 211
homosexuality 14, 16, 131, 197–9
Hopkins, Harry 24, 163, 173, 212
Horn, Adrian 18

Houston, Penelope 43, 55, 60, 92, 96, 127, 163, 202
Hudson, Rock 60, 64, 139
Hunter, Evan 82–3, 88, 91, 93, 96, 98, 103
Hunter, Kim 63
Hutchinson, Tom 125, 208

Island of Lost Souls (1932) 47
ITV 99

Jackson, Brian and Dennis Marsden 100
Jagger, Dean 190, 191
Jailhouse Rock 2, 4, 184, 186–90, 192–6, 200–3, 213, 217
  BBFC and 194–6, 200
  critics and 201–3
  promotion and publicity 186–91
James, David E. 98, 185
James Dean Story, The 139–40
Jarvis, Fred 99
jazz 19, 54, 140, 172, 192, 193, 208
Jefferson, Tony 24, 53
Johnston, Johnny 151, 160–1
Jones, Carolyn 191
Jordan, Colin
  White Defence League 25
Julius Caesar (1953) 46, 62
juvenile delinquency 7–8, 16, 23, 39, 70, 114, 115, 119–20, 153, 156–60, 169–71
  in American cinema 42, 49, 53, 54–5, 59, 66–7, 70–1, 81, 85, 88–9, 98, 111–14, 117–20, 151, 161, 203
  in British cinema 16, 17, 50, 89, 93, 127, 196–9, 228
  Senator Estes Kefauver 81–2
  US Senate Subcommittee on Juvenile Delinquency (1953) 23, 81–2, 100

Katzman, Sam 163
Kazan, Elia 14, 20, 43, 45, 96, 103, 128–9
Kennedy, John F. 235
Kenney, James 60–1, 93
Kiley, Richard 80
Kinematograph Weekly 60, 129, 187, 194
Kinematograph Year Book 89
King Creole 2, 4, 184, 190–6, 200–1, 203–4, 207, 216, 218
  BBFC and 194–201
  critics and 203–4
  promotion and publicity 190–4
Kinsey reports on men and women 14
Klein, Amanda 8
Klinger, Barbara 5, 11, 91, 111
Kosmala, Katarzyna 16
Kramer, Stanley 41, 54
Kuhn, Annette 8

Ladies Home Journal 82
Lambert, Gavin 46, 68, 126
Landy, Marcia 11, 93
  see also star text
Lassally, Walter 202
Laughton, Charles 47
Laurie, Peter 30–1, 57
League of Empire Loyalists 69
Leavis, Frank and Q. D. 18
Leigh, Vivien 45
Lejeune, C. A. 122
Lennon, John 169, 175, 216, 234
Let Him Have It 27
Lewin, David 68, 136
Lewis, Robert 20
Lewis, Virginia 202
Life 42
Lilies of the Field 98
Lincoln, Paul 232
Lindner, Robert M. 114, 121
Lion Has Wings, The 165
Little Richard 175
London County Council 99, 100

Look Back in Anger
film 228
play 17, 228
Lord Chamberlain and theatre 50, 197
Love Me Tender 186, 195, 205, 213
Loving You 188, 206
Luce, Clare Boothe 81, 91
Lumley, Joanna 209–10
Lyall, Gavin 132, 134

McCallum, David 141, 229
McCann, Graham 15
McCartney, (Sir) Paul 215, 218, 234–5
McCrea, Joel 51
McDonald, Paul 12, 13
McDonald, Tamar Jeffers 11
MacInnes, Colin 31, 206, 229–30
McLean, Adrienne L. 11
Mad at the World 161
Majdalany, Fred 115, 123, 161, 204
Malden, Karl 141
Maltby, Richard 7, 15, 22, 121
Mankiewicz, Joseph L. 13, 14, 46
Mansfield, Jayne 205
Marchant, Hilde 103, 136
Marty 131
Marvin, Lee 40, 42
Marwick, Arthur 115
masculinity
in American cinema 3, 13, 16, 55, 60, 64, 115–16, 125, 172, 184, 204, 209, 210, 215
in British cinema 16, 60, 228–9
male as spectacle 14–15, 63–4, 125–6, 204–7, 228
Massey, Raymond 128
Mass Observation 165
Matthau, Walter 190, 191
Mayer, Louis B. 83
Melly, George 25, 214
Melody Maker 8, 184
method acting (Method, the) 1, 11, 13, 20–1, 43, 45, 59, 96, 102, 112, 122, 124–5, 129,140, 193, 201, 204, 205, 228–9
MGM (film studio) 82, 83, 85, 87, 89, 186, 188–9
Miles, (PC) Sidney 26, 158
Miller, Jonathan 235
Mineo, Sal 16, 112
mise en scène 5–6, 13, 54, 86, 94, 125, 190, 198, 201, 205
close-ups 6, 54, 63–4, 87, 118–19, 126, 189
costume 49, 55, 202
Technicolor 140
voiceover 47, 51, 63, 90, 190, 199
Mitchell, Gillian 175, 214
Monroe, Marilyn 102, 161, 205
Monthly Film Bulletin 43, 92, 127, 161, 201, 202
Morin, Edgar 12
Morrow, Vic 4, 80, 91, 92–4, 96–8, 190, 192
Mosley, Leonard 92, 139, 141
Mosley, Oswald
Union Movement 25, 68–9
movies
camp 13, 174
cult 71, 174
fad 174, 202
MTV 217
Muller, Robert 64, 71, 125, 131
Mulvey, Laura 14, 63
see also gaze theory
Murphy, Mary 41, 62
musical genre 83, 194, 195, 202, 205, 216
My Teenage Daughter 127

National Film Theatre (NFT) 59, 66, 140

National Service 19, 27, 99, 164, 167
National Union of Teachers (NUT) 87, 99, 100
Neagle, Anna 127
Neale, Steve 15, 63–4, 205
new film history (historians) 5–6, 9, 59, 112
Newman, Paul 46, 140, 192
New Musical Express (NME) 8, 184
newspapers (readership) 10

Oldham, Andrew 168, 175
Olivier, Laurence 45–6
One-Eyed Jacks 71
On the Waterfront 60, 90, 96
Orwell, George 18
Osborne, John 17, 228
Osgerby, Bill 212

Palm, Delmar C. and Gilbert A. Cahill 81, 98
Paramount (film studio) 190, 191, 193, 204
Parker, Colonel Tom 193, 217, 231
Parnes, Larry 230
Payne, Jack 208
Peck, Gregory 14
Pedelty, Donovan 61, 94
Perkins, Anthony 140
Perkins, V. F. 6
Photoplay 10, 61, 94, 211
Picturegoer 10, 60, 61, 94, 95, 97, 102, 125, 130–1, 135, 164, 208, 210
  annual awards 60, 95, 97, 131, 213
Picture Post 28, 62, 103, 131, 132, 134, 136, 170, 211
Picture Show 11, 94
Piersall, Jim 141
Plant, Robert 215
Platt, Edward 112
Play It Cool 230
Poitier, Sidney 81, 98, 213
pop film, the 8, 213
Porter, Vincent 69, 165
Powell, Dilys 68–9, 92, 123, 163, 203, 205
Powell, Eleanor 94–5
Presley, Elvis 1, 2, 3–4, 151, 160, 172, 175, 183–219, 228, 230, 234–6
  acting style 184, 191–3, 201–4
  American Dream and 185, 217, 231
  army service 183–4, 192, 218
  branding and merchandise 192–3, 208
  fans and fan clubs 9, 183–5, 193–4, 206–9, 209–12, 215
  juvenile delinquency and 183, 193–4, 201, 216, 218
  sex appeal 14, 187, 203, 208–10, 214, 217
Presley, Priscilla 4
Princess Margaret 126
Production Code Administration (PCA) 21, 47, 51, 83, 115–16, 188, 201
  Catholic League of Decency and 22, 47, 83, 116
  Motion Picture Production Code 21
Prouse, Derek 126, 203

Quant, Mary 235
Quayle, Anthony 125, 196
Queen Elizabeth (II) 28, 172, 218
Quigley poll 98

Ray, Andrew 196
Ray, Johnny 208
Ray, Nicholas 16, 113, 123–4, 125, 131, 140
Rebel Without a Cause 2, 8, 13, 105, 111–42, 192, 193
  BBFC and 114–121, 139
  critics and 122–7

promotion and publicity 111, 113–14, 121–2
queer reading 15–16, 125
Richard, Cliff 10, 169, 175, 196–9, 212–13, 215, 217, 231–3
Richards, Dick 204
Richards, Jeffrey 16–17, 165
Richards, Keith 215
Richardson, Tony 125, 202, 228
Robbins, Harold 191
Roberts, Rachel 229
Robertson, James 51
Rock Around the Clock (film) 2, 4, 142, 150–75, 194, 197, 202, 203, 209, 216, 230
BBFC and 153, 157, 158–60, 161
critics and 161–4, 217
fans 164–9
promotion and publicity 160–1
song 2, 79, 87, 104, 151, 156, 168
rock 'n' roll 10, 19, 72, 86, 104, 133, 150–4, 157–68, 171–5, 183–4, 186–9, 192–6, 198–9, 202–4, 208–17, 229–34
Rock Pretty Baby 159
Rocky Horror Picture Show, The 174
Rolling Stone (magazine) 217
Rolling Stones, the 168, 215
Room at the Top 228
Rooney, Frank 41–2
Running Wild 160, 194
Russell, Ken 29

Sampson, Anthony 168
Sandbrook, Dominic 29–31, 115, 212
Saturday Night and Sunday Morning 61, 141, 228
Scala, Mim 79, 104, 168
Scott, Lizabeth 185
screen charisma 4, 6, 12, 13, 54, 165, 174, 198, 209, 217, 218
see also mise en scène
Sears, Heather 229
Second World War
gender roles 14
social attitudes 17, 170
Sequence 67
Serious Charge 196–200, 231, 232
Sexual Offences Act (1967) 131
Shake Rattle and Rock 160
Shaughnessy, Mickey 186
Shepard, Jan 190
Sheridan, Dorothy 165
Shingler, Martin 13
Shinwell, Emmanuel 67
Shulman, Milton 50–1, 124
Sight and Sound 43, 46, 92, 116, 127, 163, 201, 202
Signoret, Simone 229
Simmons, Jerold 120
Sinatra, Frank 208, 212
Slide, Anthony 11
Sloman, Tony 195
Smith, Sarah J. 51
Somebody Up There Likes Me 140
Sound of Music, The 174
Spare the Rod 88–9
Spicer, Andrew 9, 60
Springer, Claudia 16, 114
Stacey, Jackie 8, 129, 136–7
Staiger, Janet 5, 13, 111, 173
Stanislavski, Konstantin 20, 43
Starr, Ringo 235
star studies 12, 13
star text 11, 12, 93–4, 175
Steele, Tommy 7, 209, 211, 215, 217, 231
Stern, Robert 113, 140
Streetcar Named Desire, A
film 20, 45, 63, 93
play 13, 43, 45, 96
Street, Sarah 7
Swann, Charles 209
Syms, Sylvia 127

tabloid journalism 132
Confidential 11
Weekend Mail 130
Talton, Alix 152
Taylor, Elizabeth 139
Teddy boys (Edwardians) 23–9, 40, 48, 50, 52–3, 56–7, 58–9, 65, 68–9, 79–80, 87, 100, 115, 123, 142, 154, 156–7, 158, 164, 169–70, 172, 195, 210, 215, 216
girls 27, 28, 29, 79, 132, 154, 156, 157, 169, 172, 210
race riots (1958–59) and racial tensions 25–6, 65, 87
teenage consumerism 3, 10, 12, 30–1, 128, 132, 139, 141, 164, 173, 185, 211–12, 229–30, 232
cafes and coffee bars 24, 102, 115, 128, 212
cinema culture 30, 69, 155, 166
dance halls 24, 102, 104, 163, 210
Terranova, Dan 81, 97
The Men 44, 46
Thompson, Hunter S. 42
Thompson, Victor 153
Tonks, Venerable Charles 158–9
To Sir With Love 98
Townsend, John 99
Trevelyan, John 21, 47, 69, 71, 88–9, 199
Tudor, Andrew 58
Turing, Alan 197
Tyler, Judy 186, 188–9
Tynan, Kenneth 45–6

Underwood Report (1955) 116
UNESCO 28

Valentino, Rudolph 130, 132, 206–8
Van Doren, Mamie 161–2, 194
Variety 82, 117, 196
Vaughan, Frankie 170, 213
Veness, Thelma 129
Violent Playground 229

Walker, Alexander 6
Walker, Derek 210
Wallis, Hal 191–3, 204
Warner Brothers (film studio) 13, 111, 114–15, 131, 132, 134, 136, 142
Warren, Harry 132
Warth, Douglas 134, 141
Watkins, Arthur 21, 49, 52, 59, 66, 85, 90, 100–2, 115, 157, 195, 197
Watney, John 67
Wayne, John 14
We Are the Lambeth Boys 28
Wexman, Virginia 20–1
Whitebait, William 89
Whitley, Reg 161
Wilcox, John 116–17
Wild in the Country 218
Wilde, Marty 232
Wild One, The 2, 4, 81, 92, 93, 98, 103–4, 111, 116, 118, 187, 193, 195, 200, 236
BBFC and 2, 13, 14, 39–40, 47–55, 65–70, 85, 157, 158, 228
Cambridge screening 39–40, 65
critics and 65–9
hipster dialect 58
motor biker clubs and gangs 2, 16, 54, 56
Black Rebels 41–2, 48, 49, 53, 67, 87
motorcycle paraphernalia 55–8
promotion and publicity 62–5
queer reading 15–16
Williams, Tennessee 20, 45
Willmott, Peter and Michael Young 83

Wilson, Cecil 134, 183
Wilson, Sloan 57
Wolfenden Report (1957) 131, 197
Wood, Natalie 112, 122, 125–6, 131, 188
Woolwich, Bishop William 158

youth subculture 23–6, 115
  Mods and Rockers 70

Zec, Donald 203, 213

Lightning Source UK Ltd.
Milton Keynes UK
UKHW041323011021
391506UK00001B/12

9 781526 154484